SOCIAL THEORY, THE STATE AND MODERN SOCIETY: THE STATE IN CONTEMPORARY SOCIAL THOUGHT

Michael Marinetto

Open University Press

Open University Press
McGraw-Hill Education
McGraw-Hill House
Shoppenhangers Road
Maidenhead
Berkshire
England
SL6 2QL

email: enquiries@openup.co.uk
world wide web: www.openup.co.uk

and
Two Penn Plaza, New York
NY 10121–2289, USA

First published 2007

A catalogue record of this book is available from the British Library

ISBN-10: 0335 214 258 (pb) 0335 214 266 (hb)
ISBN-13: 978 0335 214 259 (pb) 978 0335 214 266 (hb)

Library of Congress Catalogue-in-Publication Data
CIP data applied for

Typeset by Kerrypress Ltd, Luton, Bedfordshire
Printed in Poland by OZGraf S.A.
www.polskabook.pl

Dedicated to Connie, Frances and Debbie

CONTENTS

ACKNOWLEDGEMENTS

Writing a book can be a highly laborious and arduous task, especially one about the state and state theory. But writing the acknowledgements is the one part of producing a book which is a great pleasure. So here goes.

I owe a debt of gratitude to many people who helped me develop the idea for this book in the first place, as well as to a number of other people who helped me get the book written once the idea was hatched. Two people were responsible for getting me started on this book project – so if you are dissatisfied with the contents, blame them. Firstly, there is Justin Vaughan, the former acquisitions editor for the social sciences at the Open University Press who nurtured the book project during its embryonic phases (proposals, initial external reviews and so on). Then there was my colleague and former head of section, Ed Heery, who encouraged me to write the book, even though the pressures of university audit have devalued book writing amongst professional academics. During the writing stage, the book benefited from the generous help of Larry Ray, editor of the Theorizing Society series at the Open University Press. As editor of the series, Larry kindly read through draft chapters of the book and gave me the benefit of numerous suggestions, corrections and insights. I also owe a debt to the referees who commented on the book proposal. Thanks for all your helpful ideas and recommendations. Linda Jones who takes care of the interlibrary loans service at the Aberconway Library at Cardiff University has been a terrific help and I appreciate all her assistance during the research for this book. I wish to thank her and all her colleagues for their kind and generous support. (Could you let me off some library fines when I am in next time!?)

I appreciate all the help and patience of the staff at the Open University Press. I would like to extend a special word of thanks, and apology, to Chris Cudmore, senior commissioning editor for media, film and cultural studies, sociology and criminology. The delivery of this book manuscript was delayed by quite some time but Chris kindly showed a great deal of patience in encouraging me to get the job done. I am also grateful to

Richard Leigh for his sharp and brilliantly informed copy editing work on the manuscript, saving my blushes on several occasions and generally helping to make the book more readable.

There are a number of Colleagues from Cardiff University Business School whom I would like to mention for their good-natured support during the writing part of this book: Jean Jenkins, Stephen Disney, John Salmon and Mark Clatworthy. Thanks to Kevin Stagg, for his insights as an empirical historian were most helpful with the historical material – I am the earlies champion, still. Thanks also to Harvey for the years of camaraderie and friendship, during which gallons of coffee have been consumed. I would also like to extend my gratitude to all those second-year students at Cardiff Business School who have taken the BS2548 module, managing public services, on whom I have inflicted readings and materials that have been used in this book. Thanks also to my colleague and co-lecturer on this module, Rachel Ashworth.

Most of the material used in this book is previously unpublished, apart from two exceptions. Some of the stuff that went to make up Chapter 3 drew from a previously published article: 'Governing beyond the centre: a critique of the Anglo-governance school', *Political Studies*, 2003, vol. 51, no. 3, pp. 592–608. My thanks to the Political Studies Association and Blackwell Publishing for allowing me to reproduce some of this material. Small sections of Chapter 2 drew from the following article that was previously published: 'The governmentality of public administration: Foucault and the public sphere – a literature review', *Public Administration*, 2003, vol. 81, no. 3, pp. 621–36.

Finally, a special thank you to my family for tolerating the fact that I was often preoccupied during the writing of this book, which was quite some time. To my wife Debbie and my daughters Connie and Frances – you are more than a family to me. Deb, you make it all worthwhile and this book is especially dedicated to you, with love. The usual disclaimer applies: any factual mistakes, poor expression, lack of clarity or errors of analysis are my own fault. For any achievements or interesting insights gained from this book the credit is shared.

Mike Marinetto

SERIES EDITOR FOREWORD

Sociology is reflexively engaged with the object of its study, society. In the wake of the rapid and profound social changes of the later twentieth century, it is important to question whether our theoretical frames of reference are appropriate for these novel configurations of culture, economy, society and the state. One of the central questions posed in this series is whether recent theoretical preoccupations – for example with the 'cultural turn', post-modernism, deconstruction, feminism, globalization and identity – adequately grasp social processes in the Twenty-First Century. One central issue here is the relationship between contemporary social problems and theories on the one hand and the classical heritage of Marx, Durkheim, Weber and Simmel on the other. Sociology is still reluctant to forget its founders and the relevance of the classical tradition is both powerful and problematic. It is powerful because the classics constitute a rich source of insights, concepts and analyses that can be deployed and reinterpreted to grasp current problems. But it is problematic because the social world of the classics is largely that of industrial, imperial and high bourgeois European societies prior to the First World War. How do we begin to relate the concepts formed in this milieu to the concerns of the globalized social world that is post-colonial, post-industrial and has seen the rise and collapse of Soviet socialism? These are some of the major challenges for sociology that this series, *Theorizing Society*, aims to address.

This series intends to map out the ways in which social theory is being transformed and how contemporary issues have emerged. Each book in the series offers a concise and up-to-date overview of the principle ideas, innovations and theoretical concepts in relation to its topic. The series is designed to provide a review of recent developments in social theory, offering a comprehensive collection of introductions to major theoretical issues. The focus of individual books is organized around topics which reflect the major areas of teaching and research in contemporary social theory, including modernity, post-modernism, structuralism and post-structuralism; cultural theory; globalization; feminism and sexuality;

memory, identity and social solidarity. While being accessible to under-graduates these books allow authors to develop personal and programmatic statements about the state and future development of theoretically defined fields.

In *Social Theory, the State and Modern Society* Michael Marinetto addresses a range of key theoretical issues in relation to state and society – classical political theory and the emergence of 'new wave' theories, especially those of post-structuralism and the Anglo-governance school; feminist theories and critique of the patriarchal state; the state and the 'cultural turn' in sociology; and the paradoxical resurgence of state theory in the context of globalization. Marinetto begins with modern theorization of the state from the 1950s (around concepts such as corporatism, pluralism, hegemony, neo-elite theory, and theories of state autonomy) and then discusses the 'new wave' of state theories that attacked shibboleths and established orthodoxies. Prominent amongst this new wave was Foucault's work and the new theoretical approaches that escaped from traditional political and social theory through the concept of governmen-tality, which sees the state policing societies through bureaucratic regimes and disciplinary powers. This displaces the state from political theory for a more diffuse, random and unintentional view of political power, a perspective that resonates with Bruno Latour's studies of laboratory scientists and Niklas Luhmann's emphasis on social differentiation and autopoiesis. He provides a thorough and innovative discussion of the contribution of Anglo-governance theories of the state.

Marinetto emphasizes how conceptions of the state in political science have changed over time. The idea of the unified state in the early to mid Twentieth Century gave way by the 1960–80s to one of the state as overloaded and failing especially in relation to the fiscal demands of welfare. In more recent times this in turn has given way to the theory of governance, where, in a context of globalization and neoliberalism, central government is less reliant on bureaucratic hierarchies than networks of agencies beyond the central state. However, Marinetto suggests that these claims might be exaggerated since the central state retains a range of powers by which it retains influence over public sector agencies. There may be a tendency towards fragmentation but the state retains its core capacities.

An important feature of this book is its integration of feminist theories of the state into mainstream analysis. He shows how feminist theories have challenged the gender-ignorance of much state theory while produc-ing new insights. While early feminist analyses largely drew from established state theories (especially Marxism) 'second-wave' of radical feminism portrayed the state as an inherently patriarchal institution. More recently, state-centred feminist perspectives have been based on detailed empirical analyses of how governments shape the relative life-chances of men and women. Marinetto however argues that a gendered theory of the state still needs to demonstrate that men and women have collective political interests, which may be pursued through the state.

Both post-structural theories and feminism have been closely involved with the 'cultural turn' in the social sciences and Marinetto provides detailed discussion of this intellectual movement. Conceptions of culture themselves differ between theorists – for some culture is understood in linguistic terms while others focus on ritual, performance and dramaturgy. Marinetto focuses on two conceptions of culture: the influence of ideas and ideology on the one hand and ritual and symbols on the other. Within each he argues, there exist different interpretations of the relationship between culture and the state, but these are nonetheless united by a concern to take culture seriously. Culture is thus viewed as a structure that provides a context for behaviour and thought of equal significance to material and socio-economic structures. These approaches have then provided state theory with a rich body of ideas but have moreover developed an alternative understanding to mainstream state theory of how the state works and how state power is reproduced. Marinetto thus brings cultural perspectives from the margins into the mainstream of state theory.

Marinetto addresses the significance of globalization for state theory, a further area in which there are multiple theories and conceptualizations. Again he guides the reader through the key issues and shows how, despite talk of globalization as spelling the 'end of the state', globalization research has brought the state back into greater prominence. In fact he argues, the debate about globalization has reinvigorated interest in the state. Bringing together many of the themes of earlier chapters, he suggests that discussion of the state and globalization have tended to concentrate on economic issues, whereas globalization is also constituted by cultural, social and political processes. These multiple processes can in some ways undermine the legitimacy and cohesion of the state but at the same time presuppose the state as an agent of globalization and party to international agreements and institutions. Marinetto shows how despite the force of power of globalization at different levels, the state retains a presence in reality and in the theoretical language of the social sciences.

Finally he notes that the practice of theorizing and debating the state does not belong simply to specialists who are academic professionals. Rather, he argues, the continued development and relevance of state theory depends on intellectual inclusiveness and the encompassing of diverse traditions. Classical theorists such as Aristotle, Marx and Hume can still be mined for their insights in to the current state of the state and their ideas melded with more recent developments. This conclusion resonates with a key theme of this series, of engagement with the ideas of classical social and political theorists. This is an important book that promises to refocus debates on theories of state and society.

Larry Ray
Professor of Sociology
University of Kent

CONTEMPORARY STATE THEORY IN CONTEXT

Jim Lee: the man who does not exist?

Jim Lee is a real person. He was born 68 years ago in Kent and now lives in London. This may be a real person – in a corporeal sense – but, to all intents and purposes, this particular individual does not actually exist. There are no available records or official documents to confirm his existence. Jim Lee is unknown to the state, for he is without a passport; has never been on the electoral roll; does not possess a national insurance number; has no birth certificate; has never been registered with a doctor. There are also no commercial records to authenticate him. Jim Lee has never opened a bank account.

For much of his life, Jim was happy to remain invisible to officialdom. Born to a traveller family and abandoned by his mother at the age of 4, he managed to fend for himself and eek out a living as a hired hand in various occupations. But old age and a lack of opportunities in the informal labour market led to unemployment. And for the first time in his life, Jim was forced to seek assistance from the state. From the state's point of view, Jim was a non-person. As such, he had no automatic rights to welfare. At the time this story appeared in April 2004, Lee was using a drop-in centre in south-east London as his refuge (see Hattenstone 2004). The management at the centre have been trying to convince those in authority that Lee should qualify for a pension and housing benefits, even though, officially, Jim Lee might as well be a figment of someone's imagination.

Jim Lee's peculiar and unusual life certainly has that 'And finally' story quality about it, the quirky news item, the lighter denouement of an otherwise apocalyptic news bulletin. But from Lee's story we can draw serious inferences, certainly as far as the purposes of this book are concerned. The long anonymity from officialdom and Lee's struggle to qualify for welfare benefits have much to say about the significance of the state in contemporary society. Jim's travails highlight that even our very existence and our identities as individuals are partly dependent on who the state says we are and what the state knows.

The state pre-dates industrialisation, but with the advent of industrial modernisation it became a ubiquitous feature of Western societies. The reach and influence of the state in modern society are all pervasive: many aspects of an individual's life from birth to the moment of death are regulated, monitored and controlled by various public authorities and organs. There are laws that we have to abide by, public institutions that we deal with and social provisions that originate from the state. The state is all around us and is an integral part of complex modern societies. The ability of the state to infiltrate many areas of our lives is nicely articulated by Bourdieu (1994: 4), who wrote the state is 'the holder of a sort of meta-capital granting power over other species of capital and over their holders'. These other 'species of capital' included the institutions of coercion and the economy, as well as the cultural, informational and symbolic spheres.

The capacity and authority of the state are important matters and have dominated recent academic discussions about the state. For instance, books have appeared on state power across historical epochs (see Hall and Ikenberry 1989), state autonomy within the international economy (see Hirst and Thompson 1996) and the relationship between the state and non-state actors (see Pierson 1996). The issue of the state's capacity and power gives us an opportunity to say something about the aims and objectives of this book.

Extant discussions about the state's authority, political sovereignty and influence are relevant to, and will be examined during the course of, this book. That said, the objective of this book is to do more than just deliberate and reflect on the capacity of the state, important though that is. The prime objective here is to commentate upon and expound contemporary theories and ideas about the state. And as with all such activities, theories of the political look to essentialise, to home in on, what are considered the most important aspects of the modern state. To begin with, for most of the theories covered in this book, the state is synonymous with the liberal democratic variety found in Western societies. But the state takes on a variety of forms. There are post-colonial state forms, developmental states and the fledgling state forms that have emerged out of the Soviet Union. Even within the liberal democratic state there are a variety of forms, as evidenced in the literature on welfare state regimes (see Chapters 4 and 6). Below I will set out a brief panoramic view of how the state has been treated historically in social and political thought. This will allow us to establish the reasons why a whole book dedicated to contemporary state theory is both germane and necessary.

A very brief history of state theory

The surfacing of Jim Lee into existence is a rather fitting allegory for what has happened to the theorisation of the state in recent years. The theoretical treatment of the state, like Jim Lee, has had a bit of an identity crisis. The field of state theory has chopped and changed, reflecting the vicissitudes of socio-political thought and the various theoretical fashions that litter the lost highway of academia. There have been occasions when some academic authors have questioned the very existence of the state, boldly announcing there is no such thing.

The state was central to classical theory, being foundational to modern political and social discourse as it emerged bleary-eyed from the Middle Ages (Bartelson 2001: xi). Given its centrality to the identity of political science as a discipline, the treatment of the state during the course of the twentieth century is surprising. What happened in the first two decades of the twentieth century is that the state became a target for criticism. And by the middle of the century, according to Bartelson (2001: 77), the concept was completely marginalised within academic political discourse.

The assessment of state theory, and its development, by Bartelson certainly has a ring of truth when it comes to American political scientists. American political scientists were at the vanguard of 'state-bashing', although early twentieth-century British political commentators such as Barker and Hobhouse were also notable state-sceptics. Amongst the chief state-bashers were those academics representing the emerging behaviourist tradition in American political science. The ambition of behaviourism as it became established in the early to mid-twentieth century was to achieve a scientific, empirically driven approach to politics. For behaviourists such as Catlin (1964), writing in the 1920s, and later proponents such as Easton (1966), abstractions like the state would have to be excommunicated from political analysis. Catlin (1964: 141) comments unequivocally that if politics is to become a science it 'must be based on the study of some act which is repeated countless times a day, not on the study of sixty states'. In other words, the scientific study of politics should concentrate on those observable and measurable properties of any political phenomenon. This would include institutional hierarchies, organisational processes and overt behaviours such as voting.

Within academic circles, by the mid-twentieth century the state had become passé. But it would be incorrect to argue that the state had become totally obsolete as a topic of study by this time. If social scientists had any lingering interests in this subject, they confined their analyses to studying how the state was a source of social equilibrium, a means for achieving political consensus in a pluralistic democracy. These concerns shifted by the end of the 1960s once the postwar consensus and faith in welfare reforms began to break down. These political changes contributed to the analytical reappraisal of political thought, especially those pluralist theories of democracy. As well as the critical lambasting of pluralism, writers explored the extent to which the state was implicated in the political and economic crises that bedevilled Western nations in this period. The writings of political sociologists and political scientists, particularly those with Marxist theoretical inclinations, were preoccupied with issues such as 'a breakdown in consensus', 'a crisis in democracy', and 'political and economic decline' (Held 1996: 241). Out of all these discussions of crises and breakdowns, the concept of the state was reinvigorated in the 1970s. The concept of the state once again became vital and relevant to political and social theory. But what of the state theory in recent years?

The death of the state?

There are diverse interpretations of how the state has fared in contemporary social and political thought. One interpretation, which has gained some ground, is the idea that the state is dying a slow death at the hands of contemporary theoreticians. Proponents of this thesis tend to be concerned with the relationship between the state and the international political economy. For instance, in her study of the global economy, Linda Weiss rued that throughout the social sciences the state is being weakened and trivialised. This is happening to such an extent that we are entering an 'era of state denial' (Weiss 1998: 2). Well before Weiss did so, other commentators registered their complaints about scholastic indifference towards the state. Peter Laslett, writing in 1956, was critical of how the deliberate embrace of positivism by political scientists had contributed to the gradual death of political theory, which is so integral to state theory. He observed: 'For the moment, anyway, political theory is dead' (Laslett 1956: vii). For Weiss, the contemporary era of state denial is more intense than in the past. The state is being 'killed off' by two separate developments: firstly, the perceived impact of socio-economic changes on a worldwide scale, especially the intensification of global integration; and secondly, the growing influence of new conceptual movements in social and political thought, especially those linked to continental thought. The observations made by Weiss also seem to chime with the dominant, neo-liberal political Zeitgeist of the past twenty years, characterised by an ideological commitment to the free market and a minimal state.

Although opinions about the imminent demise of the state, and therefore state theory, may reflect scholastic and political developments, they need to be qualified. These views simplify the current position of the state within social and political thought. Or to paraphrase Mark Twain, 'reports of the state's death have been greatly exaggerated, in certain quarters'. The state is not dead, nor is it so marginalised that it has become the concept that time forgot. In place of the 'death of the state' thesis, we need a more complete and nuanced understanding of how state theory has faired in recent times, one that is uncontaminated by entrenched sectional viewpoints.

In an article written in the late 1960s, the political scientist John Nettl commented on the relative 'statelessness of American social science'. We have already mentioned why this is the case. Despite the lack of interest in the state during this historical juncture, Nettl (1968: 559) claims it still 'retains a skeletal, ghostly existence largely because, for all the changes in emphasis and interest of research, the thing exists and no amount of conceptual restructuring can dissolve it'. The staying power of the state was made evident in the late 1970s, following the intellectual collapse of Marxist theory. The intellectual redundancy of Marxism was followed by an analytical shift towards neo-Weberian analysis. This shift was especially noticeable in the field of state theory. This contemporary application of Weber in the political field was popularised by American political scientists such as Theda Skocpol and Eric Nordlinger, who from the late 1970s onwards endeavoured to 'bring the state back in'. The concern here was to portray the state as independent institution irreducible to economic processes and as an independent determinant of political events. The pursuit of Weberian analysis was certainly prominent in Anglo-sociology. Hence, Nettle's observations of forty years ago still have relevance today. The state is difficult to dissolve and continues to form a part of the intellectual collective conscience within the social sciences.

The durability and staying power of this concept are such that there are still a healthy number of books being churned out about the state. In fact, there has been a recent glut of books about state theory. Take the following varied titles which have been published: *The Orthocratic State* (Sicker 2003), *Revitalizing the State* (Khandwalla 1999), *Rethinking State Theory* (Smith 2000), *Paradigm Lost: State Theory Reconsidered* (Aronowitz and Bratsis 2002), and *The Critique of the State* (Bartelson 2001). As these publications suggest, there is still a healthy curiosity surrounding the state. Symptomatic of such interest is the fact that theories of the state have over the years proliferated throughout a range of disciplines and subdisciplines. Social geography, feminist theory, international relations, internal political economy, cultural theory, organisational analysis, anthropology: all have made some contribution to our understanding of the state. Moreover, state theory is characterised by a creative range of perspectives and philosophical standpoints, from poststructuralism to postpsychoanalytic theory, from symbolic analysis to systems theory.

A stateless theory of the state

We also need to clear up another misunderstanding about latter-day state theory. The reason why analysts such as Weiss feel compelled to write about the death of the state in social thought is that they have misinterpreted modern theoretical currents. This is understandable, to a certain degree. There are contributions to the state that have been informed by theoretical movements committed to achieving the intellectual equivalent of 'year zero', sweeping away established ideas and concepts. In this spirit, there are people who think that the state has reached its sell-by date both as a concept and as an actual institution. Hence the late Philip Abrams' (1988) contention that the state no longer exists. But thinkers like Abrams occupy the extreme end of the theoretical spectrum, as we shall discuss in Chapter 6 on the relationship between cultural analysis and the state.

Rather than deny the significance of the state, contemporary analysts have tried to avoid fetishising the state, as Taussig would put it (Taussig 1993: 217–19). The fetishistic treatment of the state can be seen in classical thought. Here, the state was treated as a pre-eminent, even otherworldly, power: the embodiment of a universal rationality (Hobbes and Hegel), the reflection of the human soul (Plato) or the guardian of monolithic interests (Marx). As opposed to reifying the state in this way, contemporary analysts have made concerted attempts to demystify, deconstruct and revise the basis of its power, setting out the origins and limits of the state's authority. Typical of this reassessment is Michel Foucault, who called for the cutting off of the king's head in political thought (with the king's head representing the sovereign state). In this typical piece of Foucauldian rhetoric and hyperbole, he insists that our analysis of political power should extend beyond the limits of the state. That said, Foucault (1980a: 122) maintains that the state is still important. Its significance is such that it still warrants theoretical reflection. As such, we should not misconstrue attempts to review the theoretical standing of the state, and even expressions of intellectual hostility, as signs that the state is about to fall off the intellectual radar for good.

This book is testament to the staying power and continued importance of the democratic liberal state in social and political theory. The pluralistic disciplinary settings and the diverse theoretical influences of contemporary state theory will be reflected in the coming chapters. Below is a summary overview of the book and each of its chapters.

An overview of what lies ahead

This book's focus is on contemporary state theories. To appreciate recent fashions in state theory, it is necessary to have some historical appreciation of how modern conceptions of the state began and evolved over time. To appreciate the present and the future of state theory, we need to know something about its past. Therefore, the initial chapters of this book consider the philosophical and theoretical heritage of modern state theory.

Chapter 1 will begin to explore the immediate forerunners of contemporary state theory. It will initially focus on the pluralist theories of the state which emerged out of American universities during the 1950s. Pluralist analysis for a time dominated Anglo-American political analysis, inspiring further theoretical explorations of the state such as corporatist theory. But the influential and formative work of key pluralist theorists of the state such as Robert Dahl gave way to a revival of state analysis during the 1970s. Neo-Marxist analysts led the way. As well as the revival of state theory on the coat-tails of neo-Marxism, this chapter discusses the so-called 'second wave' of state theory during the early to mid-1980s. The revival of interest in the state was especially prominent in the United States. The main theoretical thrust of this revival was its attempt to bring the state back as the central actor and institution in society. It was argued that postwar social theory subsumed the state under external social forces. Chapter 1 shows us that modern state theory grew from, and built its foundations upon, classical social and political theory, especially Hobbes, Locke and later classical thinkers such as Weber and Marx. However, there were countervailing forces afoot. From the late 1970s onwards, state theory was gradually redefined according to a different set of intellectual antecedents than those which had previously dominated the field. The modern state-theoretical contributions of the postwar era relied on the classical liberal thought as well as the founding fathers of social science (Marx and Weber especially). The new wave of state theorists were less about Hobbes and Locke, or Weber and Marx, than Nietzsche and Saussure, de Beauvoir and Lévi-Strauss. The *new wave* of state theory of the past twenty-odd years amounts to a fundamental re-evaluation of politics, power and the state. The realignment forms the basis of the core chapters of this book.

The disciplinary origins of contemporary, new wave approaches to the state are diverse and characterised by quite distinct theoretical preoccupations. Despite these differences, there are certain recurring themes or conceptual narratives that can be found in contemporary state analysis. One common theme is the idea that political authority is not necessarily immanent in a centralised bureaucratic institution, such as the state. To use the fashionable parlance, the state has become decentred. The decentring of state theory has been epitomised most notably by the thought of Michel Foucault. And it is Foucault's re-evaluation of the state that will form the main theme of Chapter 2. This chapter shows that Foucault's work on power, governmentality and the state owes much to intellectual upheavals in Europe between the 1930s and 1960s. One of the key movements was the rise to prominence of poststructuralism in the social sciences. In many respects Foucault's work uses an intellectual modus operandi influenced by poststructuralism to challenge prevailing orthodoxies in state theory. The opening sections of this chapter will present a summary of Foucault's ideas on government and politics, as encompassed in his concept on governmentality. As will be shown, Foucault's ideas about governmentality are inextricably linked to the development of one of the key themes running through his work – power. From summarising Foucault's thoughts on governmentality, the chapter will turn to authors who have used, adapted and in some instances critically revaluated Foucauldian notions of the state and politics.

Chapter 3 examines the more recent contribution of governance theory. This approach may, on the face of it, be out of place in a book on the state because it seems to dispense with the state altogether. Instead of the state, the preference is to think in terms of autopoietic systems or autonomous networks of governance. Be that as it may, the contention here is that governance theory does make a purposeful contribution to a theoretical understanding of the state. In fact, governance theory has influenced the work of out-and-out state theorists. Although a relatively new enterprise, we trace the antecedents of governance theory, looking specifically at the overloaded state thesis and the interorganisational analysis developed by European thinkers. From these formative efforts, we move on to the contemporary governance theory. There are different types of governance theory, but in this chapter we focus on what can be termed the Anglo-governance school, which will be subject to a critical exposition.

Chapter 4 will consider the treatment of the state by feminist theorists. The initial sections of the chapter will discuss embryonic attempts to understand the state from a gender perspective, which was achieved by fusing Marxism and feminism. Here, the state was responsible for reinforcing patriarchy as it served the needs and requirements of the capitalist system. Early attempts to develop a feminist analysis of the state gave way to criticisms that explanatory primacy was given to capitalism rather than a distinct gendered approach to the state. From a gender perspective, the state is shaped by the imperatives of patriarchy, especially inequitable reproductive and domestic relations between men and women. In addition to patriarchal analyses of the state, there is a liberal feminist literature which has looked upon the state as having dual qualities, with the potential to both oppress and liberate women. More recent feminist theorising of the state has traversed into poststructural territory, arguing that a feminist approach needs to appreciate the complexity of the state, its discourses and technologies of power. For poststructural feminists, patriarchy is fragmented and the state is one patriarchal body amongst many. As such, the state's embodiment of patriarchal relations is seen to be variable and contingent, although state practices and discourses have come to privilege certain gendered identities.

In Chapter 5 we focus on the cultural turn in state theory. The early sections of this chapter show how culture played a part, albeit peripheral, in classical contributions to the state. However, the bulk of this chapter is dedicated to those state theorists for whom culture is an independent variable, a prime and distinct influence on the social rather than a mere condition of underlying social forces or objective structures. The interface between the state and culture has been subject to various interpretations and schools of thought. These schools correspond to different interpretations concerning to the autonomy of culture *vis-à-vis* the state. Initially we focus on the work of those thinkers who have used a cultural analysis of the state as part of an overarching theory of society. From here our analysis takes us to more culturally orientated analyses of the state – namely, to historically and anthropologically based models, focusing on the cultural rituals of the state. The latter half of this chapter spotlights what is the most radical explanation of the state–culture interface. The radical constructivist approach argues that the state is indistinguishable, inseparable from culture.

In Chapter 6 we begin to examine how the globalisation debate and the emergence of a globalised perspective in the social sciences have impacted on state theory. In many ways, state theory has been invigorated and revitalised by discussions of globalisation, throwing up fresh ideas and debates. One by-product of this is that interest in state theory has further extended its disciplinary reach beyond the orthodox confines of political science to include subdisciplines such as geography, international relations and international political economy. Equally, discussions of globalisation have challenged many fundamental shibboleths of state theory, especially the idea that the state is something that is delimited to self-contained national units. In fact, there is a central, recurring fault-line running through debates about the relationship between globalisation and the state. The main division is between those who argue that global interconnections have become so intense that autonomous states no longer exist and those for whom the state remains a fundamental political actor. This fault-line will become distinctly apparent in this chapter, as it explores debates about the global order and the state. There are three areas of the globalisation debate that have made a notable contribution to contemporary theorisation of the state. Each will be covered in this chapter, and they include debates about the global economic order; cosmopolitan and multilevel regional democracy; and the international political order and violence.

CHAPTER 1

MODERN EXPLORATIONS

Introduction

The contemporary era of state theory took off, for argument's sake, in the 1950s. Contemporary endeavours to theorise the state fall into three general categories, which will be considered in this chapter. Each theoretical category is by no means homogeneous, but the schools of thought represented within each category do share certain conceptual affinities. Under the first, there are those theories for which the state is organised around competing sets of interests. The key theoretical contributions are made by authors who subscribe to a pluralistic conception of the state and those who follow a corporatist approach. The second set of theories assert that the state reflects societal relationships and interests. These approaches are placed under the umbrella of society-centred approaches. In our overview of these approaches, we focus on sociological and neo-Marxist accounts of the state. What is interesting about neo-Marxist theories of the state is their lack of unanimity: there are different views over the extent to which the state is politically independent. The third group of theories take the view that the state is a distinct institutional entity, irreducible to social interests and structures. As such, the state operates as a purposeful and independent actor, which can bring about social and economic change. This more state-centred approach gained particular credence as a backlash against the society-centred approach popularised by neo-Marxist thinkers.

Competing interests and the postwar state

In the early years of the twentieth century, the state was largely ignored by professional political scientists in their drive to create a behaviourist discipline (see the Introduction). Of course behaviourism still exercised a prominent influence after the war, especially in American academic departments. Despite this hostile intellectual milieu, there still emerged some begrudging interest in the state amongst social and political observers in the postwar era.

The theorists who initially made the most notable contributions, ironically, were located in American academic institutions. Such thinkers were inspired in their writings, in part, by the classical sociology of Max Weber. It was the Weberian notion that social divisions can emerge from a variety of status differentials, which shaped the initial stream of postwar thought on the state. Amongst these early theories, the one that proved most influential was the pluralist school, achieving paradigmatic dominance in American political science during the early 1950s. My intention is to consider the pluralist model in conjunction with the corporatist approach that became established at the end of the 1960s. Both approaches offer highly distinct insights and arguments about the nature of the modern state. Although divergent in their positions, I have included them under the same category because they share an essentially liberal democratic view that the institutions of the state and their policy outputs are fashioned by a multitude of competing interest groups.

Pluralist analysis – a 'non-theory' of the state

Pluralism is less a self-conscious theory of the state than a general theory of society and the policy process. As a social theory, it is concerned with the fragmentation of interests and power in society; as a theory of policy, it focuses on how the democratic system adjudicates between these diverse social interests to ensure that benefits are equally distributed amongst all citizens. Such ideas can be traced to the classical liberal belief of Locke and Montesquieu that political power needs to be separated along the lines of an executive and legislature. This division is necessitated because it helps to establish a democratic counterweight to the monolithic tendencies of the state. These concerns were subsequently elaborated by the British thinkers J.N. Figgis and H.J. Laski, amongst others, who favoured the maximisation of social diversity to maintain liberty (Vincent 1987: 196–7).

It was in the hands of American scholars that pluralism became a popular and dominant theoretical force in political analysis throughout the 1950s and for part of the 1960s. We would be hard pressed to say that these political scientists were interested in the state *per se*. In fact the state barely gets a mention in much of their work. But the American neo-pluralists operated, note Dunleavy and O'Leary (1987: 42), with an implicit model of the state, a model which produced several sophisticated insights on the workings of political power.

One of the formative contributions to American neo-pluralist theory was David Truman's *The Governmental Process*, published in 1951. In this seminal book Truman sets out, principally, to study pressure or interest groups and their contribution to the 'formal institutions of government'. The governing institutions and processes have come to reflect an increasingly complex society. Social complexity has created a governing process that 'involves a multiplicity of co-ordinate or nearly co-ordinate points of access to governmental processes' (Truman 1981: 519). Such access allows interest groups to influence the formation of policy, establishing a truly open and democratic system of government.

Exactly how the democratic system, based as it is on interest groups jostling and competing for supremacy, can maintain stability is a moot point. Truman's answer is that democratic equilibrium is in part a default mechanism of social diversity. Modern democratic polities are so internally diverse and divided that it is impossible for a single political faction or sectional interest group to emerge as dominant. As a result, government policy is the outcome of a consensus between diverse political and social interests. In addition to diverse representation, overlapping membership between interest groups acts as the 'principal balancing force in the politics of a multigroup society' (1981: 520). That said, Truman admits that the openness of the political system can be problematic in practice. The multiple lines of access into government can blur responsibilities over policy-making, which can potentially result in inertia. The opportunities and risks associated with multigroup democracy were examined further by other key figures of early postwar American political science.

The contemporary popularisation of pluralist theory owes much to that doyen of American political science, Robert Dahl. Although the concept of the state rarely makes an appearance in his ground-breaking statement on pluralism, *A Preface to Democratic Theory* (1956), it is nevertheless regarded as a notable contribution to modern state theory. In the *Preface*, Dahl's principal objective was to explore how democracy should be secured and maximised by limiting the power of the state (1956: 64). Conventional wisdom has it that the 'tyranny of the state' is contained through constitutional checks and balances. If formal checks and balances are seen as the key to maximising democracy, 'we place little faith in social checks and balances' (1956: 83). Dahl tries to redress this oversight. These social checks and balances refer to how society is arranged according to various interest groups, competitively and non-hierarchically intertwined. All such groups have access to some form of political power through which they can exert an influence upon the democratic process. These arrangements form an in-built safeguard against oligarchy, either by an institution like the state or by powerful social factions such as the corporate sector.

The fragmentation of social interests produces what Dahl terms a 'polyarchal democracy'. This democratic system is effectively government by different minorities or rule by the many. Here, the system is 'marked by separation of powers: it has legislature, executive, administrative bureaucracy and judiciary … in this sense, too, every polyarchal system is a system of checks and balances, with numerous groups of officials in competition and conflict with one another' (Dahl 1956: 136–7). And the state? In a polyarchal democracy, the state exists to oversee the bargaining process amongst interest groups and to mediate between competing demands. As such, the state has little or no autonomy to follow its own independent course of action; it exists to do the bidding of external interests and to make sure that competition between these is fair and not detrimental to the public good.

Pluralist theory can be regarded as a xenophobic celebration of American democracy and its presumed superiority over other 'lesser' democratic nations, argues Margolis (1983: 116). Although pluralist theory provided an ideological justification for American democracy, this model of democracy was challenged and criticised from various quarters. Critics point to a near Pollyannish optimism. Detractors argue, contrary to pluralist insistence, that the proliferation of power across social strata would in itself be incapable of guaranteeing true democracy: a political system where all citizens had an equal say and influence. Instead of governments being receptive to a diverse range of interests, they are more likely to be influenced by powerful factions in society, factions that command sufficient resources and status from which they gain prominence in the national political arena. As Lively (1975: 59) notes, governments can be sensitive to church leaders, industrialists, military chiefs and even trade union officials, but that does not mean they are liable to popular control. These criticisms were given added veracity by developments in American society from the late 1960s onwards. The outbreak of inner-city riots, the replacement of postwar economic stability with recessionary cycles, the rise of new social movements, the spectre of poverty and the realisation of elite political corruption: these developments directed political commentators to question the taken-for-granted pluralistic notion that democratic polities are 'naturally' open and stable (McLennan 1984: 84).

Pluralist theory felt the full force of history and changing intellectual fashions. This meant the end of its pre-eminence in American political science, but not its complete extinction. As those within the school endeavoured to address these criticisms, pluralism would fragment into various competing approaches, offering distinct views on democracy and the state. One splinter faction that emerged after the halcyon days of the 1950s and 1960s was the critical pluralism spearheaded by Charles Lindblom. In his brand of neo-pluralism, Lindblom (1977) took a jaundiced outlook on corporate power, arguing that policy decisions available to the state are constrained by the disproportionate influence of the business sector. Similar critiques were pursued by Dahl in his later writings, which at times were more reminiscent of Marx than Weber (see Dahl 1985). The mature Dahl wrote about the abject failure of democratic polyarchies to address entrenched socio-economic inequalities and to curb rampant corporate power. In one article he notes that democratic pluralism has provided insufficient conditions for the redistribution of power and wealth to subordinate groups in society (Dahl 1978: 199). The failure to redistribute power and wealth has democratic implications, for it inhibits full democratic participation.

These attempts to reinvent pluralism in the face of internal and external criticisms have allowed various pluralistic offshoots and even orthodox approaches to retain a certain stature in the political and social sciences. The diversification, however, failed to restore the paradigmatic dominance this school had enjoyed around the 1950s. To begin with, it was too fragmented for that to happen. As well as problems inherent to the school itself, there were other emerging theories that were covering similar ground whilst providing distinct theoretical alternatives to those of pluralism. One prominent challenge to pluralist conceptions of the state came from corporatist thinkers throughout the 1970s.

Elite cabals and the corporatist state

The corporatist approach shares distinct filiations with pluralism: it assumes that sectional interests are an integral part of the state machinery and the policy process; it assumes that, as these sectional interests associate, they gravitate towards stability and consensus. There are, however, stark and incompatible differences between these two positions on the state. Pluralism conceives of the state as a neutral institution under constant pressure from a diverse range of interest groups. From the corporatist position, the state is controlled by an elite, or the main representatives of key interest groups, who seek agreement on what policies to pursue for the sake of social stability.

The intellectual forerunner to corporatist analysis was neo-elite theory (see Held, 1989, pp 64–7). A contemporary reappraisal of the classical elite theory of Mosca and Pareto can be found in Raymond Aron's work. In Aron's neo-elite analysis, there is a close affinity between elites and social classes. These ties are responsible for producing a pluralist elite comprised of capitalists, trade unions and politicians. As such, the process of governing 'becomes a business of compromises' as those in power are well aware that there are opponents waiting and struggling to assume the reigns of control (Aron 1950: 10–11).

The idea of power sharing amongst elite interest groups is echoed by corporatist theory. In contrast to neo-elite theory, though, political power in corporatist thought is less the preserve of an elite minority than shared amongst a broader cross-section of key social and economic groups. The groups can include professional associations, specialist interest groups, trade unions, and representative bodies of the corporate sector. Such representative groups are independent of the state but they enter a mutually dependent bargaining relationship with government, where favourable policies are traded for cooperation and expertise (Cawson 1982: 39). Corporatism is distinguished by its emphasis on inter-group cooperation. However, there is little agreement between such theorists over what are the key defining features of corporatist arrangements. Despite the lack of a clear orthodoxy, the writings of corporatist theorists do reveal certain recurring themes in their study of collaborative ties between sectional interests. Amongst these persistent themes, we will find the concepts of intermediation and incorporation (Grant 1993: 28).

Corporatist thinkers have placed a great deal of credence on how the modern system of government has a predilection towards elite inclusivity: major interest groups are brought into the system of government to share the responsibilities of power. This inclusive process has been popularly dubbed 'incorporation'. The main rationale of this inclusive approach to governing is the minimisation or avoidance of conflict, which causes instability. The origins of incorporation in Britain, notes Middlemas (1979), can be traced back to the end of the First World War. In this period, key interest groups, namely trade unions and business organisations, developed close ties with government in order to avoid industrial conflict and social instability. By the early 1920s, it was clear that a sufficient number of unions and business organisations saw common interest in the avoidance of conflict and the development of the mixed economy. Grant observes that while intervention and incorporation are central ideas in the corporate armoury, intermediation more usefully captures the nature of corporatism.

The concept of intermediation refers to the reciprocal ties that by necessity exist between interest groups and government. In return for being involved in the governing process, sectional groups are expected to regulate their members, ensuring adherence to any agreements that have been hatched. Such incorporation is especially necessary in highly decentralised political systems. For instance, Milward and Francisco (1983) found that America, as a federal democracy, has a decentralised and uncoordinated policy infrastructure, creating a network of policy subsystems. As these policy systems become firmly ensconced, government agencies intermediate closely with interest groups in an effort to steer legislative programmes and initiatives through the ebb and flow of the policy process (1983: 273). The authors observe that one notable by-product of intermediation in the United States has been the growth of interest groups across a variety of policy sectors. And what was the main force behind this growth? This expansion of interest groups was actively encouraged and supported by federal governments, looking to augment their ability to micromanage policy implementation.

The two main theoretical approaches examined under this section – pluralism and corporatism – offer a residual theory of the state which contains several important insights. The most significant of these is how the state is constrained by a series of sectional interest groups that make a whole host of demands upon the resources and authority of the state. For both pluralist and corporatist theorists the state in many ways is a bounded institution. The claim that state power is circumscribed persisted as socially centred approaches came to prominence in the 1970s under the aegis of a neo-Marxist revival. These approaches offered a concerted analysis of the state and its relationship to society. They will form the basis of the following section.

The state versus society – autonomy versus dependence

Outside of natural science disciplines, the lesson of the twentieth century is about a single phenomenon: the triumph of the social sciences. The intellectual hegemony of the social sciences has many different features and has spawned various intellectual fashions. There is one particular aspect of this hegemony that does stand out. Here, I am thinking of how society became firmly established as an object of study. Following the emergence of sociology, the concept of society emerged into the twentieth century with its own unique and distinct character. Of course there are detractors. There are those analysts who prefer to think less of abstractions like society than of individual discrete acts and behaviours that form the social whole. Still, society, or social processes, form an essential part of the social sciences, especially state theory. The interface between the state and society has featured prominently in postwar reflections on the state.

For all its executive authority and monopoly over coercive apparatuses, can we really think of the state as truly independent and autonomous? There are those who beg to differ. Such thinkers suggest that society and the state are inextricably linked. By this they mean that the state is far from being a self-contained unit but is something that operates within, and is constrained by, society. Some analysts go further. The suggestion from these is that the state is secondary to, and even derives from, society. We can dub such ideas, for want of a better term, society-centred approaches to the state. Below we will consider two related modes of analysis that come under the society-centred umbrella: sociological and neo-Marxist contributions to the state.

Sociological accounts of state development

We mentioned it in the previous chapter, but it is worth saying once more. Theories of the state have become less and less the preserve of outright political theorists or political scientists. Attempts to theorise have flourished throughout different social science disciplines and subdisciplines. One discipline that has been especially receptive to the state is sociology. Weber, Marx and even Durkheim: all had some residual interest in the state. Contemporary sociological figures, including Giddens, Beck and Habermas, have all written about the state to a greater or lesser extent.

More significantly, sociological concepts have featured and influenced modern state theory. For an interesting example of how sociological ideas came to shape academic understanding of the state, we can go back to the late 1950s and the work of the political systems theorist, David Easton. In his seminal work, *The Political System*, Easton attempts to reconcile the methodological individualism of behaviourism with the contention that real forces exist beyond the individual; his intention being to produce credible theoretical insights. To square this particular circle, Easton relied on the notion of an integrated social system, a concept informed by Parsonian structural functionalism. The Parsonian influence had implications for conceptualising the state. In fact, the concept of the state is eschewed for that of the political system. Easton (1996: 97) argues that the political system is 'an aspect of the whole social system'. So political institutions, which we might label the state, are firmly integrated with, and dependent on, various other societal arrangements and systems. These other systems can include social class, economic activities, and regional associations. From this perspective, it would be artificial to isolate the political system from other social relations, for 'social life is interdependent'. These observations about the political system serve as a useful segue into sociological analyses of the state that deal explicitly with the interface between state and society. As an illustrative example, we shall focus on Gianfranco Poggi's *The Development of the Modern State* (1978), very much a forgotten contribution to the socio-historical theorising of the state.

The early passages of Poggi's *The Development of the Modern State* contemplate David Easton's systems approach to politics. Echoing Easton's thoughts, the nature of the modern state can only be truly grasped when it is seen to be integrated with other *social systems*: 'the formation of the modern state parallels and complements various similar processes of institutional differentiation affecting, say, the economy, the family, and religion' (Poggi 1978: 13–14). So a fully autonomous and self-regulating state is out of the question. Whilst citing systems theory, Poggi does move some way from Easton's functionalist approach to the state. To begin with, he questions Easton's economistic view of politics. As well as this economic bias, this systems theory fails to identify the material and ideological origins of the modern state. The aporias of systems theory are addressed through a historically based sociological analysis of the modern state formation – a methodological modus operandi that was subsequently mimicked by other prominent thinkers in the field (see Mann 1993; Corrigan and Sayer 1985).

In Poggi's historical sociology of modern state development, what could be dubbed a society-centred account of the state is posited. To develop this societal approach, there is a historical categorisation of different types of state institutions. Four types of historical state institutions are identified: the feudal, absolutist, nineteenth-century constitutional and liberal democratic states. If we compare the nineteenth-century constitutional and modern democratic states, there is a distinct shift in the relationship between state and society. Under the constitutional state of the nineteenth century, state and society were two quite separate entities. Or rather, as Poggi notes, the state had few equals in terms of authority, power and resources, apart from other foreign states. The nineteenth-century state could govern and regulate itself without considering social interests and influences. Under these conditions, state and society were poles apart (Poggi 1978: 121). However, the dividing line between state and society became less evident over time. The closer interface between state and society has come about as a result of various internal and external machinations associated with the modern democratic state.

Historically, the civil sector in liberal democracies has forced society and the state closer than had been permitted by the nineteenth-century constitutional state model. There are specific forces at work in civil society. The civil momentum driving a closer interface between state and society was mainly economic in nature. What Poggi is referring to here is the growth of the capitalist economy. With capitalism there is the attendant rise of a powerful bourgeois class, the owners of capitalist production. The bourgeois class inevitably makes demands on, and requires concessions from, the liberal state. The end result is inevitable. The liberal state becomes less autonomous and self-regulatory and exists 'to favor and sustain through its acts of rule the class domination of the bourgeoisie over society as a whole' (Poggi 1978: 119). This relationship between capitalism and the liberal state is essentially Marxist in flavour. Poggi admits that Marxist accounts of the state may be convincing but they are partial. Marxist state theory underestimates the influence of non-economic forces and institutions – hence the conceptual limitations of this approach. As well as the pressures applied by external forces, there are other factors that exerted pressures on the state. The dividing line between state and society was also eroded by forces internal to the democratic state. For Poggi, the liberal state is a specialised political body responsible for producing and enforcing laws. It is a discrete and highly powerful bureaucratic entity in its own right. As a bureaucracy responsible for law-making, there are interest groups attached to the state who seek to extend its engagement throughout society (1978: 134–5). The momentum for state intervention is also located beyond the state as certain pressure groups may support rather than oppose the extension of state rule into new domains.

If state and society became increasingly tangled under democratic conditions, what are the repercussions for the state? There are quantitative consequences: the increased share of gross domestic product by the state; the growth in the number of state employees; and the proliferation of public agencies. Of greater interest are the qualitative changes resulting from the closer interface between state and society, particularly the effects on the legislative process and the standing of parliament. In terms of the qualitative shifts, there is a single, overwhelming message from Poggi. The greater societal engagement and responsibilities assumed by the state restricted the state's room for manoeuvre and undermined the authority of parliamentary institutions. As such, state action is characterised by crisis and *ad hoc* management, of muddling through rather than commanding and authoritatively steering policies (Poggi 1978: 145–6). For the modern state, there is much to be done but there are dwindling capabilities by which to meet such demands.

The sociological model of the state developed by Poggi makes use of different traditions to develop a society-centred theory of the state. As we have seen, it alludes to functionalist accounts of the state. This model also draws upon Marxist analysis, although, as we have seen, Poggi remains critical of Marxist theories. From these diverse traditions, what we get is a sociological account that underlines both the external and internal constraints on the state. It is notable that Poggi should refer to Marxist theory in making the case for society-centred analysis. For it was Marxist scholars who were responsible for generating considerable academic interest and debate in the state during the course of the 1970s. Marxist theorists were also responsible for reimagining the state as overrun by powerful factions and interest groups, a state that is not its own. The significant contribution of neo-Marxist analysis to contemporary state theory will be explored next.

The modern capitalist state and neo-Marxism

The prevailing orthodoxy in relation to the state within Marx's writings conforms to what can be described as a functionalist model. Here there is no separation between the business sector of civil society and government. The close relationship is both necessary and inevitable: those who own property are *de facto* the most powerful social group in society. This critical view of the state was established during the middle period of Marx's early career. In *The German Ideology* (1846), Marx and Engels argue that the state is used by the ruling class to assert its economic interests. The state also helps to create a ruling ideology, where the state's claim to represent communal interests veils the real struggles between different economic classes (Marx and Engels 1965: 45). But there are exceptions to this functionalist conception of the state as a bourgeois instrument (McLellan 1995: 210). These exceptions can be found in early works. In such writings, Marx expresses the opinion that the political realm does have an existence independent of capitalist control. We can also see this political approach in mid-period Marx; that is, in works produced after *The German Ideology* when Marx wrote about political events. The most categorical and interesting exploration of the state's relative autonomy comes in *The Eighteenth Brumaire of Louis Bonaparte* published in 1852 by the New York based *Die Revolution* (Held 1989: 34). For as Spencer

(1979) acknowledges, when Marx chronicled historical events, he unwittingly revised his orthodox view of the state as an epiphenomenon of the economy. Such unintentional, *ad hoc* revisionism comes into its own in *The Eighteenth Brumaire*, in which Marx examined the socio-political background to Louis Bonaparte's successful coup of December 1851. Marx noted how the state bureaucracy following the revolution of 1789 had become an instrument of the ruling class but under Napoleon 'the state seems to have made itself completely independent' (Marx and Engels 1977: 176).

Those authors who embraced the classical writings of Marx and Engels made the most telling contribution in the resurgence of state theory during the 1970s. For these neo-Marxist theorists, the state is pivotal to private capital and to the process of accumulating profit. In their analysis, they established a definite contemporary spin for society-centred approaches to the state. The myriad of neo-Marxist writings and theories on the state that have emerged during the course of the twentieth century can be divided, for heuristic purposes, into two separate theoretical sub-camps of neo-Marxism: proxy and contingency models of the state. These approaches, in effect, correspond to the economic and political interpretations of the state that exist within Marx's own writings (see Held 1989).

A proxy approach to the capitalist state

The proxy approach conforms to a mechanistic view of the state as an instrument of the capitalist class, a view developed by Marx and Engels in *The German Ideology*. An early neo-Marxist proponent of the proxy approach was Karl Kautsky, a leading scholar of the Second International during the early twentieth century. Kautsky was the father of 'state capitalism', a concept influenced by Bukharin's writings on the centralisation and concentration of capital (Callinicos 1990). The term 'state capitalism' was used by Kautsky to capture the close alliance between the capitalist and the administrative class of government, with the function of the latter being to oversee and run the state machine on behalf of the bourgeoisie. Kautsky's criticisms of the state are echoed by Lenin in *The State and Revolution* (written in 1917), although he did fall out with Kautsky. For Lenin, the state not only supports the capitalist class but also actively exploits wage labour through its repressive forces of the police and army. Capitalists achieve this control over political affairs by cultivating close links and alliances with the state. The prime conduit for these alliances is the executive bureaucracy of the state, rather than parliament. Lenin's analysis entails that the state is an epiphenomenon, a mere reflection of more fundamental economic laws and processes.

A latter-day elaboration of the Kautsky and Lenin state capitalist theme can be found in the writings of the late Marxist historian, Ralph Miliband. From Miliband's orthodox Marxist view, the political system in democratic societies is closely aligned with the ruling economic elite. As such, 'the state in these class societies is primarily and inevitably the guardian and protector of the economic interests which are dominant in them. Its "real" purpose and mission is to ensure their continued predominance, not to prevent it' (Miliband 1973: 237–8). This 'mission' is one shared and propounded by the political agents and civil servants in government. There is a close relationship between capitalist and civil servant, particularly as they often share the same socio-economic, educational and cultural backgrounds. Despite the close relationship, Miliband argued that there is a distinction between the actual operational control of the state machine and the exercise of ultimate control. In practice, this distinction means that the bourgeoisie, in the last instance, control the state for their own interests. But the day-to-day running of the state is carried out by the administrative apparatchiks of the governing class.

There subsequently appeared some interesting variants on the instrumental neo-Marxist approach to the state. A notable example is the work of James Petras (1977) on state capitalism in the Third World. Petras's analysis of development politics rests on the argument that state capitalism in the Third World can be attributed to market-fuelled imperialism and the intensification of class struggles in these developing countries. Past imperial exploitation impacted on the contemporary balance of these countries. As a result of imperialism, the landed and commercial bourgeoisie, orientated as they were to export production, gained favour and domestic dominance over the industrial bourgeoisie, who were focused on domestic production (Petras 1977: 11–14). Consequently, the state in Third World countries was dominated and used by the commercial and landed bourgeois classes in pursuit of their own interests (Dupuy and Truchil 1979: 5–6). The external nature of their activities meant that the commercial and landed bourgeoisie were ultimately subservient to international capitalism. The importance of international capitalism is highlighted by the fate of nationalist sentiment in state capitalist regimes of the Third World. As Petras notes, the state capitalist regimes of developing countries had to pay lip-service, initially, to radical nationalist pressures, especially with reference to economic policy. Such economic nationalism, in time, became muted as developing states were rendered subservient to the demands of international capitalism, which already had significant interests in the developing world (Petras 1977: 13). In effect, Third World states became satellites of a powerful, transnational capitalist elite. The state as 'play thing' of the capitalist class had a powerful resonance amongst state theorists during the 1970s. This instrumental appeal to the state had its detractors. Most prominently, these critics were to be found amongst fellow Marxist theorists.

A contingency approach to the capitalist state

Those neo-Marxist theories of the political that fall under the contingency approach eschew a class-dominated conception of the state. Amongst those espousing a contingency position are those postwar neo-Marxist theorists who embraced the cultural brand of Marxism found in Antonio Gramsci's writings. Gramsci's ideas ran against the grain of the crude materialism that characterised early twentieth-century Marxism. Instead of economic reductionism, Gramsci emphasised the importance of purposeful action and ideas in what he termed his 'philosophy of praxis'. Influenced by the Hegelian philosophy of Benedetto Croce and Marx's early philosophical works, he examined the contribution of ideology and culture to bourgeois domination. Capitalist rule also relies on subtle processes, working through ideas, language and moral codes, so that the masses passively comply with their own domination and exploitation (Vincent 1987: 167–8). Integral to this elusive and intricate form of domination is the state. The Gramscian perspective would disagree with the assertion that the state is colonised by, or under the direct control of, the capitalist class as it holds a relative independence from the economy. Through such independence, the state is better able to perpetuate the dominant ideology of capitalism (Gramsci 1982: 244). Thus the state is less a set of materially based institutions than a 'complex of practical and theoretical activities' through which the capitalist class manages to convince those it rules that the capitalist system is normal and legitimate.

By the 1960s and 1970s, Gramsci's thought on domination and the state was responsible for helping to redefine academic thought on the state. At the forefront of this neo-Gramscian interpretation of the state there is the towering contribution made by Nicos Poulantzas. The writings of and ideas developed by Poulantzas are considered by some commentators to be the single most important postwar Marxist analysis of the state (Jessop 1982). In positing a theory of the state, his philosophical antecedents were principally Gramsci and the French sociologist, Louis Althusser. From Althusserian structuralism, he appropriated the idea that ideological and political structures are distinct from economic forces. From Gramscian sociology, he draws upon the state's contribution to hegemonic domination: the way in which capitalist domination over the proletariat is achieved through both coercion and also, most importantly, through cultivating the active consent of those very same subaltern classes (Jessop 1982: 155).

This more nuanced and less economically deterministic brand of Marxian state theory was developed by Poulantzas in a series of texts, chief of which is *Political Power and Social Classes*, first published in 1968. In this account, the role of the capitalist state is to protect the ruling class from self-destruction. The economic elite finds itself in peril because of intense competition within the free market economy. To avert this market-induced apocalypse, the state unifies the actors involved in capitalism and disorganises the working classes, for the proletarian class is a threat to capitalist domination due its sheer size. The state manages to both unite and divide the said social factions through political and ideological practices: the various institutions of the state – including a highly centralised bureaucracy – provide a source of cohesion between different levels of society (Ponlantzas 1973: 44–5). The state's maintenance of capitalist cohesion and hegemony is only possible if it retains autonomy from the very class interests it sets out to protect. The extent of state autonomy is shaped and determined by the contradictions and power struggles that are part and parcel of the political system under capitalism. The theme of political struggle is pursued in later works, especially *State, Power, Socialism* (1978). In this study, Poulantzas observes how 'popular struggles are inscribed in the state' and have long-range effects on the state (1978: 141, 159). These struggles encompass the ruling bloc and the dominated groups. Hence, both capitalist forces as well as the popular working masses help to configure the state apparatus. As such, even the subordinate working class has a modicum of influence over the state.

What we have in Poulantzas's theoretical oeuvre on the state is an attempt to produce a model that takes into account historic variation and strategic choices but which acknowledges the class bias of the modern state. However, this endeavour to develop a flexible Marxist analysis ultimately failed to reconcile the class determinacy of Marxism with a socially contingent appreciation of the state (Pierson 1996: 79). For instance, in *State, Power, Socialism* he concedes that even if state policies come to favour the subjugated masses, the political sphere will in time 're-establish the relationship of forces in favour of the bourgeoisie, sometimes in a new form' (Poulantzas 1978: 143). In other words, subaltern classes may eek out concessions and gain political representation, but these advances ultimately contribute to their subordination.

The British social and political theorist, Bob Jessop, attempted over a number of years to iron out the deterministic shortcomings of Poulantzas's theory. In so doing, he has more than any other contemporary thinker developed and extended Poulantzas's work, ensuring the continued relevance of this major neo-Marxist figure long after his premature death in 1978. Such influence is evident in Jessop's strategic relation approach to the state. The strategic relational approach is rooted in Marxist theory but distances itself from many of the analytical excesses associated with orthodox Marxism, and to a certain extent with Poulantzas's own version of Marxism. The strategic element refers to the actions of individuals, who, to an extent, can operate free from the constraints of institutional and social structures. As such, individual action can shape the state in a number of different directions. The relational element refers to how the state is determined by the balance of forces between capital and labour. But the state form is also influenced – and this is a point ignored by Poulantzas – by past and present strategies (Jessop 1990: 269).

There is in the strategic relational model clear theoretical blue water between the economic determinism of orthodox Marxism and Poulantzas's insistence that state independence from the capitalist economy is relative. In dealing with the whole issue of economic determinism, Jessop argues that there exists a structural coupling between the political and economic dimensions. Jessop (2002: 3) equates the state and the economy without attributing a causal priority to either dimension. These complex arrangements have been conceptualised through a progressive synthesis of Marxist theory with a diverse range of new theorising. Initially this involved an appropriation of regulation theory and latterly, in Jessop's work, it has centred on discourse analysis and theories of self-organising systems (see Smith 2000: 159–60). In Jessop's refinement of Poulantzas's ideas, the state remains a system that has properties distinct from those of the capitalist economy.

The fact that figures such as Poulantzas and Jessop were unwilling to write off the state suggests there was still some mileage in a state-centred analysis, even at the height of the neo-Marxist revival of the 1970s. Moreover, as we shall discover in the next section, there was an emerging movement amongst state theorists in the 1980s which attempted to bring about a more decisive break with society-centred conceptions of the state.

The autonomous state, or 'bringing the state back in'

There followed a period of intellectual disillusionment, manifested in a backlash against, and a disavowal of, Marxist thought and practice. The crisis in Marxism that set in during the mid-1970s gave way to a revival in Weberian-inspired sociology amongst English-speaking social theorists (Callinicos 1999: 261–3). The Weberian contribution to political analysis is premised upon the independent bureaucratic authority of the state and its monopoly control over the means of coercion. Echoes of Weberian analysis were noticeable in academic efforts to invigorate the concept of the state during the late 1970s and early 1980s. This revived interest in the state was particularly associated with American political and social scientists – Theda Skocpol, Peter Evans and David Laitin, amongst others. These authors found common cause in seeking to 'bring the state back in'. This appellation captures the idea of the state as an independent institution, a purposeful policy actor and irreducible to economic processes. Within this American-led academic lobby for the significance of political institutions, there appeared two schools of thought (Mitchell 1991). The first school retreats into a subjective definition of the state: as a product of individual actions and intentions – or what is termed decision-making and policy-making. For the second school, the quintessence of the state can be found in organisations and administrative structures. Advocates of this school also acknowledge the significance of societal forces, of external pressures exerted on government. But these are secondary to the purposive actions of the state. If anything, the influence of the external environment is mediated by the political system. In this section each school is detailed in turn.

The state and purposeful actors

The case for a state-centred analysis rests fundamentally on narrowing the parameters of what actually constitutes the state. From this perspective, extraneous forces that potentially interfere with state autonomy – namely, class interests and wider social considerations – should be excluded from any attempt to theorise the state. This very point was forcefully reiterated by Stephen Krasner. As a formative contributor to the renaissance of the state amongst American political scientists, Krasner insisted on a basic distinction between state and society. This difference is premised on a fundamental separation between the state as the subjective realm, sustained by individual agency, and society as an objective order. Krasner (1978: 10) observes: 'it is useful to conceive of a state as a set of roles and institutions having peculiar drives, compulsions, and aims of their own that are separate and distinct from the interests of any particular societal group'. What is being implied here is specific interpretation of the society–state dichotomy, which is further elaborated upon. Although the needs of society and the state are intertwined, it would be a mistake to assume, *vis-à-vis* Marxism, that the state represents the interests of society or powerful social factions. Rather the state is an autonomous actor, albeit one that faces domestic and international constraints.

To explore and develop this autonomous approach to the state Krasner focuses on American foreign policy and raw material investment between the early twentieth century and the 1960s. In terms of foreign policy, the key actors are the president and the secretary of state, both of whom enjoy a certain level of insulation from societal pressures. This personalised view of foreign policy befits an autonomous and subjective conception of the state. To underline the subjective basis of America's international strategy, Krasner draws the analogy between foreign policy and psychological theory. Drawing on Maslow's hierarchical model of motivation, state foreign policy is akin to an individual who after satisfying basic physical needs looks to fulfil a series of ever more metaphysical psychological needs: 'so hegemonic states can indulge in ideological foreign policies because their core objectives are not in jeopardy' (Krasner 1978: 342). The central protagonists in American foreign policy, by adhering to ideological over pragmatic objectives, weakened the position of the USA, both domestically and internationally. Invariably, countries that follow an ideological foreign policy become imperialist, and imperialists become embroiled in all sorts of perilous struggles. Krasner argues that America's involvement in the Vietnam war is a case in point.

The adoption of a micro-level analysis to flesh out a politically centred analysis of the state is forcefully demonstrated by Eric Nordlinger. The state, unlike society, argues Nordlinger, is a personal entity that behaves like a purposeful actor. The state is simply the aggregate of decisions made by individual officials and politicians: 'The state is made up of, and limited to, those individuals who are endowed with societywide decision-making powers' (Nordlinger 1987: 362). As such, state autonomy can be explained in behavioural or subjective terms as a function of the beliefs and perceptions of officials. State officials, though, are still exposed to societal pressures that are beyond control. And the extent to which state officials are constrained by society depends on their malleability, insulation, resilience and vulnerability in relation to societal forces (Nordlinger 1987: 373–84).

The autonomy enjoyed by state officials is far from homogeneous or constant. Autonomy can vary between states. Variation in state autonomy is shaped by four structural features: the state's boundedness, differentiation, cohesion, and policy capacities. But these features, argues Nordlinger (1978: 384), only have a marginal impact upon the subjective variables of the state. For instance, a vulnerable state will avoid acting on decisions because it perceives itself as lacking the wherewithal to implement policies effectively. This consideration of state vulnerability is less an examination of how society shapes or delimits the options available to state officials than a reconfirmation of how individual perceptions and ideas form the basis of state action. In this deft piece of thinking, Nordlinger transforms something that might impinge on the state (societal pressures) into factors that are part of the cognitive processes involved in decision-making.

The state may be an autonomous and subjective actor, but it would also be difficult to completely ignore society-centred explanations of the state. (We have already seen this in the above paragraph.) So Nordlinger argues that taking the state seriously means bringing societal and subjective accounts of the state together. Subjective variables allow us to understand the behavioural autonomy of the state. But Nordlinger speculates that these same variables could also be the 'theoretical beachhead' from which to identify those social forces that impact on state autonomy. Is Nordlinger really contemplating a society-centred explanation? Although society forms a notable context for state action, society-oriented accounts often lead back to the state. What may seem like impositions and encroachments can in fact enhance the independence and authority of the state (Nordlinger 1987: 388). Representative monopoly bodies like employer or professional associations, such as the British Medical Council, can impress demands on the state. By the same token, they also provide institutional mechanisms for micromanaging the implementation of state policies. This is a case of state autonomy will out.

Skocpol and the political organisation of the state

A noteworthy attempt to extend the statist thesis was undertaken by the sociologist, Theda Skocpol. But this statist analysis rejects the psychologism associated with Nordlinger and Krasner. Skocpol adopts an 'organisational' and 'realist' perspective on the state. From this perspective, there is a refusal to treat the state as the product of economic forces or class relations. Rather the state is a political organisation that controls territories and communities of people – a view which is the theoretical progeny of Weberian sociology (Skocpol 1979: 31–2). For Skocpol, the state operates in a social context, where non-state actors potentially engage in the policy process. Despite this greater openness to social forces, Skocpol makes a case for state autonomy based on a basic institutional distinction. This is a basic division between fundamental state organisations (administrative and coercive agencies), where power and authority are located, and political systems where non-state interests seek influence. By separating state organisations from political systems, the unique organisational characteristics of the state are upheld, hence protecting the state from over-socialised accounts (Held 1989: 47).

The state-centred thesis developed by Skocpol is worked out through a series of historical case studies of revolutionary events. *States and Social Revolutions* (1979) compares pre-revolutionary society and post-revolutionary state-building in Russia (from 1917 until the 1930s), France (1787) and China (from 1911 until the 1960s). To comprehend these political upheavals, Skocpol eschews social explanations, which attribute revolutions to social and economic interests outside of the state. She also avoids explanations that attribute revolutions to the actions and motives of political leaders. Whilst taking into account class and interstate relations, Skocpol insists that the state organisation should be integral to the aetiology of revolutions.

Historically, the social conditions that produced revolutions in France, Russia and China were, according to Skocpol, the outcome of policies deliberately pursued by states, or rather autocratic-imperial states. In all three case histories, revolutions were precipitated by the way despotic leaders used their monopoly powers to amass material resources for military campaigns and state-controlled economic initiatives. One example of this is the revolutionary collapse of France in the late eighteenth century, an event attributed to the French state's involvement in expensive colonial and market-led wars. In detailing the reasons for French involvement in these wars, there is little mention of the state's organisational links with colonial companies or other states. This involvement is explained primarily by recourse to the desire of the French monarchy to protect France's honour and status abroad (Skocpol 1979: 60). Although the case example of the French revolution stresses the autonomy of the state, such independence was subject to external constraints. For instance, in pursuing military campaigns and state-sponsored economic projects, an autocratic-imperial state such as pre-revolutionary France invariably faced political and social obstructions. Significant opposition came in the guise of the landed classes. The imposition exerted by a powerful agrarian elite also applied to the Russian and Chinese cases. In particular, 'conflicts of interest between monarchs and the landed upper classes … could have the unintended effect of destroying the administrative and military integrity of the imperial state itself' (Skocpol 1979: 49). The implication of this statement is clear: whilst Skocpol is insistent that the state organisation remains distinct from society, this distinction is difficult to maintain in practice (Mitchell 1991: 87).

Similar tensions between state-centred and society-centred explanations persist in the second half of *States and Social Revolutions*. In this part of the study, Skocpol looks at how and why highly centralised and authoritative post-revolutionary states emerged. The proffered explanation for the rise of these strong states again prioritises the independent actions of state actors, namely, the penchant of post-revolutionary political leaders for state-building. But once again, the examples of state-building garnered from the three case studies underline that broader socio-economic factors should be part of any explanation. As Skocpol (1979: 170–1) observes, socio-economic conditions 'create specific possibilities and impossibilities within which revolutionaries must operate as they try to consolidate the new regime'. This realisation that there are limits to state autonomy is alluded to by Skocpol in later writings. An example is her recent study of American social policy under successive Clinton administrations. She bemoans the inability of state-led initiatives to solve the widening socio-economic inequalities in the 1990s. She steers clear of blaming these social policy failures exclusively on deficiencies within the state, as would be expected from theorists who believe in the autonomy of democratic processes and political systems (Skocpol 2000: 7). Rather, progressives in the Clinton governments were forced to deal with the intractable problems of budget deficits and reactionary business opposition to progressive social initiatives.

The overview contained in this section underlines some important lessons about state theory. Our analysis shows how the drawing of boundaries between state and society in the name of creating a theory that privileges the autonomy of the former is potentially difficult to sustain. As we shall discover in subsequent chapters, there have been efforts to completely redefine the relationship between state and society.

Contemporary state theory: the story so far and to come …

Our story in this chapter began in the 1950s when modern theorisation of the state took off. Such contemporary theorising of the state operated within theoretical parameters established by classical social and political thought. Corporatism, pluralism, Gramscian analysis, neo-elite theory, and theories of state autonomy: these various positions were informed by the early classical political thought of such figures as Locke, Hobbes and the later, nineteenth-century social thought of Marx and Weber, amongst others. The customary practice has been for modern state theory to draw upon a classical intellectual lineage. In recent years, however, a growing number of analysts have embraced alternative philosophical and intellectual precepts in theorising the state. In drawing upon these alternative influences, the result has been the impromptu rise of a new wave of state theory. The 'new wave' state theories are characteristically fragmented and diverse. However, they are very much united by the task of attacking the shibboleths and orthodoxies of established approaches to the state. Prominent in this new wave of state theory is poststructuralist-influenced analysis led by the likes of Foucault. But there are other theoretical movements and disciplinary innovations that have contributed towards the redefinition of state theory. As we shall examine in the subsequent chapters, the assortment of theoretical approaches that have emerged from governance and systems perspectives, feminist theory, cultural analysis and globalisation debates have contributed to this alternative state canon.

CHAPTER 2

THE POSTSTRUCTURAL STATE

Introduction

The founding fathers of modern social and political thought have lost their lustre for a growing band of contemporary social and political thinkers. Here, the great thinkers of the nineteenth century – Marx, Weber and Durkheim – have been overlooked in favour of Nietzsche, Bakhtin and Saussure, amongst others; these philosophical figures for much of the twentieth century remained on the fringes. The key development responsible for this shift in tastes has been the rise of poststructuralism. The radical shift in ideas brought about by the emergence of poststructuralism has been captured by bold declarations, often prefaced by the word 'death': 'the death of the subject', 'the death of history', 'the death of metanarrative' or, curiously, 'the death of Marx'. Since the late 1970s the intellectual Zeitgeist has been a poststructural one, and by the 1990s its ideas and practitioners were firmly ensconced in prestigious academic institutions, especially in the English-speaking world. Poststructuralism came to influence a diverse range of academic disciplines, including architecture, literary criticism, philosophy, and social and political theory. Even the traditional field of state theory was not immune from the poststructural effect. Indeed, this whole book testifies to way new thinking in state theory was in part down to the impact of thinkers influenced by various strands of poststructuralism. This chapter will specifically trace how poststructuralism was brought to bear on state theory through the work of the celebrated French philosopher, Michel Foucault.

Since his death in 1984, Michel Foucault has become an influential and ubiquitous figure in contemporary social thought. As a self-proclaimed historian of systems of thought, his work examined areas often neglected by mainstream historians. This celebrated oeuvre is as capacious as it is voluminous, covering such areas as madness and asylums, the medical clinic, prisons and sexuality. He wrote from what for historians proved to be an unconventional perspective and adopted a distinct philosophical approach, influenced by the philosophy of Friedrich Nietzsche. These works were responsible for popularising poststructuralist themes in the social sciences. Although he would reject the poststructuralist label, there was a distinct poststructuralist undercurrent to his work: Foucault was an ardent critic of liberal humanism, the modernist project and the metatheorising associated with classical thinkers such as Marx.

Foucault's later writings applied his poststructural concerns, or what is termed the 'genealogical approach', to the mainstream academic themes of politics and the state. In what is typical of his iconoclastic style, the main rationale of these writings was to eradicate the state from political and social theory. This was an act Foucault likened to 'beheading the king'. As part of this endeavour, Foucault investigated the 'rationality of government' or, to use the neologism he devised to capture this exercise, governmentality. Although his writings on the state do not form part of the core Foucault experience, his ideas about governmentality are inextricably linked to his theory of power. This chapter will show how Foucauldian governmentality looked to broaden political theory to include a variety of practices and ideas that do not necessarily originate in the state. The chapter will also explore how Foucault's poststructural approach to the state and power attracted the interest of contemporary thinkers. Within social science research, especially sociology, a growing band of writers have extended Foucault's original work on governmentality.

Before dedicating ourselves to Foucault's position on the state, it would be worth reflecting on the development of poststructuralism from the earlier works of structuralist thinkers. This will require a diversion into the historical development of modern philosophical inquiry, and into the internecine squabbles of postwar French academe. A background overview of structuralism and the evolution of poststructuralism will provide us with a philosophical context by which to understand Foucault's contribution to state theory.

A structural diversion, or the rise of structural man

Structuralism emerged as a counterforce against existential philosophy, which was the dominant philosophical tradition in France for much of the 1940s and 1950s. As the pre-eminent philosophical approach in this period, it drew upon the classical phenomenology of Husserl and Heidegger to emphasise the importance of subjectivity in shaping existence (Schrift 1995: 3). Existential thinkers such as Sartre and Merleau-Ponty gave primacy to the individual as a purposeful and constituting actor. One of the first major French intellectual figures to break rank with, and challenge the dominant orthodoxy of, existentialism was the French anthropologist, Claude Lévi-Strauss. Rising to prominence as one of France's leading intellectuals in the late 1950s, Lévi-Strauss became an ardent critic of existential philosophy, which is berated as 'shop girl metaphysics'. Instead of a philosophy where human freedom is valorised, the underlying intention of Lévi-Strauss's structural anthropology was to dissolve the idea of the purposeful individual. He looked to how human action is shaped by universal mental constructs and structures. In this respect, Lévi-Strauss owed a great debt to the linguistic theory of Ferdinand de Saussure. From a Saussurean perspective, language is treated as a system of signs, and of rules and conventions on how these signs interrelate. So the emphasis is on the objective structure of language, independent of purposeful action, rather than on how people creatively employ language. Structuralism appealed to practitioners outside of the linguistic field, with Lévi-Strauss using Saussurean insights to study the culture of tribal societies. Culture, for Lévi-Strauss, is a system of communication that constrains more than it allows for the creative free expression of individuals.

The structural moment in French academe in the 1960s proved hugely significant. Structuralism began to replace existentialism as the pre-eminent intellectual force in France. But it also contributed to the rehabilitation of social science disciplines at the expense of philosophy. Philosophy had dominated the elite academic establishments of postwar France, but under the aegis of Lévi-Strauss's *anthropologie*, the social sciences came to the fore again. The importance attached to the social sciences was a politically sensitive matter in France due to their Anglo-American connotations (Bourdieu 1988: xx–xxi). Nevertheless, structuralism, for a time, usurped the dominance of philosophy. Such was the standing of structuralism that it had an influence on thinkers who, due to their political and theoretical predilections, would routinely be averse to such a position (the neo-Marxism of Louis Althusser, for instance). Structuralism would also have a profound and lifelong influence on emerging intellectuals during the early 1960s; figures who would eventually form the vanguard of French intellectual life after the structuralist moment – namely, Michel Foucault, Jacques Derrida and Gilles Deleuze. For this nascent group of pioneering thinkers, the main attraction of structuralism was the focus on language and, more broadly, culture. They were also attracted by structuralism's take on human existence, specifically the notion of the decentred subject. This is the idea that self-identity is formed out of a dispersed system of signification rather than from individual consciousness or purposeful action.

There were key aspects of structuralism, however, which the emerging cadre of philosophers repudiated. Their challenge was prompted by what they perceived to be a number of contradictions and limitations inherent in structuralism, a challenge which opened on analytical space for poststructural philosophy. One concern was the idea of structure derived by Lévi-Strauss and others from Saussure's linguistic theory. Such thinkers conceived of structure as closed, but within this delimited structure the process of signification was seen to produce an infinite range of possibilities. The dual nature of language was trumpeted by Saussure himself. Within the Saussurean scheme of things emphasis is placed on linguistic systems and structures rather than on how individuals draw on language. The users of language, nevertheless, still get a look-in with Saussure's formative structuralism. His ontology 'still retains a concept of active agency' (Tudor 1999: 63). This relationship between the stability of structure and the infinite possibilities of language was questioned particularly by the deconstructionist Jacques Derrida. Instead of attempting to reconcile the apparent contradiction between the structure and free use of language, Derrida rejected the notion of a stable, unchanging structure, preferring a decentred conception of structure. This is all down to signification, a process based on the infinite play between signifier (mark or sound) and signified (the concept or idea). The signification process is impossible to supplant. And neither is it possible to become detached from its generation of opposites; for everything depends upon and is mediated through language (Callinicos 1999: 275). The primacy given to language is a moment when, according to Derrida, there is a collapse of the transcendental signified or the possibility of a centre or central point of origin. As such, everything becomes ambiguous, constantly shifting and unstable, because everything is mediated through discourse or text.

For the generation of thinkers who followed Lévi-Strauss – the *post*structuralists – structuralism suffered from additional problems. The difficulties, this time, were of a disciplinary nature. Their chief point of contention was the lack of historicity inherent in the synchronic analyses of structuralist authors. There were also concerns over the privileging of the human and social sciences over philosophical inquiry. With reference to the latter point, Bourdieu (1988) notes in *Homo Academicus* how philosophy declined in French academia following the structural turn. In attempting to revive philosophical inquiry as well as historical discourse, those key philosophical successors of structuralism were influenced to a large extent by the nineteenth-century German philosophy of Friedrich Nietzsche.

The poststructuralist embrace of Nietzsche was made possible, *inter alia*, by the structuralist appropriation of Marx and Freud. There was also Heidegger's recovery of Nietzsche, as evinced by a two-volume text published in 1961 (Schrift 1995: 4). The appeal of Nietzsche for the new generation of French intellectuals was also precipitated by the politics surrounding the philosophical establishment in France. The traditional philosophical elite had overlooked Nietzsche. Instead of this idiosyncratic thinker, they preferred the classical thought of Descartes, Kant, Hegel and Husserl (see Foucault 1990: 33). As such, the embrace of Nietzsche by a younger generation of philosophers enabled them to keep a political and theoretical distance from the philosophical high priests of France's most prestigious seat of learning, the Sorbonne. These high priests, in turn treated the up-and-coming generation of French philosophers, represented by the likes of Foucault, Derrida and Deleuze, 'like religious heretics' (Bourdieu 1988: xix). This meant that professionally they were given few of the privileges accorded to senior French scholars. Because of their pariah status, this new generation of philosophers established links with the avant-garde journals, the media and American academe (Bourdieu 1988: xix). By developing these alternative networks, they were able to gain a celebrity status as public intellectuals of repute not only in their native France but also internationally.

The appeal of Nietzsche had its theoretical repercussions. Nietzsche allowed poststructuralist thinkers to reconcile the structural dissolution of the subject with questions concerning agency and historical change and comparison. In developing these questions, these analysts rejected existential considerations of the purposeful subject whilst not ignoring the notion of agency completely. Here agency is seen to operate in a complex network of dispersed power relations that intersect with knowledge and discourse, socio-historical forces and regulatory practices (Schrift 1995: 6). These philosophical concerns, when applied to the macro level of social or institutional life, question the existence of unified or centralised social entities. Instead of unity and centrality, the preference is for the fragmentation and the decentring of social life. Such ideas would help to redefine, as will be made clear, the state and political power. A key figure in this poststructural redefinition of state power was Michel Foucault.

Foucault and power: an evolving theory

Foucault's contribution to state theory grew out of his theoretical contribution to the subject of power. Power is a constant theme throughout Foucault's work. Such a preoccupation was in part due to the pursuit of a critical agenda contra Marxism and what he termed its sovereign conception of power – that is, the presumption that power is a centralised force, used intentionally to oppress and proscribe. The theme of power was also vehicle for pursuing his other philosophical crusade: that of exposing the taken-for-granted assumption which equates post-Enlightenment society with human progress and freedom. Power operates in a manner which is not readily conscious, it proves highly diffuse and progressively delimits through the very humane practices, and freely pursued activities, that underpin Western democracies. And it is Foucault's developing theory of power that eventually led to an interest in the state and the exercise of political power.

In Foucault's writings, this reconceptualisation of a subject that has been at the heart of the human sciences – power – was inextricably bound with the development of his own thought. As such, his treatment of power underwent a number of distinct shifts. The approach to power utilised in the study of the psychiatric profession in *Madness and Civilization* (1961) was one that would be subsequently rejected in later writings. *Madness and Civilization* examined how modern psychiatric institutions and practices were responsible for excluding those deemed mentally ill from mainstream society: they were both physically removed into closed institutions and denied an independent voice by a medical profession which sought to control the diagnosis and treatment of their condition (Foucault 1967). Here, Foucault by his own admission conceived of power as a purely repressive force used to render silent, interdict and ostracise oppressed minorities such as the mad (Foucault 1980b: 184).

Following *Madness and Civilization*, Foucault distances himself from the repressive approach to power. A new formula emerges – one that conceives power as more intricate, enabling and unpredictable. His little-mentioned analysis of transgression makes the point that the experience of contesting repression in social relations is not the preserve of oppressed minorities, such as the mentally ill. Rather this transgressive experience is more ubiquitous and diffuse as it is located in language and thought (McNay 1994). His subsequent dalliance with structuralism, in Foucault's so-called archaeological period, points to another milestone in the progress of his thought on power. In the structuralist-inspired *The Order of Things* (1966), Foucault's rejection of a monolithic conception of power is signalled in his approach to discourse and language, which are regarded as diffuse (McNay 1994). Discourse is seen as independent of centres of power, which forms a 'dense and consistent historical reality' that are part of 'the unspoken habits of thought' (Foucault 1989: 297).

By the mid-1970s, Foucault's thought had moved on from the archaeological and into the genealogical phase. It was here that he began to tackle the matter of power more systematically, constructing a profound critique of Marxist theory for which power is centrally located and the preserve of elite ruling groups. In his most celebrated work of this period, *Discipline and Punish* (1975), a microphysics of power is advanced. The central theme of *Discipline and Punish* is how penal systems in Western societies underwent a dramatic transformation between the mid-eighteenth and early nineteenthy centuries (Foucault 1977). The form of punishment meted out to criminals changed from one dominated by public executions and torture to one where a system of incarceration prevailed based around 24/7 surveillance – the Panopticon. The transformation of punishment was symptomatic of a new type of power – disciplinary power – emerging in the fledgling modern society of the nineteenth century. The modern form of power relied on the surveillance of individuals, the generation of knowledge and discipline and regulation of bodily movements. This form of power proved essential to the emergence and maintenance of capitalism and the nation state. Indeed, Foucault argues in *Discipline and Punish* that there is a carceral continuum. There is a carceral texture running through all manner of social institutions, from the military barracks to the factory floor. Power is conceived as a heterogeneous force, penetrating subjective as well as structural aspects of social organisation, being constructive and elusive. So just as the incarcerated prisoner is subject to 24-hour surveillance and control, modern power disciplines and regulates the minutiae of existence, is all-knowing, is everywhere in society.

Foucault's historical analysis of the penal system focuses on the operation of disciplinary techniques. The onus is on how power dominates, how it totalises in social relations. The proliferation of disciplinary methods, which are at once punitive and intrusive, produces docile bodies incapable of resistance. The notion of disciplinary bio-power, subsequently elaborated in the first volume of *The History of Sexuality* (Foucault 1978), individualises as well as disciplines in that it seeks to maximise efficiency from the human body. Just as the Panopticon disciplines, so the confessional is central to the individualising force of bio-power. The ancient Christian confessional has been embraced and used in all types of professional discourses (medicine, psychiatry, social work) to form regimes of truth that categorise individuals as either normal or deviant. In an interview, Foucault conceded that his explorations of bio-power ultimately concentrate on the 'objectivising of the subject' whereby the individual becomes a docile object. Relations of power in this respect are insidious: 'power relations can materially penetrate the body in depth, without depending even on the mediation of the subjects own representations' (Foucault 1980b: 186). As Brenner (1994: 702) explains, this view of power is socially problematic: it fails to explain how centres of domination are created, reproduced, resisted and transformed by diverse forms of individual and collective action.

In the later phases of his oeuvre, Foucault seemed to recognise these problems. Indeed, Foucault addresses these self-identified shortcomings in his studies of ethics and practices of the self in posthumous volumes of the *The History of Sexuality*. In these volumes, he attempted to rise above the idea that individuals are merely pliable objects of power relations; for power is also about 'the way a human being turns him − or herself − into a subject' (Foucault 1982: 208). The subjective side of power is contingent upon freedom of choice and autonomy of the individual. Hence, social order and regulation are not achieved simply through discipline − the corporeal impunities of power. For power to be effective, it requires self-regulation and self-mastery by the individual. The ability of individuals to shape their subjective life is compatible with the 'manifold relations of power' that permeate the social body. Foucault's study of ethics and the self in these subsequent volumes on the history of sexuality also conceive of the possibility of resistance in the promotion of 'new forms of subjectivity through the refusal of this kind of individuality which has been imposed on us for several centuries' (Foucault 1982: 216). That said, even critical friends of Foucault question whether these later volumes really do justice to human agency. For McNay, Foucauldian references in the later volumes of *The History of Sexuality* to practices of existence may show a greater willingness to recognise the autonomous and creative elements of human agency, but such concerns are 'asserted rather than elaborated in detail' (2000: 9). However, his study of power and its relationship to subjectivity covered a broader range of analytical interests.

Foucault explored the subjective nature of power in areas other than the history of sexuality. The fields of political authority and government were also vehicles by which to understand how power works through individual agency. And the key concept in this phase of Foucault's theorisation of power was that of governmentality. The Foucauldian notion of governmentality, argues Dean (1999: 13), 'provides a language and a framework for thinking about the link between questions of government, authority and politics, and questions of identity, self and person'. And it is in his pronouncements on governmentality that we get the semblance of a Foucauldian theory of the state and politics.

Politics, governmentality and the state in Foucault's thought

Can Foucault be regarded as a political theorist? Allen (1998: 164) acknowledges that politics had little prominence in Foucault's early writing career. There are critics who question the suitability of Foucault's ideas for an understanding of the political. Those on the left note that Foucault's assertion about the ubiquitous nature of power is bereft of any theory of resistance (Poulantzas 1978: 149). Similar points were raised by Habermas (1994: 95–6) in an ongoing debate with Foucault during the late 1970s. Habermas goes further by arguing that such is Foucault's theory of power that critique is another form of power and as such undermines itself. Feminist authors, such as Grimshaw (1993: 53–4), note that the usefulness of Foucault's views on the construction of subjects for a political critique of patriarchy is tempered by his undertheorisation of resistance.

Certainly questions have been raised against Foucault's suitability as a political thinker. But these concerns have failed to prevent a growing number of political theorists from treating Foucault as one of their own (Bevir 1999: 351). In terms of a Foucauldian political theory, a nascent version came to the fore with *Discipline and Punish*, a book in which Foucault begins to deal more explicitly with the regulatory forces of industrial society. In an interview debate with Noam Chomsky, Foucault notes that '[t]he essence of our life consists, after all, of the political functioning of the society in which we find ourselves' (Foucault and Chomsky 1997: 128). Of course Foucault has been embraced by those whose take on political theory is some way from the mainstream.

Foucault's approach to politics is far removed from orthodox themes of government institutions or the practices of the state. Foucault emphasised the micropolitical – the often taken-for-granted, the ordinary and hidden practices that make up political power (Arac 1986: xi). Simons (1995: 102–3) notes how studies on the self and ancient ethics underlined the importance of identity and culture to new social movements and to contemporary conflicts. Connolly (1993) traces the value of Foucault's work on identity for radical liberal democracy, pointing to the tension between individuals as purposeful agents and as subjects of domination. The importance of Foucault to identity politics has not been lost on feminist authors (McNay 1992) and analysts interested in race (Malik 1996). European thinkers and philosophers have been apt to read Foucault as a political theorist. There is Dario Melossi's work on social control and the state. In *The State of Social Control* (1990), Melossi draws in part on Foucault's key theoretical work on power – *Discipline and Punish* and the first volume of *The History of Sexuality*. These works are used to understand how social control operates and works primarily through the state. Another European thinker who has employed Foucault as a political theorist is the Italian philosopher, Giorgio Agamben. In *Means Without End* (2000), he embraces Foucault's notion of bio-power, which views power relations as carefully interwoven into, and dispersed throughout, society. For Agamben, there is now little distinction to be made between domestic life (*zoe*) and political life (*bios*). Hence the private biological body is now indistinguishable from the body politic. With *Homo Sacer* (1998), Agamben's Foucauldian-inspired philosophical inquiry reaches the pessimistic conclusion that the liberal state, although recognising rights and liberties, simply exerts sovereign power over life itself. For Agamben, there is an inner solidarity between democracy and totalitarianism. These varied writings have attempted to identify the political relevance of Foucault's major published works. This is a valid exercise and shows the breadth and significance of these studies. The relevance of Foucault to political theory is not just confined to his main works.

Crucially, Foucault set out a distinct and explicit approach to politics and government in discussions on governmentality during the latter part of his career. Much of Foucault's thought on governmentality and the state is not set out in formal writing but is published in lectures and interviews. These lectures and interviews on governmentality echo Foucault's views concerning the operation of political power in society (McNay 1994: 117). Let us now turn to what Foucault had to say about governmentality and, by implication, the state. As already mentioned, much of this exposition is based on fragments of interviews and lectures.

Researching governmental rationality

In 1970, Michel Foucault was appointed to a specially created professorial chair in the History of Systems of Thought at the prestigious Collège de France. As part of his professorial duties, Foucault was required to deliver a course of 13 annual lectures on themes relating to his ongoing research.

The majority of lectures given between 1970 and 1984 provided exploratory outline of subjects he would subsequently develop in more detail in his books. Certain themes, however, were never elaborated into book form. Two such courses of lectures were given in 1978 and 1979, respectively entitled 'Security, territory and population' and The 'birth of biopolitics'. In terms of the chronology of Foucault's work, these courses were delivered after the publication of what many see as Foucault's *magnum opus*, *Discipline and Punish*. Although there is undoubted continuity between *Discipline and Punish* and the subjects covered in these lectures, Foucault sets out a new course of research into what he termed government rationality, or, to use his own personal neologism, governmentality. Foucault did not work on this topic alone. One notable *éminence grise* was Gilles Deleuze, who contributed to seminars at the Collège de France which complemented the governmentality lectures.

Foucault did not return to governmental themes in his subsequent lectures during the 1980s. He chose, instead, to pursue ideas of ethics and sexuality that would form the basis of his final volumes on *The History of Sexuality*. Even so, Foucault maintained his interest in government. He commented on governmentality in interviews and the odd book chapter here and there. In addition, he used his visiting professorships in the United States during the 1980s to discuss such ideas. Many of these lectures, seminars and interviews on governmentality found their way into published form, following the interest in 'new' Foucault work in the wake of his untimely death. Hence, despite any substantive book study, Foucault has left a notable body of work on the state, government and the public realm through his explorations of governmentality.

Foucault's brand of political theory provides a corrective to the primacy of the state in political theory. Marxian thinkers, and also those who are liberal pluralists by persuasion, portray the state in 'sovereign' terms. In liberal thought, the state is pitted against the defenceless individual, whilst Marxists regard the state as embodying capitalist power (Foucault 1991: 104). In other words, the state is regarded as a unified and centralised authority. Foucault's intention was to displace the state from political theory for a more diffuse, random and unintentional view of political power. In effect, just as the decentred subject was pivotal to Foucault's anti-humanism, so the decentring of political institutions and structures was integral to his anti-statism. By implication, the state has to be marginalised in the study of power or, as Foucault graphically put it, political philosophy needs to 'cut off the King's head' (1980a: 121). Foucault concedes, 'I don't want to say that the State isn't important' (1980a: 122), although he adds two caveats. First, the power apparatus of the state may be all-present but it is unable to dominate all power relations. Secondly, the authority of the state is dependent on existing relations of power, forms of power that do not necessarily originate in the state. Such ideas on the workings of political power were developed further in studies of governmentality.

What Foucault has in mind when referring to government is the 'conduct of conduct'. This is an activity that aims to shape or affect the conduct of a person or persons. Such government activity can potentially encompass personal conduct, interpersonal relationships, relations within an institution, or the exercise of political sovereignty (Gordon 1991: 2). Preoccupation with government, in the sense used above, is traced by Foucault to the mid-sixteenth century. A whole range of political essays were written on the subject of government in this period. These discourses examined the matter in relation to a broad range of issues, including the pedagogic government of children, correct government over oneself, as well as more orthodox considerations regarding the government of the state by the monarch. The interest in government came as a result of major historical transformations in this period – namely, the eclipse of the feudal order that laid the foundations for the modern secular state and the counter-reformation against the prevailing religious hegemony of the Catholic Church.

Between the sixteenth and eighteenth centuries a whole series of political treatises were produced. These writings did not seek to establish advice to the sovereign ruler or 'the Prince' or to produce treatises on political science. Rather they attempted to provide nuts-and-bolts guidance on the art of running governments. Much of this literature on government either explicitly or implicitly established its position in contradistinction to Machiavelli's *The Prince*. Foucault shows that the main point of contention was the sovereign conception of power encompassed in Machiavelli's figure of the Prince (Foucault 1991: 88). For Machiavelli, government is immanent in the singular and transcendental figure of the Prince who is concerned to maintain personal control over his principality. In anti-Machiavellian literature, government activity is multifarious and located throughout the state and society (Foucault 1991: 91). Early texts, such as that by Guillaume de La Perrière's *Miroir Politique,* were also trying to define a particular art of government. By the end of the eighteenth century, writings on the art of government rescind sovereignty and fully embrace liberalism. Here, the principles of government are no longer part of some divine, quasi-theological order (Kerr 1999: 185). The art of government is about maintaining the power of the state rather than the sovereign.

The concept of governmentality embraces the idea of power as a multidimensional entity, infiltrating even the minutiae of everyday life, which is just as much able to be constructive as to constrain. This is clearly evident in discussions of those governmental techniques that compose the modern state. In a lecture entitled 'Omnes et singulatim: towards a critique of political reason', Foucault outlines and details those techniques that fall under the rubric of 'apparatuses of security', notably those of the police (see Foucault 1990: 58–85). Reference to a 'theory of the police' was made during the seventeenth and eighteenth centuries when the European nation state was emerging. These references were mostly evident in the writings of predominantly German and Italian political thinkers. Foucault argues that what authors like Turquet de Mayenne, Delamare and Huhenthal regard as 'the police' is less a penal institution within the state than 'a governmental technology peculiar to the state; domains, techniques, targets where the state intervenes' (1990: 77). For instance, the German writer von Justi's *Elements of the Police* (1756) defines the purpose of the police in terms of its social and moral role, overseeing how individuals live in society. From considering rudimentary demographic aspects of people occupying territories, von Justi dedicates the final part of his book to the conduct of individuals: their morals, their capabilities, their level of honesty, and their respect for the law. Foucault notes something important about the police as a rational form of political power wielded over individuals: 'the role of the police is to supply them with a little extra life; and by so doing, supply the state with a little extra strength' (1990: 79). Foucault anticipates possible objections: 'but that's only the utopia of some obscure author. You can hardly deduce any significant consequences from it' (1990: 79). However, books by the likes of Turquet and von Justi were typical of the ideas circulating throughout Europe in this period. These ideas were popularised during the seventeenth and eighteenth centuries as a result of government policies and educational growth.

Foucault's historical analysis of government echoes his views on the operation of social power in society (McNay 1994: 117). Instead of a centralised view of government, modern government adopts a range of different practices, undergoing what Foucault terms the 'governmentalisation of the state'. This refers to how modern government has positioned itself and augmented its position through deploying a range of practices and rationalities of rule that neither originate in the state nor are used intentionally. Government draws upon heterogeneous strategies and techniques. These are not used to dominate individuals by suppressing their freedoms but operate through the agency of the governed (Gordon 1991: 5). In Foucault's (1991: 102) words, governmentality is the 'ensemble formed by the institutions, procedures, analyses and reflections, the calculations and tactics that allow the exercise of this very specific ... form of power'. Political power in this respect is totalising, overseeing and caring for the population and individuals for the sake of security.

Political power from this perspective must be located beyond the state, as governmentality is far removed from the central executive activities or formal law-making bodies. Rather Foucault (1991: 102) offers a decentralised theory of politics in which the power of the state is an effect of both social and self-imposed forms of regulation. The state is simply one amongst many power relations. In contrast to classical theory where the state is put on some theoretical pedestal, Foucault (1991: 103) argues that it 'does not have this unity, this individuality ... this importance; maybe, after all, the state is no more than a ... mythicized abstraction'. Hence, it is governmentality which makes the state possible, which defines the functions of the state, and not vice versa (Kerr 1999: 189). Hence, it is the governmentalisation of the state rather than the state itself which should be central to political theory. But for Foucault, as we have already stated above, the state still retains its importance. Foucault (1982) seems to contradict the main thrust of his governmental approach: he concedes that the state is the most important form in the exercise of power, with governmentalised powers gradually coming under the auspices of the state. Kerr asks whether this caveat offers a new or different spin on the prevailing governmental view of the state. In Foucault's governmental analysis, Kerr (1999: 189–90) responds, the state is still displaced and reduced institutionally to something that is vague and indeterminate.

What impact have Foucault's governmental ideas had in the intellectual firmament? It was only belatedly that governmentality came to the fore in social science research, forming an integral part of an Anglo-Foucauldian approach. Sociologists have been in the vanguard in elaborating and expanding the concept of governmentality, with the likes of Nikolas Rose and Mitchell Dean being major figures. In the next section, we will examine these neo-governmental efforts in a little more detail.

Governmentality and the decentred state after Foucault

The concept of governmentality, as we saw, cropped up during the mid-1970s mainly in Foucault's lectures and interviews. It is only belatedly, however, that governmentality has come to the fore in social science literature and research. Much of this is down to the fact that governmentality never received a book-length study. And it was Foucault's published books that were the most celebrated and primary vehicles for proselytising his ideas. In later years, after Foucault's death, publishers and scholarly acolytes began mining his unpublished work for further reflections on established themes or even to gain new insights. As a result, the 1990s saw the concept of governmentality rise in prominence amongst Foucauldian disciples. Sociologists have been in the vanguard in elaborating and expanding the concept of governmentality, with names such as Nikolas Rose and Mitchell Dean being major proponents. As well as the sociological field, governmentality has proven a conspicuous influence on research within human geography and rural studies. Murdoch (1997), for instance, applied a Foucauldian governmental approach to the study of rural communities, agricultural politics and government planning in rural areas. MacKinnon (2000) adopted the very same approach to the study of of local economic governance in the Scottish Highlands. There was also a fledgling interest in governmentality from organisational and management authors, with Jackson and Carter (1998) employing governmentality to explore the management of labour. There are those practitioners in the broader social science family who have researched aspects of public administration using a governmental perspective (see McGreggor Cawley and Chaloupka 1997). Some of the more significant and fruitful post-Foucauldian governmental studies have focused on the state. Here, the concept of governmentality has been employed to uncover and expose the inner workings of the governing process. In focusing on the governing process, authors using a neo-governmental approach have produced some notable work on the subjective side of state power and the often taken-for-granted practical techniques of the state. Below, these two features will be examined in turn.

Subjectivity, power and the state

As we have seen in his later works on the history of sexuality, Foucault was concerned with how the operation of power is intimately tied to subjectivity. Foucault is certainly not alone in attempting to accommodate the subjective life of the individual within broader social and political relations, although scholars are normally 'ontologically partisan' in their prioritisation of either the individual or structural features of social organisation. Hennis (1987) maintains that the classical sociology of Max Weber offers a systematic historical exploration of *Menschentum*, or human conduct. He was especially concerned with how social forces – economic relations or religious systems – mould individual subjectivity and lifestyles (Rose 1992: 160). Much later, Jürgen Habermas (1986) conceived of the 'lifeworld', an heterogeneous social entity, which relates the subjective realm and self-identity formation to the institutional, cultural and economic structures of society.

The theme of subjectivity forms a significant part of Foucauldian governmentality. The governmental position places a distinctive spin on the interrelationship between subjectivity and power (Simons 1995). On the one hand, the subjective aspect of governmental power is regarded in orthodox terms as being able to shape individuals and their ideas (Foucault 1982: 214). In this respect, external authorities manipulate individuals or their identities are shaped by prevailing social norms and values (McNay 1994: 123). On the other hand, the subjective influence of governmental power is contingent upon the free choices and liberty of the individual. Social order and regulation are not achieved simply through discipline – the corporeal impunities of power – but also through self-regulation and self-mastery.

The governmental literature has been especially productive in subjecting neo-liberal government regimes to Foucauldian scrutiny, especially their penchant for using policy to influence lifestyles and identities. Just how far the neo-liberal project used policy to transform identity and subjectivity is highlighted by UK governments under the leadership of Margaret Thatcher in the 1980s. In a *Sunday Times* article from May 1989 the then prime minister noted: 'I used to have a nightmare for the first six years in office that, when I had got the finances right, when I had got the law right … the British sense of enterprise and initiative would have been killed by socialism'. A year later she was quoted as saying: 'Economics are the method. The object is to change the soul'.

The sociologist Nikolas Rose (named one of the top five UK social scientists by the *Guardian* newspaper) produced, during the course of the 1990s, a considerable body of neo-Foucauldian analysis of Conservative regimes and the modern state. For Rose (1992), the neo-liberal Conservatism that dominated the 1980s was more than a political philosophy; it was also a mentality and a technology of government. These governments used the reform process to intervene in the regulation of personal existence. Rose pinpoints the endeavours of successive Conservative administrations to promote enterprise culture as an especially powerful instance of the interface between government and self-formation.

The idea of an enterprise culture entered the popular vernacular of the 1980s. The popularisation of enterprise helped to forge a link between the way individuals are governed by political institutions and the way they regulate and govern themselves (Rose 1992: 145). The enterprise culture, at its heart, valorises certain personal attributes and qualities. This includes those psychological characteristics suited to wealth creation, such as initiative, personal drive and ambition. This personal profile does not stop at a purely utilitarian economic man of the type epitomised by Gordon Gekko in the film *Wall Street*. It also encompasses virtues with moral and ethical overtones, including self-reliance, prudence and a work ethic (Heelas 1991: 80). The language of enterprise and the adoption of policies to develop an entrepreneurial society formed part of the technology of government. As is the case with modern techniques and mentalities of government, enterprise culture is preoccupied with the autonomous and independent self. Rose argues that the emphasis on personal independence underlines how governing the liberal-democratic way is done through the freedom of subjects. This is made possible by the proliferation of practices in which 'the self-governing capabilities of individuals can be brought into alignment with political objectives' (Rose 1992: 147).

The relationship between state authority, subjectivity and free choices of individuals is highlighted by Dean (1995). Here, Dean studied a series of reforms to the administration of unemployment benefit in Australia during the early 1990s. The reforms, devised by the government of Bob Keating, had a definite neo-liberal flavour. They attempted to radically alter the administration of unemployment benefit towards a more active system of 'employment seeking'. Active job seeking entailed the integration of income support with job retraining programmes. As well as the onus on job training – on getting the supply side rather than the demand side right

– the Australian government planned to replace universal welfare benefits. Instead of universal provision, the government introduced a differentiated system of benefits tailored to distinct social groups, particularly those 'at risk' of long-term unemployment. Dean examined a number of different technologies in the government of the unemployed that were used to generate knowledge about their subjects. This included: the administrative structure and integration of various departments and agencies involved in the government of the unemployed; the various schemes for training civil servants; and the forms of expertise that they had to acquire for the administration of programmes.

The technical means for governing the unemployed are not just formally located in constitutional states. They have their provenance in agencies and groups that exist both within and outside the parameters of the central state, such as businesses, employers, academics, community associations and technical colleges. Crucially, 'the complex linking of state bodies with heteromorphic practices, authorities, agencies and institutions' is implicated in the problematisation of identity and the formation of the unemployed self (Dean 1995: 571). This can be seen in the way the active system of unemployment benefit would expect the subject to exercise choice in engaging with various agencies that assist the process of self-analysis and training. What emerges is a government intervention in, and support for, particular kinds of ethical and ascetic practices. As McGreggor Cawley and Chaloupka (1997: 40–1) put it, the practice of administration is not a value-free phenomenon: 'the reforms and assumptions we now apply to administrative practice might not represent as clear a vision for progress ... Every development in public administration – no matter how thoroughly cloaked in the terms of apolitical progress – has power implications'. The will to knowledge thus can be found in the most technical and mundane administrative practices which form part of the government of conduct.

The practical techniques of the state

There is another dimension of neo-governmental research of interest to state theory. This is the work covering the technical aspects of govern-ment. Miller and Rose (1990), in a seminal paper on governmentality, argue that in orthodox political analysis forms of rule are understood through grand, sweeping concepts such as state control, nationalisation or the free market. The reality, according the authors, is that humble and mundane activities make it possible to govern. In the governmentality literature, the term 'technologies of government' is used to refer to 'the actual mechanisms through which authorities of various sorts have sought to shape, normalize and instrumentalize the conduct, thought, decisions and aspirations of others' (Miller and Rose 1990: 8). The practical technologies of rule, according to Miller and Rose, can include a heterogeneous and seemingly endless list of practices: techniques of notation, computation; procedures for examination and assessment; the use of surveys; standardised forms of training; and even building design.

From the position of Foucauldian governmentality, practical and technical issues are integral to the process of government, as is borne out in a comparative study of privatisation in the UK and New Zealand by Larner and Walters (2000). The authors maintain that the likely success of a policy programme is contingent only in part upon political mobilisation or putting forward a convincing argument. The successful realisation of policies is also dependent upon the skilful use and manipulation of the technical aspects of governing. Privatisation initiatives in both countries required inventiveness and improvisation on the part of politicians and financiers to implement novel policy initiatives. However, privatisation, particularly in Britain, was far from a coherent and carefully orchestrated plan, although invariably portrayed as such by key protagonists of the era in memoirs and other personal recollections. In contrast to these official accounts, Larner and Walters point to the ambiguous and *ad hoc* nature of neo-liberal regimes. Initially, the policy was shaped by practical concerns rather than ideological predilections. As Dean (1999: 31) makes clear, 'technical means are a condition of governing and often impose limits over what it is possible to do'.

The privatisation of British Telecom, the first and most influential utility sell-off under Margaret Thatcher, was driven by the question of how to modernise the telecommunications infrastructure. For instance, Treasury rules prevented the public sector from raising external finance. This led to the ground-breaking decision to sell shares in the company, a strategy that was helped by increased economic confidence and growth in the value of share prices throughout the stock market. The ensuing £4 billion sell-off was seven times bigger than any previous attempt to privatise. The successful floatation of the company was made possible by the technical infrastructure provided by the London stock market, one of the major trading centres in the world economy. In order to secure finances for this massive float, the political decision was taken to popularise the marketing of shares beyond the financial institutions to include British Telecom's employees and customers (Larner and Walters 2000: 366). Here, the government and expert advisers adopted and devised a range of techniques to sell the company's shares to the wider public. Amongst the methods used were staggered payments to make share purchasing affordable, share shops and advertising campaigns were organised to raise public awareness. And the clawback option was used to balance retail with institutional demand.

This governmental treatment of privatisation policy underlines the contingent, fragile and often tenuous nature of neo-liberal reforms. Larner and Walters observe how the governmentality literature underlines the way modern government is often dominated by functional matters of whether policies are workable or not. The success or otherwise of policy initiatives such as privatisation depends less on convincing key decision-makers or mobilising political forces. Rather it depends on the technicalities of government. And by focusing on the mundane features of government the authors destabilise 'the hegemony of neo-liberalism in that it reveals that not everything is in the control of political programmers' (Larner and Walters 2000: 374). In fact, the neo-liberalism policy agenda often proved expedient and based around short-lived experiments, not all of which succeeded.

A critique of Foucauldian governmentality

The Foucauldian concept of governmentality has its detractors. Szakolczai (1993: 4), however, argues that any conventional criticism of Foucault's use of governmentality would be improper as the term was never used in proper print. This argument is unconvincing. Governmentality as a political and theoretical concept has its problems and shortcomings, which in many ways reflect difficulties with the general Foucauldian theoretical schema. A notable point of contention is that the concept of governmentality offers a decentred notion of government: the fact that governing practices do not originate in the state but are dispersed throughout society. Thus, the governmental approach intentionally marginalises the role of the state, neglecting the import of government and the continued significance of orthodox politics. Reflecting this, Neocleous (1996) argues that the process of governmentalisation makes for a passive state, bereft of constitutive power. From a Foucauldian and neo-governmental perspective, the state is one power centre amongst many. The state's authority and regulatory influence are dependent upon relations of power that exist outside the state. The result of all this: 'for all the claims made by Foucault and his followers to be effecting a major break in social and political theory, their new conceptual apparatus leaves them with an essentially liberal conception of the state' (Neocleous 1996: 79). For Neocleous, the legal order and the public administration are inextricably linked to state institutions. The 'Foucault effect' on social and political theory denies this *reality*.

It is possible that the denial of the state applies to Foucault's followers more than to the man himself. Bruce Curtis raises this possibility in relation to the neo-Foucauldian work on governmentality, especially the contribution of Rose and Miller. As we have seen, these authors are highly critical of traditional theories of the state – theories which regard the state as the monopoly power, with its control over force and taxation. For Miller and Rose, power is located beyond the state. It depends on various mechanisms and technologies – often taken-for-granted and seemingly unnoticed. But, Curtis (1995: 575) observes, 'Such a conception is inadequate to the reality of politics and government in liberal democracies'. For this particular critic, Rose and Miller distort Foucault's position on the state and political power. Whilst Foucault acknowledges that regulatory social power do not originate solely within the state, he does show how the state performs various roles and is still vital to the exercise of political power. But, as Curtis argues, Rose and Miller present Foucault as having no interest in the state.

For other critics, particularly those on the left, it is noted that governmentality, whilst addressing significant issues, promotes a depoliticised and value-free conception of social relations. Here, the individual is transformed into an object of government, which eliminates the possibility of contradiction and critique (Kerr 1999: 178). In fact, there is little sense of how the state from Foucault's point of view suffers from the inherent contradictions that come from being located in the global capitalist system. We only get an impression of state power continually perfecting itself, of the continuity of state regulatory power. These shortcomings appear because 'Foucauldian governmentality is derived from a top-down conception of power that externalizes and marginalizes social subjectivity' (Kerr 1999: 197). This results in a positive and productive system of power and governmentality which can be subject to modification but rarely cancelled. But if governmentality is productive, argues Kerr (1999), this is only because it helps to reproduce the ideology of the market. Thus, governmental studies of neo-liberal policies in the West have failed to engage critically with these political configurations. Indeed, Kerr argues that authors such as Rose have positively embraced neo-liberalism.

Even some of those operating within this neo-Foucauldian approach have acknowledged problems with the governmentality literature. For instance, O'Malley et al. note that, by epistemological design, governmentality literature treats the official pronouncements and texts of government as representing the governing process. This neglects the 'messy actualities' of governance. It overlooks how government is a contested terrain, shaped by diverse social relations. This analytical strategy according these insiders leads to an overly abstract view of the governing process, with politics reduced to a rationality or 'mentality of rule' (O'Malley et al. 1997: 504–5). As such, governmentality studies have been insensitive to the multiplicity of voices that exist in the process of rule. These comments should be kept uppermost when deciding upon the relevance of governmentality for state theory. But to dismiss Foucault's work out of hand would seem unwarranted. Foucault himself assiduously exposed his work to self-criticism, looking to reformulate and revise ideas in the light of such reflection (Foucault 1990: 14). As shown above, the traversing into governmental territory provoked important shifts in Foucault's thinking.

Conclusion

Giddens (1987) wrote that the philosophical concerns of poststructuralism are a transient intellectual fad. This is contestable. As Clegg (1989: 150) notes, poststructuralism is still influential and continues to provoke debates, particularly in the areas of power and politics. The poststructuralist suggestion of language as a conduit for power relations and the related concept of the decentred subject are integral to the intellectual lexicon of the social sciences today.

One of the most celebrated figures to have popularised such themes is Michel Foucault. Foucault stands as one of the most influential thinkers of recent years. His studies delved into aspects of social life often neglected by mainstream academe, covering such areas as madness and asylums, the medical clinic, prisons and the ethics of sexuality. One feature of Foucault's later writings that has belatedly gained recognition is his analysis of politics and the state. The main rationale of this move into 'traditional territory' was unorthodox: to eradicate the state from political and social theory. Here, Foucault investigates the 'rationality of government' or, to use the neologism he devised to capture this exercise, governmentality. The concern is to broaden the idea of government to include the variety of practices and rationalities that form the basis of rule rather than focusing exclusively on the inner workings of the state. The concept of governmentality shows how the state goes about policing societies through bureaucratic regimes and disciplinary powers. These strategies include mundane practices to do with hygiene and the regulation of labour, as well as scientific disciplines such as demography, criminology and medicine. The poststructural state is one that is fragmented and decentred – it is one of many power centres and draws its authority from existing centres of power. From this, there are valuable insights to be gained about how taken-for-granted processes and activities often contribute to the regulatory power of the state.

Foucauldian governmentality provides a corrective to the primacy of the state in political theory. Marxist and even pluralist theorists portray the state in 'sovereign' terms, according to Foucault, as a unified and centralised authority. His intention was to displace the state from political theory for a more diffuse, random and unintentional view of political power. Foucault, however, is not alone in advocating a decentred position on the state, as thinkers from other disciplines have made similar assertions. There is the concept of governing at a distance developed by Bruno Latour's (1987) studies of laboratory scientists which has been applied to social regulation and the operation of political power (Law 1986: 15–17). Another notable example is the work of Niklas Luhmann (1982), with its emphasis on the differentiated society and the related concept of self-regulating autopoietic systems.

So what is the value of Foucault's poststructural conception of the state? It would seem that a theoretical approach which endeavours to minimise the role of the state would be inimical to social and political theory. In recent years, though, state theory has become increasingly open to a range of competing theoretical approaches. Moreover, the complexities of mass industrial society have led analysts to go beyond prevailing approaches in order to explore the changing functions and structures of the modern state. As such, Foucauldian governmentality would not be entirely out of place in contemporary writings on social and political theory. In fact, a growing preoccupation in the field has been the weakening of the state in the face of internal and external developments. In addition, governmentality has attracted the interest of contemporary thinkers. Within social science research, especially sociology, a growing band of writers have extended Foucault's original work on governmentality. Although such work does not form of coherent school of thought, it has been used to explore a wide range of themes. There is also research within governmental literature which is highly prescient to contemporary state theory and analysis, especially studies of neo-liberal policy interventions.

Even at the height of Foucault's popularity, there were critics who were prepared to go against the grain. Questions were raised about the way Foucauldian governmentality had sidelined the state for being no more than the reification of various cultural and social practices or the product of discourses. These concerns are justified. For all the fragmentation of power and the deceptive influence of culture, the state's regulatory power and monopolisation of force cannot be theorised away. With respect to the power beyond the state, a number of writers who ran with and extended governmental analysis proved to be more Foucauldian than Foucault himself.

CHAPTER 3

GOVERNANCE AND THE DECENTRED STATE

Introduction

The seventeenth-century political philosopher, Thomas Hobbes, believed the modern state to be a *leviathan* – an absolute institution with the power to intervene in the affairs of citizens, seemingly at will. But in contemporary social thought the state is at best one amongst many *leviathans* – institutions with power to control and normalise – or at worst an increasingly powerless force in society. The prospect that changes to the state impede its ability to regulate and control society is a theme that lies at the heart of governance theory. In fact, governance is now a byword for the way the state has undergone a dramatic transformation to its structures and institutions. The concept of governance and allied theoretical offshoots have gained a popular foothold. Most prominently, since the early 1990s, governance theory has found a welcome home in political science and public administration circles. There is now a substantial body of work on governance. Although the most prominent work in this field, as we shall discover below, focuses on the transformation of government in Britain, it has a wider relevance to state theory. As already mentioned, the themes covered by governance theory chime with much current writing about the state, spotlighting the way modern conditions have impacted on the ability of governments to steer policy. Moreover, governance theory is grounded in the 'new wave' of state theories that emerged during the 1970s.

The first half of this chapter examines the emergence of so-called governance theory. The intellectual precursors of this model of governance are traced to two separate academic contributions during the 1970s: the interorganisational analysis of northern European scholars within the policy and administrative sciences and the sensationalist theories on the overloaded state. These contributions show that the state has become either overburdened by too many responsibilities or fragmented into a vast network of semi-autonomous organisations. Either way, the impression is of a state that is failing and enfeebled. Such ideas have formed the basis of contemporary governance theory. And it is to this subject that the second half of the chapter turns.

Possibly the most prominent and influential account of governance theory is what can be dubbed the 'Anglo-governance' tradition, associated principally with the British political scientist, Rod Rhodes. His more recent writings have embraced governance theory to explore theoretically the institutions, actors and processes of change within the central state. Rhodes' Anglo-governance model has formed into an authoritative theory of how new methods of governing society have emerged. As part of this analysis, he examines the contribution made by actors and institutions beyond the central state to the process of governance. This theoretical approach challenges the conventional wisdom of constitutional theory which portrays government as a strong centralised executive or a unified state. Significantly, according to governance theory, a distinct shift has taken place in government from a hierarchical bureaucratic organisation to a fragmented and decentralised entity. To capture these changes, this model has relied on a range of aphorisms and concepts: hollowing out the state, networks, core executive, fragmentation. There is a great deal of value in this work both from an empirical and theoretical standpoint. Such analysis has reinvigorated the study of governing institutions, producing a sophisticated theoretical account of the modern British state. Evidence from academic literature would suggest that the Anglo-governance model has gained a wide currency in both political science and cognate disciplines. There are some points of critical interest – a task left to the latter parts of the chapter. The emphasis placed on the transformation of government institutions is at the expense of chronicling how the central state has maintained and even reinforced its position. This analytical blind spot is in part due to the way such analysis utilises aspects of post-bureaucratic analysis. And yet it stands as a significant contribution to contemporary state theory.

A paradigm shift in political science

It is possible to understand governance theory as part of this ebb and flow of paradigms within the discipline of political science – specifically, paradigms about the nature of the central state. Although governance theory has a close attachment to politics as a discipline, it resonates with the 'new wave' of theoretical currents on the state. And, more significantly, the theoretical precepts of governance, and even the linguistic terms used, have resonated beyond the discipline of politics.

The dominant intellectual paradigm during the formative development of politics as a professional academic discipline in Britain was concerned with the formal institutions of government. This traditional approach has been labelled the Westminster model (see Smith 1999). For nineteenth-century constitutional scholars such as A. V. Dicey, this mainly entailed a preoccupation with parliamentary government. This intellectual position dominated the first half of the twentieth century. For prominent political scholars in this period, namely John Mackintosh (1977) and Anthony Birch (1964), the key tenets for the study of politics boil down to parliamentary sovereignty, cabinet government, executive authority (through the positions of prime minister and key ministerial figures), the parliamentary conventions for legislation, and a neutral civil service.

The traditional Westminster model was from the 1970s onwards subject to increasing scepticism and attacks from within the discipline of political science. Questions were raised over the perceived ability of the state to manage policy effectively. In conceptual terms, critics argued that a preoccupation with the formal governing institutions results in a highly circumscribed view of politics. Political scientists increasingly drew upon American- and European-inspired political theories, including behaviourism, neo-Marxism and neo-pluralist policy analysis. The result was a broadening of politics beyond an exclusive concern with parliament and the central executive. But more than this, political analysts questioned whether true political power, authority and sovereignty rested with the central state. Two models stand out in this respect: the Scandinavian approach to interorganisational policy-making and the overloaded state model. Both theoretical contributions were at the forefront of a new dominant paradigm for understanding and researching how central government works. Let us look briefly at each one in turn because they were the forerunner to – and the inspiration for – governance theory.

Crisis of the liberal state: from 'overloaded' state to interorganisational inertia

The postwar rebuilding of conflict-traumatised societies also coincided with the systematic reinvention of the liberal democratic state. The extension of universal welfare provision – the so-called Keynesian welfare settlement – resulted in the historically unprecedented growth of the state sector, with the state extending its reach into uncharted areas. But after the extended postwar binge of state intervention across Europe and North America, there ensued a protracted hangover. The postwar mood of optimism and confidence was followed by a dose of reality, where gloom and pessimism became the order of the day. The ambitions of the state, no matter how progressive or well intentioned, at times failed to materialise. The sense of crisis surrounding political institutions was especially acute in Britain. After a period of reconstruction and boom, British society experienced socio-economic near-paralysis during the 1970s: industrial relations were in meltdown, inflation was on the rise and economic growth on the decline, and there was the onset of deindustrialisation and all the urban blight that followed the decline of heavy industry. There was also a growing sense of disillusionment with the Keynesian welfare settlement, which had resoundingly failed to eradicate the five key wants – contrary to what the Beveridge report of 1945 had predicted (Skelcher 2000: 5).

The apparent sluggishness of the liberal state during the course of the 1970s could be subject to all manner of conjecture. Maybe this was a temporary blip after the great reconstructive efforts of the postwar years. Or possibly, the liberal state had become a victim of its own postwar success in establishing universal welfare and social provision, with the public expecting too much. But for a growing band of commentators and academics, there existed a deep structural malaise in the liberal capitalist state. The state was becoming structurally hamstrung, undermining its long-term viability and effectiveness. This was the position of those commentators who put forward what became known as the 'overloaded state' thesis. Arguments about an overloaded state gained much prominence in Britain, where economic and social dislocation seemed especially acute. For prominent government commentators such as Anthony King and Samuel Brittan, the British state was overburdened by demands and obligations. As social problems had become more entrenched, the size of the state machine that exists to deal with these societal demands would have to expand: 'Complexity added to scale yields further complexity' (King 1975: 295). The end result is a state machine so overloaded that it is rendered impotent to act effectively at a policy level. King (1975: 288) observed: 'Governments today are held responsible for far more than they ever were before'. The growing burden of responsibility would not be a problem if there were sufficient resources available to meet the ever growing list of demands. But the capacity of the British state diminished at a time when its reach was being extended.

There were good reasons why the resources available to the state were on the decline. The overloaded state thesis starts from a pluralistic conception of the modern liberal state. From this perspective, political power is spread across various interest groups who bargain, jostle and manoeuvre for advantage. In this competition for resources, governments faced demands from all quarters (Held 1996: 242). In Samuel Brittan's words, there are excessive demands made on the 'sharing-out' function of governments. The sharing-out function refers to how public authorities distribute resources through taxation and spending plans. The state used fiscal and economic policy to keep all parties on board and retain popularity (votes). Such public spending made for costly programmes and unwieldy bureaucracies that often failed to achieve their objections. This vicious spiral of ever bigger government only made effective intervention more difficult. All of this undermined public confidence in government. According to Anthony King, foretelling the rise of the neo-liberal new right, the inverse relationship between state growth and policy effectiveness would result in clamours for radical change. And the demand for change not only resulted from the perceived failings of the state. For Brittan (1975: 130–1), the sharing-out function of government reached breaking point in the mid-1970s, with social expectations outstripping society's willingness to pay through higher taxation.

Of course, the growing sense of malaise and pessimism surrounding the modern polity was not unique to Britain. The erosion of legitimacy for state institutions was spreading throughout western Europe. The academic community seemed to respond, producing assorted explanations and further research into why industrial democracies seemed so difficult, if not impossible, to govern. Whilst overloaded thinkers looked to the escalation of interest-group demands on the state, other commentators blamed the *organisation* of the state (Hanf 1978). This emergent field was variously dubbed the 'interorganisational', 'intergovernmental' or 'transnational' approach to policy-making. The leading proponents of interorganisational policy analysis were European for the most part, but not exclusively so; in the United States the talk was more of subgovernments than interorganisational policy-making (Rhodes and Marsh 1992: 9).

For scholars reviewing the field, interorganisational policy studies, though growing in scope by the late 1970s, lacked a common paradigm. Public choice theory, corporatism and neo-pluralist theory seemed to jostle side by side within the interorgansational policy family. Although without a general theory, the studies conducted under the interorganisational umbrella would come to the same conclusion: it is unlikely for policy to be strategically directed by a single agency located in a neat hierarchical system of authority. The processes involved in making and forming policy 'are inevitably the result of interactions among a plurality of separate actors with separate interests, goals, and strategies' (Scharpf 1978: 347). All this organisational disaggregation makes for an administrative state system where the ability of government to guide and shape socio-economic developments is heavily impeded. A good example of how intergovernmental relations impact on policy-making is Scharpf *et al.*'s case study of the Federal Republic of Germany. The pre-unification Federal Republic of Germany is characterised as a multilevel governance system, involving federal, local and state government bodies. The authors note that under certain circumstances a fragmented and decentralised decision-making system like Germany's can produce suboptimal results (Scharpf *et al.* 1978: 67–70). Does this mean modern governance is an uncoordinated free-for-all? As Hanf observes, even fragmented politico-administrative systems like Germany possess a certain degree of order. That said, ordered interactions tend to stem from the way units voluntarily coordinate their actions (Hanf 1978: 2). Such coordination occurs without deliberate steering on the part of a central authority or overarching power.

The overloaded state thesis and the interorganisational policy approach signalled a major shift away from the idea that political power resides with a single power authority. Both models did much to undermine the somewhat antediluvian, constitutional-obsessed assumptions of the Westminster approach to political institutions. Central government was not as powerful as once thought. And there was more to political power than the sovereignty of parliament and ministers of state. The paradigm shift away from the Westminster model constituted an important development in the discipline of political science – the traditional home of state theory. And the demise of the Westminster approach was a definite signal that the state was being rethought and revised within and without the discipline.

Governance theory and the state in political science

Interorganisational policy analysis would evolve and develop. The approach would have its firm advocates, who would eventually become major figures in governance theory. The insights of interorganisational policy studies were used most notably by the British political scientist, Rod Rhodes, who in time would be at the forefront of governance theory (see Rhodes and Marsh 1992: 8). These theoretical insights were used by Rhodes (1988) to study the interface between central and local government. His work focused on the structural characteristics of central–local relations, focusing on the emergence and nature of policy networks. In the late 1980s, Rhodes's work responded to the claim that his analysis of policy networks failed to take into account the context in which policy networks operate and change. As such, he started to look at the changing relationships between central and local government. In this analysis of central and sub-central government, it was maintained that central government conditions the way policy networks operate (Rhodes and Marsh 1992: 14). But detractors of Rhodes's central–local studies have argued that it failed to outline an adequate theory of the state (Rhodes 1997: 11).

It was accepted by the leading lights of policy network research in the UK that such work had to be located in the context of a state theory. In fact, Rhodes's later writings adapted his analysis of networks and central–local relations to outline a theory of the state in transition, where new governing structures have evolved. The key notion in this theoretical evolution is that of governance. The theoretical language of governance was already in circulation in the early 1990s amongst European academics looking to explore the changing organisational structure of the state. These explorations had a clear affinity with earlier interorganisational approaches. And like their predecessors, European governance theorists were vexed by the struggles and complications of governing which confronted modern democracies. Such matters were taken up by Jan Kooiman and others from Erasmus University in Rotterdam, dubbed the 'governance club' by commentators. The writings of Kooiman and his colleagues in the early 1990s, like the other theories detailed in this chapter, formed an influential alternative to orthodox thinking about the state. For these early trailblazers of governance, the regulation of society is achieved less by hierarchical control or decentralised markets than by networks of policy organisations (Kooiman 1993: 252). Marin and Mayntz (1991) note that there can no longer be an a priori assumption of a crucial, central, hegemonic actor. Political governance is less about central state control of society than something which involves a network of governing actors. And these policy networks may be interdependent but they are far from harmonious and cooperative (1991: 17). Government is some way from being the key policy-making institution in modern democracies. The central state is one amongst many organisations responsible for making and implementing policy.

Kooiman's writings established a theoretical touchstone for Rhodes's exploration of governance. Rhodes acknowledges that the term 'governance' has several definitions and uses, potentially rendering it meaningless as an analytical tool. Rhodes integrated the notion of governance into a conceptual model of contemporary government, its evolution and its relationship to political and wider social processes. These ideas, for want of a better term, constitute the Anglo-governance school. In this context, 'governance refers to self-organizing, interorganisational networks' that are typically interdependent whilst enjoying significant autonomy from the state (Rhodes 1997: 15). Since the early 1980s, the policy networks of government have undergone important changes. Rhodes (1997: 57) argues that networks located around functional departments grew with the incorporation of new policy actors from the private and voluntary sectors. This has resulted in a decentred government, where the central state's ability to steer and control policy has been weakened due to the growth, complexity and independence of interorganisational networks. One of the implications of this development is that central government has become increasingly dependent upon governance to effect policy implementation and service delivery. Now actors and agencies beyond government, rather than central departments, are integral to the policy network.

Why has the transformation of the central state taken place? Analysts attached to the Anglo-governance school have adopted striking phrases such as the 'hollowing out the state' to capture the shift from government to governance. 'Hollowing out' refers, very crudely, to the way the state has been eaten away and fragmented. Smith (1999), in a study of the key actors and institutions within the executive (the core executive), underlines how internal and external forces are responsible for the movement towards a hollowed-out, fragmented polity. The internal hollowing-out of the core executive came about through the consolidation of market-style policies initiated in the 1980s – namely, privatisation, contracting out services, the setting up of quangos and quasi-markets. The acceleration of globalisation in recent years has resulted in the external hollowing-out of the nation state, with the internationalisation of finance and production placing especial pressures upon the ability of central government to manoeuvre freely. The central state is not hollowed out to the point of powerlessness

(Rhodes 1997: 100). Rhodes acknowledges that government does retain extensive control over the financial levers of policy. However, such control mechanisms oversee an increasingly shrinking policy intervention base.

The Anglo-governance school

The intellectual dominance of that political tradition which views British government as a unitary system has long since passed. Clearly, there are critical alternatives to such conventional thinking. The question to ponder now is this: to what extent has the Anglo-governance school itself, where the onus is on a state structure hollowed out of its powers, gained intellectual ascendancy? The argument here is that a form of paradigmatic consensus has formed around this model. The Anglo-governance school has achieved a degree of intellectual credibility and influence, as shown by the great volume of writings it has spawned. More than this, the willingness of political scientists and other social analysts to apply governance theory in their research is symptomatic of the said model's ubiquitous acceptance.

Writings on the core executive constitute an important developmental marker for the Anglo-governance school. Their starting point is the fragmentation of the executive, admittedly regarded as axiomatic in contemporary political literature. An early article by Dunleavy and Rhodes (1990) expounded the notion, showing that what counts as the executive cannot be limited to the prime minister and cabinet. The term 'core executive' was introduced to show that central government is splintered into a variety of institutions, interorganisational networks and informal practices, which all contribute to the coordination of government policy. Dunleavy and Rhodes (1990: 5) crucially question the assumption of core executive control over the state apparatus. A collection of articles on the core executive was subsequently published, which analysed such issues as ministerial responsibility, the joining of the Exchange Rate Mechanism and the influence of cabinet committees under John Major (Rhodes and Dunleavy 1995). Hay and Richards (2000) analysed the transformation and evolution of strategic policy networks in the core executive. The authors note that the core executive is reliant upon a complex network of arrangements composed of diverse organisations 'with clearly divergent strategic intentions and motivations, criteria of success or failure, time-horizons, and strategic resources' (2000: 19). This 'tangled web' of political networks has notable implications for the coordination of policy and the ability of governments to attain strategic control.

Much of the early core executive literature was confined to Britain, but later studies drew comparisons with other executive systems. Goetz and Margetts (1999), for instance, discuss the core executive in the emerging parliamentary democracies of central and eastern Europe. The centres of government in these emerging democracies have not formed core executives that have been able to coordinate policy with any great effectiveness. This is not only a characteristic of former communist states; core executive studies in Western societies show that executive institutions in mature democracies face similar problems in steering policy (Goetz and Margetts 1999: 444).

The early literature on the core executive, as Rhodes (1997: 15) notes, only describes what is happening in government. More explanatory theoretical work emerged with the literature on the hollowing-out of the state. Again, there has since the mid-1990s been a proliferation of literature expounding and applying these ideas. Peters initially adopted the phrase 'hollowing out' to underline the loss of state power and influence at three levels: at the macro level where there has been a loss of legitimacy resulting from a growing tax burden; at the meso level where services are no longer solely provided by the state but through a mixed economy; and at the micro level in which civil servants have become less and less influential in the policy process (Peters 1993: 47–50). In a *Political Quarterly* paper on the hollowing-out of the state, Rhodes (1994: 149) not only made reference to fragmentation, as alluded to in the core executive concept, but also to the loss of central capacity. He points to new forces which have circumscribed government's capacity for governing: the European Union, the emergence of political controls and new forms of managerial accountability. In addition to these initial contributions, an edited collection entitled *The Hollow Crown* brought together a number of notable writers in the areas of politics, public administration and policy analysis to discuss hollowing-out trends in the Netherlands, Germany and Britain. Bakvis (1997) examined the role of think tanks and consultants in hollowing-out core executive functions. Wanna (1997: 150), on the other hand, does not question the hollowing-out thesis but shows how budgets are used to centralise control in the midst of hollowing out. At a sub-central level of analysis, Patterson and Pinch (1995) embraced the concept of hollowing out to theorise the changes in local government wrought by privatisation, through the practice of compulsory competitive tendering.

From government to governance: the emergence of a new orthodoxy

The same pattern of intellectual proliferation and consensus has followed the argument concerning the transition from government to governance. Rhodes (1996) notes that hollowing-out trends at the heart of government during the 1980s served to multiply the number of self-administered interorganisational networks within the state, especially in the delivery of services. This has resulted in a new form of governance without government, a trend, notes Rhodes (1995:18), that 'is not widely recognised' and which 'has important implications for the theory and practice of British government'. By the latter part of the decade, there was certainly greater recognition of these developments. Smith (1998) adopts a similar vernacular and imagery to the organising perspective developed by Rhodes. He suggests that changes as a result of reform, globalisation and the loss of sovereignty to external authorities have led to new political relationships. Here, there is governance without central government (1998: 59–61). For Richards and Smith (2002), policy-makers operate in an era of governance, in which there has been a shift from government to governance. The authors outline these views in a textbook of key governance themes, giving proof, if any were needed, of the academic orthodoxy and 'establishment' position of the governance approach.

The government to governance narrative has reached beyond the disciplinary boundaries, in a strict sense, of political science. Bob Jessop, who is probably one of the foremost contemporary sociological theorists of the state, makes some telling points about the political system in a piece about the future of capitalism. In one passage, which does not quote key governance theorists but yet reproduces their exact sentiments and vernacular, he observes: 'there is a trend towards the destatization of the political system. This is reflected in a shift from government to governance on various territorial scales and across various functional domains' (Jessop 1997: 574). Jessop goes on to argue that the state apparatus is no longer the sole focus of policy-making. Rather, in an echo of Rhodes's views on the self-administered networks within the state, it has to steer a multiplicity of diverse and operationally autonomous agencies, systems and institutions. This is not unique, he concedes, as governments have long relied on external agencies. But the nature of this interdependency has changed both substantively and quantitatively, suggesting a break with past configurations. This same governance narrative is applied in studies of public sector institutions other than the state. Loader, in an examination of the institutional provision of policing and security services, uses what he terms the 'new sociology of governance' – essentially the work of Rhodes and Kooiman. The changes in public policing are better understood in relation to the 'emergence of dispersed, multilevel governance', involving complex interoganisational networks (Loader 2000: 332).

The above testifies to the intellectual status – dominance even – of the Anglo-governance school. Such pre-eminence is reflected in the prominent contribution of Rhodes to the Whitehall Programme of the Economic and Social Research Council (ESRC), the most extensive study undertaken of central government in Britain (Rhodes 2000a). For some academic commentators, the dominance achieved by the Anglo-governance model was a product of the political milieu of the day. Holliday (2000), one of the few dissenting voices to be found in the literature, argues that real political events conspired to give this theoretical contribution a sheen of plausibility. He notes: 'It would seem that the rather eccentric politics of a passing (now past) era in British politics have been confused with real structural change' (2000: 175). The eccentric politics that Holliday refers to is the radical programme of reform undertaken by successive Conservative governments during the 1980s. Privatisation of utilities, the use of competitive tendering in the delivery of public services, the establishment of internal markets and the anti-trade union legislation, *inter alia*, give credence to the assertion made by Rhodes and colleagues over the transformation of the British state. As Smith (1998: 58) observes, such 'reforms have produced major changes in the organizations and functions of government'.

The changing political environment of recent years, however, does not wholly account for the paradigmatic orthodoxy achieved by governance theory. There also exist intrinsic disciplinary matters worth considering. To paraphrase Foucault (1991: 262), governance theory exists in twentieth-century political thought like a fish in water: that is, it would be unlikely to breathe elsewhere. In other words, governance theory is compatible with the intellectual thrust and direction of contemporary social and political thought. The key development was the proliferation of poststructuralist thought beyond the realm of language. The suggestion of language as a conduit for power relations and the related concept of the decentred subject are now an integral part of the social sciences. One of the most celebrated figures to have popularised such themes, as shown in Chapter 2, was Michel Foucault. An ardent critic of liberal humanism and the modernist project, Foucault turned his critical rhetoric in later works to political and state theory. His ideas on power and governmentality, as we have already shown, provide a corrective to the primacy of the state in political theory. Marxist and even pluralist theorists portray the state in 'sovereign' terms, according to Foucault, as a unified and centralised authority. His intention was to displace the state from political theory for a conception of political power as fragmented and diffuse. This position certainly shares an intellectual affinity with governance theory (see Smith 1999: 67–8).

Thinkers from other distinct and cognate disciplinary traditions have made similar assertions about the shift to a decentred polity. The contribution of new institutional theory is relevant in this respect. One of the main assumptions of new institutionalism in political science, which emerged as a reaction to dominant behavioural approaches, is the disaggregated nature of relations between governmental and non-governmental actors (Lowndes 1996: 189–90). Another notable example is the thought of the late German sociologist, Niklas Luhmann. In his neo-functionalist theory, Luhmann (1982) developed an account of a differentiated society and the related conception of political institutions forming a part of self-governing autopoietic systems. Rhodes, underlining the Anglo-governance school's semblance to the prevailing intellectual climate within the social sciences, quotes Luhmann's view that society is a centreless entity. The implication for government is that 'there is not one but many centres linking many levels of government – local, regional, national and supranational' (Rhodes 1997: 3).

There is a great deal of value, both empirically and theoretically, in the writings associated with the so-called Anglo-governance school. The emphasis on policy networks provides 'a sensitive tool for examining relationships between interest groups and government departments' (Kassim 1994: 19). The governance approach also highlights the contribution of private and public actors in the policy process. Moreover, it has reinvigorated the study of the functions and institutions of central government. Such is the consensus that has formed around the Anglo-governance school's ideas that it has attracted few critical analyses (for exceptions, see Saward 1997; Holliday 2000). Although governance theory, as outlined above, carries considerable import, this should not in any way preclude critical analysis of its key proposition: the superordinate role of central government in the policy process is now redundant as a result of changes within and without the core executive. The discussion below questions this assumption by considering three issues: the nature of contemporary institutional arrangements within the central executive; the role and autonomy of state and non-state actors beyond the central core; and the comparative historical development of governance forms in the British polity.

(Re)instating the centre

The Anglo-governance school forms a valuable corrective to the conventional, monocentric view of the state. The state is deemed to be centred on the constitutional sovereignty of parliament and the executive. The argument that government is a unified and sovereign institution is rebutted by a more realistic appraisal of the state's authority to manage policy. Assertions concerning the fragmentation of the core executive and the growth of self-organised networks form the basis of substantive, yet contentious, theoretical conclusions: that there has resulted a diminution in the powers and legitimacy of government and a muddling in the lines of accountability. The impression is of a central state impeded in its ability to coordinate and influence other state actors.

Advocates of the governance approach are sufficiently astute as theoreticians not to dismiss the central executive as completely powerless. Central government is still an important policy-making body. Smith (1999: 253) notes that the core executive may have given up some of its main capabilities but it is still 'more highly resourced in terms of authority, finance, and control over coercion than any other domestic institution. Therefore, its centrality and control of resources means it continues to have dominance over other organisations and networks'. Rhodes (1997) notes how the central state in the UK has relinquished a certain degree of direct authority over services as a result of market reforms. But the government has extended financial controls so that public agencies and institutions are dependent on the centre for resources.

At the same time, the centralisation of financial resources in government is unlikely to recapture properly ground that has already been ceded. As Rhodes (1997: 16) observes, 'hands-off controls may not provide enough leverage for the centre to steer the networks'. Much of this is due to the transformation of government, constituting a fundamental break from past configurations: 'Dramatic changes are taking place in British government. The shift from government to governance may not introduce the post-modern era, but it is impossible to refuse the invitation to ponder the direction and pace of change at the end of the twentieth century' (Rhodes 1997: 198). Hence, the creation of agencies, contracting out, the creation of quasi-markets, and the reliance on quangos have led to a proliferation of networks, which by their very nature have become increasingly complex and independent from central government. The state, whilst not impotent, is now dependent upon a vast array of state and non-state policy actors. The state is regarded as the first among equals; it is one of many centres.

The pessimistic tenor concerning the state's loss of authority and autonomy can, and has been, questioned. Holliday (2000: 173) states that 'in the thirty years Rhodes surveys in tracing the hollowing out of the British state, enhancement of core executive capacity has been consider-able'. In terms of the number of personnel and resources at its disposal, the central core of government is far from being diminished. The numbers employed in the Prime Minister's Office, for instance, increased by 40 per cent between the last Conservative administration of John Major and the new Labour government of Tony Blair in 1997. The Cabinet Office, which is responsible for coordinating policy across government, employed 2467 civil servants in 1999; in 1974 it had 600 staff members (Holliday 2000: 169). Although this is not irrefutable, such evidence suggests that the core retains substantial capacity (Holliday 2000: 170).

There is evidence beyond such statistical data. Further detailed exami-nation of the central 'architecture' underlines, if anything, further centrali-sation rather than the haemorrhaging of power and authority. Symptomatic of this trend are the efforts of recent Labour administrations to bolster the capacity of the Cabinet Office to coordinate policy. Under Tony Blair, the Cabinet Office is headed by a minister who has a seat in the Cabinet as Chancellor for the Duchy of Lancaster. Holliday (2000) notes how several specialist Cabinet Office units were formed to facilitate joined-up action on cross-cutting policy issues: women, drugs, social exclusion, performance and innovation. The Social Exclusion Unit was identified by the Performance and Innovation Unit as a model to be used throughout Whitehall (Taylor 2000: 56). The Cabinet Office also has overall responsibility for managing the Civil Service and its influence extends to the legislature, with the Parliamentary Business Support team coming under the Cabinet Office's sphere of influence. Developments in the Cabinet Office intimate that the trend, to use Taylor's (2000) term, is more towards 'filling in' than 'hollowing out'.

The tendency for 'filling in' is evident in the core networks, the web of organisations and actors centred around departments, cabinet committees and managerial departments such as the Whips Office (Holliday 2000: 170–1). These core networks in the British state cover 11 key policy responsibilities of government, from tax and budgeting to national security. This would intimate that there is a certain level of fragmentation, resulting in distinct problems for the coordination of policy. Holliday notes, however, that the potential difficulties should not be overblown. Most of these policy networks cover specific areas of core activity. As such, partial integration is generally sufficient or, in other cases, policy networks can run in parallel with minimal integration. Closer coordination, when required, can be attained by key ministerial figures who tend to be members of several core networks. What Holliday seems to be arguing is that fragmentation and specialisation are an inherent part of modern government. However, the core is far from resigning itself to a permanent state of incapacity but is striving for strategic coordination across the public sector.

Even under the pressure of reform and organisational restructuring in the 1980s, the centre in the UK resisted complete fragmentation. Take the Department of National Heritage (DNH) – now the Department for Culture, Media and Sport – as a case in point. Taylor (1997) suggests, using the DNH as a case study, that the restructuring in central government towards smaller, policy-focused central departments has not diminished the centre's importance in the policy process. DNH, when formed in 1992, brought together diverse policy networks. The DNH, in what is a microcosm of wider developments in Whitehall, adopted an arm's-length principle when it came to managing networks. This gave the distinct impression of a self-organised network pitted against a hollow centre. The DNH, like other departments, adopted this arm's-length principle to avoid being drawn into the pressures of being directly engaged in the implementation of policy. Despite appearances, the DNH was still able to exert considerable control over these policy networks (Taylor 1997: 451–2). It chose to do this not by direct intervention, but by manipulating the conditions under which policy networks operated. Powers such as ministerial activism, financial controls, policy guidance and monitoring give this central department significant capacity to control its immediate policy networks.

The centre and autonomous local networks

Although there is an apparent level of cohesion at the very centre, the core is still dependent on a range of local state and non-state agencies to deliver policy. The governance perspective looks upon the political process as being preoccupied with managing the proliferation of complex functional interdependencies between actors and policy networks (Taylor 1997: 447). That said, recent studies of street-level actors and local policy agencies highlight the ability of governments to monitor and steer these local agencies.

In a consideration of policy partnerships at a local level, Skelcher (2000) maintains that Rhodes and colleagues from the Anglo-governance school might be correct in arguing that governments coordinate networks in a loose and flexible arrangement. This is not so with formal partnerships in policy areas such as urban regeneration, training, and health improvement. These partnerships are actively created and closely regulated from the centre. The steering instruments at the government's disposal are not confined to financial mechanisms. Governments may shape partnership networks by utilising statutory instruments, or by acting as the gatekeeper to other, non-financial resources. Governments can also monitor partnerships through the creation of bureaucratic infrastructures and through the power of patronage.

The ESRC's Local Governance Programme of 1993–7 produced a welter of evidence revealing how local policy networks operate under exacting bureaucratic demands. The centre establishes these conditions, suggesting that the core executive still retains a variety of mechanisms by which it can steer policy. A study of local crime strategies by Benyon and Edwards (1999) reveals undoubted tensions between decentralised local partnerships and centralisation. The authors point out that crime prevention policy was reorientated towards a multilateral strategy, involving the courts, police and prisons working in partnership with the community. The rationale was to cultivate a policy that is responsive and tailored to local crime prevention needs. The prospect of these local partnerships forming into self-governing networks is jeopardised by top-down, centrally imposed accountability structures, performance criteria and bureaucratic procedures. One such outcome of this was that police involvement in community-based crime prevention partnerships proved secondary to the pursuit of centrally imposed key performance indicators for crime control (Benyon and Edwards 1999: 158).

In a study of local economic development networks in south-east Wales and the West of England, Morgan et al. (1999) question the idea that new governance constitutes governing without governing. The case studies from these two subregions show that central government has a more detached role in local economic development. Even so, the authors note that central government 'continues to exert an extremely powerful influence, not least in structuring the environment and in defining the rules under which local institutions interact' (1999: 196). The existence of vocational education and training networks, in which collaboration is based on more profound criteria than the mere exchange of information, was impeded by central funding and policy imperatives. The conclusion from this and other research projects in the ESRC's Local Governance Programme is that networking has been flourishing at a local level. But it does not resemble the autonomous system of governance which Rhodes argues has been ushered in by the transformation of government. One of the main reasons for this is that the central state, contrary to the exhortations of the Anglo-governance school, still places exacting political controls on local policy networks and institutions (Davies 2000: 425).

Practitioners of the governance position would, against such criticisms, point to the force of empirical evidence: that the radical neo-liberal reforms undertaken by successive Conservative administrations transformed the relationship between the central state and policy institutions beyond the centre. The creation of quangos, policy agencies and numerous regulatory bodies independent of the centre has contributed to greater fragmentation in government and reinforced the dependence of the centre on a complex array of policy networks and local agencies. But, for Müller and Wright (1994), the changes in the instruments of public policy, resulting from the public management revolution of recent decades, should not be equated with the diminution of central government authority. The lesson of the 1980s might be one which shows the difficulty of limiting the power of government: 'Future historians may well point to the fact that the 1980s and early 1990s have involved less a reallocation of authority than a switch from public management back to more traditional modes of state regulation' (Müller and Wright 1994: 10). The position of the centre in relation to local policy networks and actors was in many respects strengthened rather than weakened by public management reforms. Financial controls were not merely augmented to compensate for the loss of control to policy networks, as Rhodes argues. The central state also amassed greater political and administrative control during the course of the 1980s.

The introduction of quasi-markets in the health service is telling in terms of how the state retained political control. Successive reforms in the 1990s attempted to transform the health service from a bureaucratically managed organisation to one where quasi-market operations and local decision-making became more prominent. Schofield (2001), in a study of new capital accounting mechanisms introduced by the 1990 Health Act, found that legislation required National Health Service middle managers to implement autonomous investment policies. This, it seemed, proved a classic example of bureaucratic delayering. Despite the introduction of decentralised investment strategies, strong hierarchical control from the centre remained to ensure central accountability over the use of resources (Schofield 2001: 86). It was also suggested that bureaucratic practices furnish the predictability and attention to detail required to transfer political ideals into practical action for the central state – see Hughes and Griffiths (1999) for similar conclusions about the National Health Service.

The above sections question the extent to which government has entered a new era of governance – with the supposed attendant loss of power and authority. The growing capacity of the central state and its continued presence over local policy networks does not necessarily entail a state free from constraints and dependencies on non-state actors. That said, the following section draws upon historical evidence to demonstrate how the context and environment in which the British government operates have long been pressurised by fragmentation and complex interdependencies. As Holliday (2000: 175) notes, 'it is hard to see that the changes of the past thirty years have made a really dramatic difference to the co-ordinating capacity of the core'.

A new governance?

Rhodes (2006: 256) maintains that governing without government has become 'the defining narrative of British government at the turn of the century'. Rhodes's stated position echoes what Hassard (1993) terms the epoch orientation or periodisation position associated with the emergence of a postmodern society. Rhodes (1997: 188–9) is adamant that a postmodern epistemology, although hard to ignore and influential, should not be used to define and interpret such changes. Yet the resounding message from the Anglo-governance school is that there now exist discontinuities with past governmental structures. Here, the British polity is no longer moulded around a strong central executive as it was in a previous era. Smith notes that after the Second World War central government was characteristically a large and centralised bureaucratic edifice. By contrast, following the political and economic crisis of the 1970s, there took place 'a shift from bureaucratic management towards decentralised and delayered management' and a 'concern with managing networks rather than directing state bureaucracies' (Smith 1999: 250).

Portraying change, whether it be societal or institutional, in terms of a radical disjunction with prior modes of organisation has attracted its detractors. As Best and Kellner (1991: 280) maintain: 'postmodern theory exaggerates the break or rupture in history and thus covers over the extent to which the contemporary situation continues to be constituted by capitalism, gender and race oppression, bureaucracy, and other aspects of the past'. One prominent example of postmodern theorisation centres on debates about the transformation of capitalist economies, such as Lash and Urry's (1987) account of the decline of organised capitalism brought about by digital technology, consumerism and globalisation. Contra Lash and Urry, and their ilk, Callinicos rhetorically asks what else is new: despite claims of radical social change, the staple features of capitalist economies –

investment, production and the division of labour – have remained remarkably stable since the end of the Second World War through to the present (Callinicos 1989: 136–7).

Can analogous observations be made about theories of governance? Do the ontological aporias of postmodern periodisation also apply to the theorising associated with the Anglo-governance school? Changes in the organisation of the state in the past twenty years have been highly prominent. Yet, it remains questionable whether the changes traced by the likes of Smith and Rhodes amounts to the dawn of a new era for government in Britain.

Lowe and Rollings's history of the core executive seeks to dispel 'assumptions about a unilinear increase in state intervention after 1900 or in the hollowing-out of the state after 1945' (2000: 117). To a certain extent, Lowe and Rollings concur with the governance model's position. The early years of the twentieth century saw the British state amass considerable powers, abetted by the absence of constitutional checks and its potential administrative capacity. Reforms after the First World War resulted in the creation of a highly centralised bureaucratic Whitehall institution. The establishment of a permanent Cabinet secretariat and the Treasury's role as a central coordinating department gave the core executive the potential to be highly interventionist. Such centralised power came into its own during both world wars (Lowe and Rollings 2000: 103). However, the British state during the interwar years remained highly constrained. The limited support network of civil agencies for promoting policy and the lack of popular support for state intervention, except in crises such as the war, imposed particular constraints on government. Thus, for the authors the characteristic features of governance – fragmented and relatively powerless core executive – precede the years of Thatcherite government and the emergence of powerful international bodies.

The prevalence of governance continued from the 1940s to the mid-1950s. Although this was an era when central government amassed formal responsibilities, central intervention was in fact circumscribed by fragmentation in the core executive. The process of fragmentation was aided and abetted by external interest groups and internal departmental factionalism. A case in point was the planning machinery across government, namely, the Central Economic Planning Staff (CEPS). The CEPS was formed in 1947 to draw up and oversee the implementation of the annual plan for government, the Economic Survey. From the off, the CEPS was challenged by the Treasury and it was bereft of the administrative capability to overcome departmentalism (Lowe and Rollings 2000: 107). Hence, Keynesian demand management – that great totem of the universal welfare state – has been interpreted as a modest form of government intervention, protecting the conditions of the market without dictating what should be done. Even the use of permanent economic controls by the Attlee Labour government was less about the long-term development of industry than the short-term management of the economy (Rollings 1992: 28).

The toing and froing between government and governance continued under Conservative administrations during the 1950s. Despite the pressures from within and without the polity, the Conservative administration of Harold Macmillan between 1957 and 1964 made definite moves to strengthen the capacity of central government (Lowe and Rollings 2000: 109). These Conservative policies challenged governance. Internal fragmentation was tackled through the fusion of ministers, party officials, civil servants and party advisers into a single policy-making community. To strengthen the core executive's influence over external interest groups, corporatist agencies were formed, for example the National Economic Development Council. However, these efforts to augment the position of the central state were undermined by the political and administrative fragmentation within the core executive. Symptomatic of this was the standing of the Treasury. Although the Treasury had a direct influence over welfare policy, this influence was generally limited and confined to a network of cabinet committees. The Treasury's weakness was also a product of its reluctance, born in part out of an ideological predilection, to adopt a proactive role. Due to the Treasury's inertia, departments resorted to factionalism.

This history of the core executive shows that there is nothing especially new about 'governance', as opposed to 'government'. The process of governance is far from being a unique feature of the present or the past twenty years. In fact it has been a feature of the UK government machine for some time. Lowe and Rollings note that the course of the twentieth century has not witnessed a periodic break between government and governance. Rather they maintain there has been a 'longstanding tension in Britain between centralisation and fragmentation, or between the rival concepts of "government" and "governance" ' (2000: 100).

Conclusion: alternative governance models?

Paradigmatic consensus in political science over how to conceptualise government – its institutions, actors and processes – has changed over time. The early to middle years of the twentieth century witnessed the dominance of a perspective that regarded the state as a wholly unified and autonomous institution, which equated political power with the constitutional sovereignty of parliament and a centralised executive. But if there was a dominant paradigm from the 1960s to the 1980s, it was characterised by the idea of the state as a failing institution; a number of writers attributed this to an 'overloaded state', overloaded by the demands of the welfare state. This took place against a background of political and constitutional crises and experimentation by analysts with various strands of neo-pluralist, Marxist and elitist theory. If there is a dominant organising paradigm within political science in recent decades, it is concerned with governance. British government has institutionally entered a new phase, one that is quite distinct from institutional configurations of previous eras. This has come about due to external (globalisation) and internal pressures (market-style reforms). Thus, central government is less reliant on bureaucratic hierarchies than on networks of agencies beyond the central state. It has also moved from being a large, dominant bureaucratic entity to one of many public sector agencies engaged in the policy process. As a result of these developments, central government has become increasingly weakened or, to use the in-house term, hollowed out.

What governance theory has to say about the transformation of political organisations seems highly convincing in view of the market-style reforms of the 1980s. However, a closer inspection of evidence from studies of central government and local policy networks, as well as historical research of government institutions, suggests that such claims may be exaggerated. Central government is still highly resourced and has, at its disposal, a range of powers by which to retain influence over public sector agencies. There is also the possibility that any changes emanating from within the centre have reinforced the power of government, although the impression on the surface suggests otherwise. Historical evidence also shows that the British polity has long been decentralised. Thus it is difficult to see how recent developments have in any way transformed the capacities of the core executive.

The above critique of the Anglo-governance school should not in any way be seen as the pretext for arguing that government is an independent and unified institutional entity. The strength of the Anglo-governance school has been its theorisation of how, in contemporary society, governments cannot do what they want to do but do what they can. The core executive is under pressure of fragmentation, it is dependent upon a variety of public sector agencies and it has to manage interorganisational policy networks that are intrinsically complex. These characteristics of modern government should not be equated with the permanent paralysis of the state.

At this point, it is not so much further evidence and research that is required but alternative ways of conceptualising the institutions and processes of change in the state. Recent efforts to develop an organising perspective, within the intellectual parameters of governance theory, offer a more conceptually cautious treatment of the central state. Marsh *et al.* (2001) propose an 'asymmetric power' model of the British polity. This approach recognises the changes wrought by governance which have contributed to the segmentation of the state. This model also contends that political power tends to be concentrated within the core executive. Governments may depend upon a variety of state and non-state actors to deliver policy, but the centre at the same time retains a unique set of powers and resources that are not available to those actors beyond the centre. Similar observations are offered by local government expert Chris Skelcher (2000). To conceptualise the contemporary state, Skelcher relies on the image of a 'congested state' which focuses on a fragmented and plural forms of governance. The preponderance of collaborative institutional arrangements is symptomatic of the congested milieu in which modern governments operate. In contrast to Rhodes's governance model, these plural networks are closely tied to and regulated from the centre. The question whether these emerging theories of government assume paradigmatic dominance is open to debate.

CHAPTER 4

THE GENDERED STATE

Introduction

Gendered scholarship is now firmly ensconced in academe. For all its significance to the study and theorisation of society, feminist analysis has made only a reticent contribution to one of the cornerstones of the social sciences – the state. This may have something to do with the nature of state and political power. State politics revolves around institutions where women have only a shadow presence. As such, so the argument goes, there seems little point in actually pursuing a feminist analysis of the state: feminist scholars should concentrate on areas that are more relevant to gender theory and more appropriate to the political aims of the women's movement. This may include areas such as the family, sexuality, reproduction politics, and gender discrimination. This is the very point made by Judith Allen, who contends that a theory of the state is not 'an indigenous feminist need' and that feminist analysis would have more to gain from resisting a theoretical enterprise dictated by those who have no concern with gender issues (Allen 1990: 34). But there are feminist analysts for whom the state is of vital significance: not only does the state have a decisive impact on gender relations but gender has also proven central to the development of the state, even when women have not always been equally treated and represented in political institutions.

The intention of this chapter is to examine how feminist authors have attempted to revise existing theories of the state by incorporating gender. The actual feminist theorisation of the state has undergone three general phases of development. Early feminist contributions to state theory mainly drew from existing theoretical approaches, particularly Marxism. Marxist-feminist theories of the state proved inchoate, eventually being superseded by a 'second wave' of radical feminist analysis of the state. In this second wave, authors viewed the state as inextricably linked and contributing to the system of patriarchy. Theories of patriarchy challenged malestream political theory (Burstyn 1983: 80), but the state was still regarded in quite instrumental terms, as something dominated by capitalist interests. The functional shortcomings of patriarchal analysis were addressed in part by subsequent developments in gendered analyses of the state. By the 1980s, what can be termed state-centred feminist analyses became prominent, especially amongst northern European academics. State-centred feminist approaches amassed detailed empirical material to explore the advancement of women's interests in state institutions and the impact of state policies on women's lives. Such research acknowledged the persistence of gender oppression and inequality, but it would deliberately avoid the conclusion that patriarchy is inherent to the liberal state. Such empirical analysis falls short of a fully fledged theory of the state. Nevertheless, it provided significant pointers towards a more nuanced understanding of how gender interests are constituted in the state. In a similar vein, recent gendered approaches have adopted insights from contemporary social thought, especially poststructuralism, cultural analysis and Foucauldian theory. For contemporary gender analyses of the political, poststructrual theory underlines the fragmented, contingent and contradictory nature of the state, as a site of political struggle, oppression and liberation.

A marriage of convenience: Marxism and feminism

According to Jessop (2001a: 157–8), feminist contributions to the state are some way from the cutting edge of state theory. Gendered contributions to the state have tended to borrow from outside of feminist theory. They have failed, argues Jessop, to establish a distinct gender analysis, as with explorations of social relationships and institutional sexism. If Jessop's observations are accurate, they really apply to those embryonic attempts, in the late 1970s, to develop a feminist theory of the state. Early feminist critiques of the state were by no means prolific or original. These formative efforts relied predominantly on Marxist theory to develop a feminist critique of the state. For those early feminists interested in the state, the reliance on Marxism was aided and abetted by the rediscovery of Engels's classic text, *The Origins of the Family, Private Property and the State*, a Marxian account of how the family is implicated in supporting capitalist production and exploitation (Siim 1988: 183). The gravitation of feminist theory towards Marxism was also indicative of the times. The neo-Marxist revival of this period – the early to mid-1970s – meant it became a natural theoretical home for any academic author with critical or radical pretensions. Indeed, the marriage of Marxism and feminism typified not only early feminist accounts of the state but also seminal endeavours to develop general feminist critiques of society (see Kuhn and Wolpe 1978).

A central theme running through early feminist state theory is the mutually reinforcing relationship between the capitalist class structure and the sexual hierarchy (Eisenstein 1979: 5). A notable attempt to graft patriarchy onto a class critique of the state came in an influential article by Mary McIntosh, 'The state and the oppression of women' (1978). In this piece, McIntosh acknowledged that women's oppression is not unique to or confined to capitalist societies. That said, women's oppression under contemporary capitalism is qualitatively distinct from other societies. The key distinction is the active engagement of the state in the economy and society at large, as an instrument of the capitalist class. Here, the state contributes to the suppression and exploitation of women. The state's oppression of women is determined less by patriarchy than by capitalism. In McIntosh's (1978: 259) view, the capitalist class may be predominantly male but its power is based on the economic exploitation of working people, as opposed to men exploiting women. As such, the state's oppression of women is determined by the capitalist system's need for a healthy and fit workforce. In order to reproduce malleable (exploitable) labour for the capitalist economy, the state helps to cultivate family households where women are dependent upon, but also support and care for, their male breadwinners. The state intervenes to ensure that women remain dependent on the male breadwinner; for by remaining tied to the home, there exists a constant source of cheap domestic labour that is crucial to the reproduction of the capitalist workforce (McIntosh 1978: 264). The state's intervention in the family also ensures that women form a flexible reserve army of labour should it be required by capitalism. This interrelationship between labour reproduction, families and gender oppression was pursued further in Marxist feminist critiques of the welfare state.

Neo-Marxist critiques of the welfare state were especially prominent as the postwar Keynesian consensus broke down from the mid-1970s onwards. The welfare state attracted the critical ire of neo-Marxist authors for its perceived institutional backing of the nuclear family, an institutional setting regarded as the prime site for replenishing cheap, pliant labour. The welfare activities of the state – including the provision of health care and social insurance – far from liberating subaltern classes, held the 'potential for capitalist control of the working class' (London Edinburgh Weekend Return Group 1980: 128). Typifying this position, Ian Gough notes the welfare activities of the state emerged historically against a background of burgeoning urbanisation, disrupting traditional familial relations. Welfare services were put in place to 'support the family in its role of reproducing and maintaining the population' (Gough 1979: 48).

A similar logic was pursued by Marxist feminists in the late 1970s. Except for these theorists, there was a greater focus on how the welfare state forces women to take on the role of carers within the home. A key work that pursued these arguments was Elizabeth Wilson's *Women and the Welfare State* (1977). In this text, Wilson traces how the confinement of women to cheap domestic labour was integral to the historical development of the welfare state. The historical emergence of state-controlled welfare activities established policies, ideologies and legislation that discriminated against women, ensuring that they remained dependent on the male breadwinner. This state-sponsored oppression of women is inscribed in the Beveridge report, which established the foundations of the postwar welfare state (Wilson 1977: 150–1). The report did address certain anomalies such as the equal status of women's insurance, but married women were not accorded the same degree of autonomy as men. As such, the report recommended that the national insurance contribution of women should be lower than that of men. Such inequitable treatment in welfare provision takes place for what Wilson acknowledges are crude, functionalist reasons: to ensure that women remain dependent on the male breadwinner, thereby assuming their customary responsibility of nurturing current and future workers.

The prevailing view of early Marxist feminist accounts of the welfare state was that the state contributes to both gender and class oppression. But these early efforts also took into account the ideas of emerging Marxist thinkers who eschewed a one-dimensional conception of the state as the instrument of capital (see Chapter 1). Here the emphasis was on the contingent nature of the capitalist state, or the relative autonomy of the state, in Poulantzas's much used phrase. For instance, Elizabeth Wilson's staunchly instrumental study of the welfare state acknowledged that the welfare system is not under the complete control of a monolithic capitalist order. Capitalism is riddled with competing factions. As such, the welfare state makes certain economic concessions to subordinate groups (Wilson 1977: 13). As well as alluding to the autonomy of the state, certain Marxist-feminist accounts conceded that state action can benefit and advance women's social position. There are national variations and differences. There are differences as to whether welfare systems reinforce women's dependency on the household or whether they promote gender autonomy (Charles 2000: 18). This is a feature of Mary Ruggie's structural Marxist comparison of Swedish and British welfare systems. Here she concludes that the Swedish state has benefited working women. Such improvements, though, are seen to be the result of a strong labour movement in Sweden rather than gender-specific factors (Ruggie 1984: 294–5).

The marriage between Marxism and feminism was far from harmonious. It generated, inevitably, theoretical strains and tensions. This is recognised even by advocates of the Marxist-feminist project. One such proponent, Michèle Barrett, notes how attempts to fuse Marxism with feminism tended to conflate patriarchy with economic exploitation. By equating the two in this way, male power and dominance were never considered properly (Barrett 1986: 29). The marriage between Marxism and feminism contained inherent tensions which were only resolved by giving explanatory priority to the former. The analytical dominance of Marxism, according to Hartmann (1981: 30), is a consequence of

Marxism's analytical status and of the influence exercised by men within the left. The deference accorded to Marxism was certainly a characteristic of early feminist analyses. But such deference in time became more critical – even contemptuous.

The (messy) divorce from Marxism

If the growing weight of feminist criticism directed at Marxism was symptomatic of anything, it was symptomatic of changing paradigmatic fashions within social and political theory from the late 1970s onwards. At this historical juncture, the decline of Marxism was matched by the intellectual and political ascendancy of feminism. With the growth of feminist analysis and literature, thinkers ventured to disown the classical forefathers such as Marx. There were feminist thinkers who were highly critical of Marxism, who asserted the primacy of patriarchy over class in explaining women's oppression. For instance, in her essay 'The traffic of women', Rubin (1975) criticises Marxism for providing an incomplete explanation of women's oppression under capitalism. In constructing a feminist discourse contra Marxism, the likes of Rubin did not totally abandon Marxist vernacular and Marxian concepts. These concepts were merely given a gender spin.

By the late 1970s and early 1980s, women's studies and feminist critiques of Marxist analysis were firmly established. Even those authors committed to a strong union between socialism and feminism were beginning to accept gender as a separate category, independent of class. A notable illustration is provided by the American political scientist, Zillah Eisenstein, in her dual-systems theory of oppression. Despite her commitment to fusing Marxism and feminism, Eisenstein notes that patriarchy precedes capitalism. Rather than reducing patriarchy to capitalism, the point is that women's oppression is not only shaped by class but also determined by the sexual ordering and hierarchy of society (Eisenstein 1979: 25–6). In a similar vein to Eisenstein, the socialist feminist Varda Burstyn found affinities between class and gender. But there are also contradictions between the economic and sexual division of labour. Indeed, Marxist theory and categories are seen to obscure masculine power and dominance. Such male supremacy is a characteristic of mature capitalism and is sustained in late capitalism by social institutions, key among which is the state. The modern state, for Burstyn (1983: 45), acts as an 'organiser and enforcer of male supremacy'.

Exactly how the state 'enforces' male dominance was a matter taken up in the second wave of radical feminist analysis. Radical feminism, unlike Eisenstein and Burstyn's dualistic efforts, attaches greater prominence to an exclusively gender-specific explanation of oppression. From this perspective, a perspective for which oppression is the product of gender rather than class relations, it is a logical step to view the state as the bastion of patriarchy. Hence, radical feminist approaches to the state drew less form non-feminist theoretical discourses such as Marxism. Rather they drew from theories which attempted to specifically explain and understand patriarchy and male dominance.

Conventional political analysis – which includes traditional state theory – does not easily lend itself to feminist theory. The reason for this is that these fields of intellectual endeavour have radically different conceptions of how power works. For the former, political power is located in, and operates through, institutions such as the central executive, parliament or the administrative structures of the state. For the latter, power works through personal relationships, it is exercised and is evident in relations between men and women. These ontological differences have not prevented feminist theoreticians from contributing to political theory and analysis. One notable figure is the feminist political philosopher, Carole Pateman (1979), whose writings on classical political theory and analysis hold relevant insights for the feminist theorisation of politics, including the state. A key assertion made by Pateman in her work on political obligation is that the state has traditionally been conceptualised in liberal democratic theory as a vertical entity. The state is a sphere occupied and dominated by representative politicians, professionals, experts; it is separate from citizens. It is separate from the private domain and only regulates this sphere as an impartial umpire. Because of these assumptions, political analysis and concepts relate and apply exclusively to men and consciously exclude women. Contrary to this position, Pateman makes the point that the state is more than a mere umpire but is a set of governmental institutions that are an integral part of everyday life. More than this, the state is 'part and parcel of the mechanisms that maintain and reinforce the inequalities of everyday life' (1979, p. 173). This includes gender inequalities.

Pateman's general political philosophy inspired feminist authors to employ a similar approach to theorising the state. Whilst questions have been raised by radical feminists such as Judith Allen against a feminist state theory, there are those for whom such an enterprise is not only relevant but also necessary. The reasoning behind this is straightforward. The state impinges on women's lives in various ways, and women are more dependent on state provision than men. The state undoubtedly impacts on women's lives in different ways. But the point is, how do we conceptualise and interpret the state as a gendered force? Radical feminism offers a distinctively gendered approach – as demanded by Pateman – to the state. Below I will outline two such radical feminist approaches: one focuses on the patriarchal state and the other on the position of the sado-state as a supportive linchpin of the violent male oppression of women.

The patriarchal state: a domain of male power and interest

Parallels can be drawn between Marxist and radical feminist theories of the state. Such analogies are informative and shed a good deal of light on feminist approaches to the state. In Marxist theory, the state as a neutral entity is an ideological fantasy. The same is true for those theorists who have propounded the idea of a patriarchal state. Here, the state reflects and becomes a patriarchal institution, providing support for relations of gender domination that exist in society. These forms of domination, from a radical feminist perspective, are not based on a socio-economic or class position as in Marxist analysis, but on sexual divisions in society – a division of inequality where women collectively form a subaltern group dominated by men. Because of their sensitivity to gender, radical feminist theorists are highly critical of Marxism. They are especially critical of those attempts to fuse Marxism and feminism because of the tendency in Marxist theory to treat women's oppression as subservient to class. To paraphrase Hartmann (1981), Marxism and feminism are the one same thing and that one same thing is Marxism.

Those feminists who have written about the state from a patriarchal perspective have particular views about the relationship between the state and society. For theorists of patriarchy, male domination over women can exist independently of the state. The state may be a significant institutional power in society, but sexual divisions and hierarchies in society stem from masculine power and dominance. This is the position of the legal scholar and radical feminist, Catharine MacKinnon. For MacKinnon, male domination over women was safeguarded, socially and economically, even before the emergence of proper legal and state systems. Male domination is secured in the personal, intimate contexts of everyday life, where the state is without an input (MacKinnon 1989: 161).

A similar point is made by Amy Allen in her discussion of Hannah Arendt's conception of power. In this discussion, Allen notes that the power exercised by the state is not the same as that exercised by men over women. Male power, the power exerted by husbands over their wives, operates through both personal and impersonal structural mechanisms, namely, the institutional sexism that confronts women in all social spheres (Allen 1999: 110, cited in Hoffman 2001: 95). Although patriarchy can exist without the state, the view from radical feminism is that the state does not conform to some liberal ideal as a neutral arbiter, as being separate from the interests of men. Contra the liberal view of the state, the feminist position maintains that the state expresses the interests of men: 'The liberal state coercively and authoritatively constitutes the social order in the interest of men as a gender – through its legitimating norms, forms, relation to society, and substantive policies' (MacKinnon 1989: 163).

Underlying classical liberalism is the assumption that citizens enjoy equal status and treatment before the law. This contrasts with medieval society, where monarchy was indistinguishable from the state and landowners enjoyed a supreme legal position. From MacKinnon's radical feminist perspective, the liberal assumption of legal equality is gender-blind: it takes no account of how modern societies are structured and divided by gender. In a gendered society, the state actually sustains male power. The state's support of male power is expressed primarily in the way the law is created and enacted. The male domination over legal processes can be seen in what MacKinnon terms 'negative' and 'positive' law.

The operation of negative law is most apparent in the founding democratic constitution of the United States. The US Constitution is based on the idea that governments should not interfere with existing social arrangements, it is founded on the idea of the negative state. From the position of negative liberty, people should be left to do what they want without interference from others or from government. Judicial or government intervention should be resisted in favour of maintaining the status quo (MacKinnon 1989: 164). But no amount of negative freedom, as MacKinnon argues, will address the oppression and inequality faced by women because civil society has been put beyond legal safeguard. The principle of negative freedom only helps to maintain the status quo, whether this is legal, economic or gendered; it does nothing to redress the imbalance of power that exists in society.

Although the US Constitution is committed to securing individual freedom from state interference, legal processes also rely on positive law. This effectively relates to the policies of the state. The content of positive law, or state policy, protects male power by securing male domination over women at all levels of society. State policies will either protect male authority or such policies will appear to curb its excesses in order to legitimate male power over women (MacKinnon 1989: 167). MacKinnon illustrates this point with reference to laws covering obscenity, sexual discrimination and rape. For example, obscenity laws regulate and prohibit the availability of pornography without ever issuing an outright ban. Such regulative practices ensure the continued interest in, and desirability of, pornography. Here, the law embodies the male point of view and, as such, it institutionalises male power over women. The institutionalisation of sexual relations, concludes MacKinnon, shows that the liberal state may be independent of class relations but it is not autonomous of gender.

Radical feminist authors may agree about the patriarchal nature of society, but there are different interpretations about how the state contributes to patriarchy. For feminist authors such as MacKinnon and Allen, the state comes to reflect and embody the patriarchy that exists in wider society; it is one patriarchal institution amongst many. Patriarchal relations are more the result of male domination over women in the private sphere and not just the product of the institutionalisation of male power by the state. In other words, patriarchy would still exist whether or not it was supported by the state. But is it possible, therefore, for male dominance to exist independently of the state? Support for such a position is by no means unanimous. For some radical feminist theorists, the state is more integral to, and directly engaged in, the exercise of male power than is assumed by the likes of MacKinnon. Why is the state presumed to be so indispensable to the existence and reproduction of patriarchal relations? The reason is that the state has at its disposal the use of legitimate violence and force. It is the state's legitimate propensity for violence, its legitimate control over multifarious forms of institutional force, that enables it to intrude in the private sphere of everyday life, a sphere where sexual relations are enacted and reproduced.

The sado-state: state violence and male dominance

The state, whether ancient or modern, has a propensity for using force. Throughout history it has revealed itself to be a perpetrator of mass atrocities, ruthless violence and human rights abuses of all kinds. State-sponsored violence of this kind is part and parcel of recent government action in Israel, Bosnia and Rwanda. The use of violence is second nature to the state. It is a natural part of how the state asserts its sovereignty. But just as force is central to the modus operandi of the state, it can be said, with some justification, that violence is inherent to patriarchy. In fact, the subjugation of women, as a form of oppression, relies on the use of physical force and violence. The incidence of rape, domestic violence and sexual abuse shows there is a distinctly violent physical expression to patriarchy. The issue is whether male violence and state force are more than analogous but mutually reinforcing. Radical feminist theorists have asserted that it is through its legitimate monopoly over force that the modern state contributes actively to the oppression of women. For example, the radical feminist theorist and theologian, Mary Daly (1987: 185), has made reference to the sado-state and to the sado-state's involvement in the torture, dismembering and murder of women who deviate from societal norms. Daly's observations are made with reference to the ancient, historical past. The question is whether such arguments are relevant to the state in contemporary society.

The matter of whether the state's control of force is implicated in the maintenance of patriarchy is pursued in a study of state sovereignty and gender by the political theorist, John Hoffman (2001). Central to Hoffman's argument about sovereignty is a Weberian-influenced definition of the state in which violence is a key defining feature. Here the state is that institution with monopoly control over the legitimate use of force in a specified territory. The state's monopolisation of force supposedly helps to secure cohesion and order in modern societies. Without such order, modern societies, which are essentially divided, would be hazardous places in which to live. This is questionable. As Hoffman (2001: 84) notes, historical evidence shows that order and cohesion are possible without a single institution claiming monopoly control over the legitimate use of violence. Hence, it follows that there is an underlying political rationale behind the state's monopolisation of force: that of maintaining existing relations of domination and oppression.

One such instance of oppression is the system of patriarchy. Patriarchy is secured and maintained by male force over women, and such force is institutionalised by the state. Thus, patriarchy is a system that is dependent on the state's dominant control of legitimate violence. To support these theoretical claims, Hoffman (2001: 100–4) makes reference to historical anthropology, tracing the sexual division of labour back to Neolithic societies. Historical evidence shows that, whilst the sexual division of labour prevailed in stateless societies, the formation of the nation state led to the institutionalisation of patriarchy. One area of state activity which has institutionalised sexual violence is war. Feminist critiques of international relations have maintained that the state's propensity for war naturalises gender oppression and sexual violence (Hoffman 2001: 119–20). To make the point, Hoffman shows, through existing research, how women and children suffer disproportionately during times of war, whether this is in terms of their actual physical suffering or of their physical displacement as refugees.

The state's institutionalisation and instigation of sexual violence can assume a variety of forms. Women obviously suffer violence at the hands of states in times of war. Women's experience of violence and force can also be perpetrated by the routine domestic policies and practices of states. Such themes are pursued by Judith Butler, the American poststructural and Foucauldian feminist. Her 1997 book, *Excitable Speech*, examines the role of the state in the violent subjugation of women in modern society. The state's role in gender oppression is traced by Butler through a study of the relationship between the language of hate and censorship. For Butler, the censor is far from being an independent arbiter who, according to conventional wisdom, exists to eradicate hate speech or vile images. Instead an alternative view of censorship is set out to that of radical feminists such as MacKinnon who support state censorship of pornography. For MacKinnon, ordinances against pornography are not censorship but forms of equality policy. Censorship is an extension of state power, which according to Butler (1997: 133) 'seeks to produce subjects according to explicit and implicit norms'. Here, the state intervenes as a censor, it defines what is hate speech and therefore what is acceptable in discourse. In fact, she goes on to argue how the extension of state power through censorship can threaten the cultural operation of certain forms of gender and sexual politics (1997: 22). The state, it is argued, is not fit to make such regulatory interventions. The state is already too powerful. It is too arbitrary in its exercise of this power. And it is too unreliable. When making such regulations in the past, the US government has pursued a conservative and anti-progressive agenda. To make the point about the reactionary implications of censorship, Butler uses examples of censorship in the military and of gangsta rappers such as NWA. In addition to posing questions about whether the state is fit to regulate hate speech, Butler makes the more substantive and controversial claim – using Foucault, Derrida and Lacan – that the promotion of hate speech relies on the support of the state. In other words, when the state intervenes to censor hate speech, it inevitably ends up helping to support and reproduce that very same language of hate.

Radical feminist writings on the state are far from extensive or detailed. And yet they are of interest and worth some consideration. The radical feminist approach has made a compelling argument for seeing the liberal state as a patriarchal institution. Contributions by the likes of MacKinnon have introduced a much needed gender focus to malestream state theory. However, these writings are still guilty of depicting the state as an instrumental or one-dimensional institution. What we have here is this: instead of subsuming the state under the category of class, it is subsumed under patriarchy instead (Jessop 2001a: 158). The state is conceptualised as an instrument of patriarchy, much as in Marxism the state is viewed as an instrument of capitalism. Here, the state functions to serve, support and maintain the system of patriarchy; it does this at the expense of other considerations. This is evident in both writings about the patriarchal nature of the state and more recent theories concerning the state's involvement in the physical exploitation of women. Here, the state is seen as integral to the logic of patriarchy. For Walby, the argument that the state is inherently patriarchal relies on the same crude, deterministic logic that has dogged Marxist state theory: 'This is parallel to the problem of instrumentality, which is often considered a flaw in the analysis of the capitalist state in the writings of Marxists' (Walby 1990: 157).

The a priori assumption that states are patriarchal leads to their characterisation as monolithic, homogeneous and one-dimensional (Mills 2003: 266). Clearly they are not. That said, this should not distract us from how they contribute to the institutionalisation of gender bias. States do act against the interests of women and do actively reinforce masculine power. But is it true to say that the state is intrinsically patriarchal? It may be possible that some states are more gender-oppressive than others. It may be likely for certain states to promote gender equality and progressive policies for women. Hence, whilst being mindful of how the state can manifest and institutionalise patriarchy, it is necessary to avoid the same theoretical deficiencies associated with instrumental Marxist accounts of the state. The following section reveals how gender theory and analysis have progressed from essentialist notions of the state as the patriarch-general.

The relative patriarchy of the state

Feminist theorisation of state is far from being in a patriarchal stasis. During the 1980s and 1990s, feminist scholars raised their heads above the patriarchal parapet. In so doing, they entertained the possibility that the state is not always the 'woman's enemy'. Gendered analysis of the state has progressed from essentialist notions of the state as patriarch-general to embrace the relative patriarchy of the state; that is, the state can make a difference to the material, political and social lives of women, whilst taking into account the constraints imposed by patriarchal social structures. For instance, Franzway *et al.* (1989) note that the state has a constitutive role in gender relations. The idea here is that the state, as a central power, is involved in reproducing gender inequalities and oppression. But this falls short of supposing the state is an inherently patriarchal institution, for state action and structures are not straightforward (1989: 53). Although involved in the reproduction of gender inequalities, the state creates historical possibilities for abolishing sexual inequalities.

The appreciation of the state's relative patriarchy was an outcome of intellectual trends in both feminist scholarship and mainstream political analysis. In terms of the former, Connell argues that the growth of feminist analysis in universities led to a burgeoning of empirical research into gender and the state. Prior to this boom in feminist research, theoretical debates about the patriarchal state were driven less by the academic requirements for rigorous empirical analysis than by the strategic needs of the women's movement, by how it should respond to the modern liberal state in a post-Marxist era (Connell 1990: 518). The political rationale of radical feminist theory resulted in a crude portrayal of the state. The emergence of academic-based feminist studies produced a more nuanced and balanced grasp of the state. As well as developments within feminist scholarship, the empirical analysis of state policies from a gendered perspective was also influenced by efforts to 'bring the state back in' within mainstream political analysis (Stetson and Mazur 1995: 6). This neo-Weberian resurrection of the state, led by political scientists such as Skocpol, Nordlinger and Krasner, was a factor in inducing social scientists to reconsider the impact of the state on women's lives. Two fields of gender-orientated empirical investigation became prominent, as will be explored below: firstly, the field of state feminist research, which has concentrated, in the main but not exclusively, on how northern European states have embraced progressive gender policies and practices; and secondly, there have been studies of how the welfare state has affected the lives of women. Although these contributions tend to be empirical, they offer certain theoretical insights about the relative patriarchy of the state.

State feminism

The effect of public policies on women's lives was a matter of growing empirical speculation throughout the 1980s. This body of research has been variously dubbed 'femocracy', 'feminism from above' or 'state feminism'. The aim of state feminist studies was to assess, through empirical analysis, the extent to which the state can transform the material, social and political circumstances of women. In addition, state feminist studies sought to investigate how far state agencies have promoted a woman-centred policy agenda. The issue of how far states have embraced a feminist agenda is something that a growing number of social scientists have attended to in recent years. The ensuing research has produced a wealth of evidence from both national-based and comparative studies. Especially prominent in this corpus of research are studies focusing on the gender policies and practices of northern European states.

The prominence of northern European states is no accident, considering that these states have been at the vanguard of enlightened gender policies. The gender-friendly policies of Scandinavian countries should be seen, in part, as an outcome of how women have become an ever growing presence in the state apparatus of these nations (Hernes 1987). Amongst the Scandinavian states, all levels of government, from leading executive positions through to parliamentary seats, have witnessed a significant influx of women. It was calculated that by the mid- to late 1980s one-third of all Scandinavian parliaments were made up of women and that eight of Norway's 18 executive ministers were women. Because of the high representation of women in these political institutions, Hernes (1987: 15) argues that 'Nordic democracies embody a state form that makes it possible to transform them into woman-friendly societies'. A woman-friendly state is one that enables women to move seamlessly from the sphere of work to motherhood and then to public life. In other words, it would support women in their life choices rather than confining them to particular spheres, whether the home or workplace.

State feminist studies have also demonstrated how far woman-friendly policies have been instituted across different states, especially in northern European countries. Countries such as Denmark, Norway and the Netherlands are considered by Mazur and Stetson to have reached the highest level of state feminism. These states have integrated gender equity into a diverse range of policy areas and government institutions (1995: 276–80). In 1975 Denmark formed its Equal Status Council (ESC), a corporate body responsible for coordinating gender issues within the executive policy-making machinery. The ESC has successfully pursued the representation of women's interests in new legislation and continually polices the implementation of existing equal opportunities legislation (Borchorst 1995: 59). Critics would invite some caution when estimating the extent to which Scandinavian-style policy interventions have transformed women's lives in northern Europe. Hernes (1987: 20–1) contends that progressive change in the treatment of women came about through a combination of economic development and women's activism as well as governmental policies. Government policies, for this critical author, regulate rather than initiate change already under way.

As well as the progressive policies of individual states, there are feminist scholars, albeit limited in number, who have considered the feminisation of parastate or transnational governing agencies. Prominent amongst such transnational institutions is the European Union (EU), which for Walby (1999) possesses significant regulatory powers above those of individual member states. The EU's legal apparatus has since its inception pursued a progressive social agenda, the prime feature of which is gender equality (Walby 1999: 130). Gender has been a prominent feature in various treaties and legal articles issued by the EU. There are the formative Articles, including the founding Treaty of Rome, that established the principle of equal pay between men and women. Recent EU directives have attempted to broaden gender legislation. Such EU legislation now includes a commitment to eliminate gender inequality. To ensure the enforcement of equality legislation, the European Court of Justice and the European Commission scrutinise the practices and activities of individual member states.

What do these state feminist studies offer in the way of a gendered theory of the state? If they do provide a theory of the state – more implicit than explicit – they embrace what Franzway *et al.* (1989) have to say about gendered theories of the state: any reasonable theory of the state should be able to inform how the state can assume both patriarchal and progressive practices. The state feminist studies demonstrate how the integration of women's interests within the executive machinery constitutes a significant political development. Whether such institutional change results in real material differences is a moot point. The question of how the state impacts upon the material interests of women is one that has interested students of social policy. Specifically, there is a growing body of gender-sensitive social policy research that has focused on welfare provision and the welfare state generally.

Gender and the welfare state

The welfare state is central to the history of the late twentieth century. And despite the political reversals of recent decades, the welfare state remains a constant across the industrialised world. There are feminist social scientists who argue that the welfare state is more important for women than for men (Hernes 1987: 37). The importance of the welfare state for women has not escaped the analytical attention of feminist social scientists and social policy experts. The welfare state, as shown above, was central to early efforts to develop feminist accounts of the state, albeit Marxist in orientation. The contribution of the welfare state in fashioning, shaping and reproducing gender relations has been subject to growing empirical analysis. Elements of this work hold implications for a gender-focused theorisation of the state.

Contemporary studies of the welfare state have progressed somewhat from earlier generic accounts, where all different types of welfare state were seen to converge around a single institutional model. Recent studies have emphasised the institutional diversity in welfare provision. The buzz term is that of welfare regimes. To comprehend this diversity and to compare the welfare institutions of different nation states, researchers have come up with various typologies. One of the more influential categories is that of Esping-Andersen (1990) who classifies welfare states according to liberal, corporatist and social democratic regimes. This typology has been adopted by feminist researchers to explore the gendered policies of different welfare regimes (see Haney 2000: 654). However, critics argue that Esping-Andersen's classification is not sufficiently gender-sensitive. This is an argument made by Leira (1989) in her study of women and welfare state policies in Scandinavia. She notes that Norway, which is classified as a progressive, social democratic welfare regime by Esping-Andersen, is closer to conservative regimes such as Britain when it comes to women's policies.

But how can we be sensitive to the gender variations of welfare states? There is one notable answer. For Jane Lewis (1992), welfare states can be classified in terms of how much they embrace a male-breadwinner ideology. That is, the popular belief that the public sphere is predominantly and rightfully male. The private sphere, in the meantime, belongs to women. The ideology is operationalised in terms of stereotypical assumptions about women's roles that underlie social policies. A male-breadwinner model of the family, Lewis (1992: 161) suggests, cuts across all other established welfare typologies. This *über*-typology is used to compare the gender-relevant variations of social policies in Britain, Ireland, France and Sweden. Ireland and Britain are examples of historically strong male-breadwinner states; France is a country with a modified breadwinner welfare state, in that the welfare system has recognised the interests of women as both workers and carers; and Sweden is classified as having a weak male-breadwinner ideology because of the way policies have integrated women firmly into the labour market.

A recent comparative study by Mary Daly and Katherine Rake establishes relevant empirical as well as theoretical insights on welfare and gender. In their study, the authors note that Lewis's breadwinner model offers a useful framework for understanding and explaining gender-specific policy variations between welfare states. But they add that Lewis's model is rudimentary (Daly and Rake 2003: 30). It assesses states along the single-breadwinner ideology axis, overemphasising similarities between welfare states. As such, the model fails to do justice to the complexity and differences between welfare regimes – a point that has been reiterated by other feminist scholars of the welfare state (O'Connor 1993: 515). In contrast, Daly and Rake utilise a more open approach that avoids placing countries into particular typologies. Instead the authors assess the peculiarities of different welfare regimes. They consider differences and similarities across various welfare states in order to underline the complexities of each national case. The comparison here is based on: a relatively large number of comparative cases (eight countries); a sample that juxtaposes cases that are both distinct (the USA versus Sweden) and similar (Germany versus the Netherlands); a diverse range of variables and criteria for 'measuring' the gendered repercussions of social policies (Daly and Rake 2003: 166–7).

Daly and Rake identify patterns in how welfare shapes the position of men and women within and between different nations. In terms of the effect of welfare on the sexes, intrafamilial gender differentials have persisted amongst the various nations covered by the study. A significant portion of women have no independent income whatsoever, despite years of welfare intervention. These disparities are by no means uniform: such intrafamilial inequalities are especially entrenched in Ireland and the Netherlands, with a high proportion of women having access to limited resources. The situation in these countries contrasts with Britain and Sweden, where state provision has given women independent resources and incomes (Daly and Rake 2003: 136–7). This empirical investigation by Daly and Rake attests to how the welfare state reaches deep into the social and gender order, structuring the resources and power relations between men and women (2003: 165). The implication of this is that the welfare state is a site of struggle between cultural, economic and other power relations that penetrate welfare processes.

Both state feminism and gender-sensitive research into welfare regimes have furnished a rich source of empirical data on the advances of women's interests at the level of the state. But these explorations of the state have attracted detractors. One such critic is Nickie Charles, who notes that 'feminists have tended to concentrate on social policies and their effects on gender relations rather than the way in which gender interests are constituted and represented at the political level' (2000: 17). That is, these studies seem to lack political insight and theoretical rigour. Such criticism may be justified. But it is justified only up to a point.

Feminist research into the welfare state, and state feminism for that matter, do provide some significant pointers for a gendered theorisation of the state. In particular, these scholarly endeavours take into account the complexities of the state and its relationship to gender. One notable feature to emerge from such work is that the gender repercussions of welfare policies are not uniform. It is possible for the state in one policy area to take from women and in another policy arena to give to women. State provision in Britain, for instance, has given women financial independence from men, but state policy has not addressed gender inequalities. In fact, in certain areas, it has reinforced these inequalities. The research also underlines that even if a state promotes women's interests and woman-friendly policies, these have to contend with wider social structures. Daly and Rake (2003: 177) observe that 'persistent gender inequalities in power and other resources continue to limit the extent to which women's claims are heard and met'. Whilst taking into account the constraints imposed by patriarchal structures, the state can make a difference to the material, political and social lives of women. What this body of research on the welfare state and state feminism seems to demonstrate is that when it comes to gender, the policies and practices of the state are not fixed – either in a patriarchal or pro-women direction. The gendering of the state is ambiguous – it can both militate against the interests of women and promote these very same interests. The equivocal nature of the state as a gendered institution is a theoretical position that has been taken to new levels by feminist theorists who have embraced poststructuralist theory. Let us take a closer look at this school of thought in the discussion that follows below.

Poststructural feminist analysis and the state

With the decline of Marxism, gender theorists looked elsewhere for inspiration. By the 1980s, feminist thinkers were being drawn to postmodernism – it seems there was a natural affinity. But there were those who resisted, and continue to resist, poststructuralism's advances – the perception being that when the Emperor was looking for new clothes he shopped in Paris (see, for example, Benhabib 1995). That said, Coole argues that the relationship between feminism and postmodernism is ambiguous and full of tension but also has a good deal of potential. Feminists are obliged to engage with postmodernism, such is the logic of feminist theory (Coole 1993: 221). This cultural approach has been particularly appealing to contemporary feminist theorists as they look to show how gender identities, as well as patriarchy, are reproduced. Julia Kristeva, for example, used the ideas of Freud and Lacan to demonstrate how the discourse of maternity helps to shape feminine identity. Indeed, language has assumed a central mantle in poststructural feminist thinking, most notably in the writings of leading feminist thinkers such as Judith Butler and the late Mary Joe Frug, for both of whom gender is a prisoner of language. And there is also Luce Irigaray's Lacanian- and Derridean-inspired feminist exposé of the masculine ideology that underpins the system of language and communication.

Thinkers who draw upon the varied poststructuralist cannon have waged an offensive against notions of a unified totality in the social sciences, what Lyotard (1979) terms 'unicity'. In so doing, they have challenged conventional ways of thinking about the individual and society. These poststructural thinkers explored how social control and order as well as truth claims are established through cultural processes, especially language. Postmodern theory moved from the margins to become something of an orthodoxy in academic departments and institutions. As we have seen in other chapters within this book (see Chapters 2 and 5), poststructural theory has inspired alternative ways of thinking about political processes, and institutions have proven especially prominent in this respect. Poststructural-informed analysis of the state offers notable insights on the way states are far from being unified structures but highly complex and disaggregated institutions. This makes states vulnerable to various pressures and forces. Such ideas have been seized upon by feminist thinkers, especially those who have ventured into feminist political and state theory.

Decentred patriarchy and the state

As we have already seen elsewhere in this book, the intellectual trend of poststructuralism came to exert an influence on political theory. One of the recurring themes found in contemporary state theory is that political power and authority have become decentralised. In particular, the writings of Michel Foucault on power, as shown in Chapter 2, were responsible for bringing inventive and original insights on the operation of power in modern society. According to Foucault, power is less concentrated in the hands of central institutions or the preserve of figures of authority than it is diffuse, fragmentary and elusive.

The poststructural insights on power and specifically the workings of political institutions have attracted the attention of feminist thinkers (see Yeatman 1994). This should be expected considering the burgeoning popularity of poststructural feminist analysis, headed by the likes of Butler, Kristeva, Paglia, Frug and others. Most importantly, the theoretical as well as the political repercussions of contemporary philosophical currents have not been lost on feminist thinkers interested in the state. Bryson (1999: 100) spells out exactly why feminist thinkers have been attracted to the idea of a *postmodern state*, of a fragmented non-unified state: 'although there might not be a state in the sense of one central body serving patriarchal and/or capitalist interests, the state can be more loosely conceptualised as an arena of conflict ... within which feminist gains can be won and resistance expressed'.

How do these theoretical concerns form into a substantive gender critique of the modern state? Pringle and Watson (1992) provide some pointers. For them the state is constructed out of a series of practices and discourses, and has never been a boundless and unchanging institution. Echoing Foucauldian ideas of power and governmentality, the state is portrayed as a fragmented structure, a structure that has fractured under the weight of different political struggles. The struggle inscribed in the state inevitably means that it also becomes a site of resistance (Pringle and Watson 1992: 67). Though questioning conventional notions of the state, the authors are keen to avoid a knee-jerk, postmodern abandonment of it. Here, the state – from a poststructural feminist position – is comprised of different arenas where 'men use a variety of strategies to construct their interests and women can use various strategies and counter-strategies to constitute their interests' (Waylen 1998: 9). The state is an arena where unequal gender relations are institutionalised. But the state, as a fragmented institutional site, is also an arena in which those same unequal relationships can be challenged (Cravey 1998: 538). Hence, the myriad of established state institutions, bodies and agencies are implicated in this political struggle between gender groupings.

One interesting instance of how gender politics works through the existing, fragmented architecture of the state is highlighted by Monica Threlfall. In her research, she demonstrates how political parties help to create the political opportunity structures for advancing feminist objectives. Threlfall demonstrates this through an analysis of social democratic parties in Spain, specifically the Spanish Socialist Workers Party (PSDE) which formed various governments from 1982 to 1996. The PSOE was central in facilitating access to the state apparatus for feminist policy activists (Threlfall 1998: 71). The significance of political parties in advancing gendered interest was also a factor in regional and local government.

Another good illustration of the way organisational contradictions in the state open up opportunities for progressive gender policies is given by the socio-legal feminist theorist, Davina Cooper. In her study of radical sexual politics in the local UK state during the late 1980s, Cooper utilises a poststructural framework for understanding the state as a 'multifaceted phenomenon with no fixed form, essence or core' (1995: 60–1). As something without fixed institutional boundaries, it becomes possible to undermine state power and access state resources. Whilst facing innumerable internal and external constraints, lesbian and gay activists in the local arena were able to utilise state authority – bureaucratic processes and state discourses. Activists were able to establish a state base from which to enact progressive change (see Cooper 1995: 112–17). Cooper notes from her study that progressive change occurred in AIDS policies, adoption and fostering initiatives, housing rights and support for cultural events. All this was made possible by the ambiguous nature of the state.

The opportunities for pursuing gender-friendly policies afforded by the institutional configuration of the modern state also extend to non-democratic states. Take Htun's (2003) study of the Latin American dictatorships of Chile, Brazil and Argentina from the mid-1960s through to the 1980s and the development of gender politics in these military-led societies. The author acknowledges that her study came up with some unexpected findings. For instance, these conservative military governments introduced progressive family law reforms, including changes to civil codes that allowed women greater property rights. But this was counterbalanced by the fact that divorce laws in these dictatorial states remained highly restrictive. Htun emphasises in her study how progressive reformers – from the elite segment of society – were able to hook into disaggregated state institutions in pursuit of gender equality policies. This included the organs of the military authoritarian state.

Political engagement at the level of the state is a complex and contradictory business. This is so as far as gender is concerned. As Franzway *et al.* (1989: 55) suggest, if the state becomes too closely aligned with feminist or women's interests this is likely to alarm masculine strongholds. Hence, significant advances in women's equality in the labour market are likely to undermine masculine dominance – a development that will elicit reactions from such male citadels as trade unions and corporations. As well as contradictions, the gender struggle inscribed within the state invariably means that progress towards women's equality will remain uneven; any challenges to patriarchy are likely to experience certain vicissitudes. One notable instance of this is outlined by Mervat Hatem in a historical study of state feminism in Egypt. In the 1950s and 1960s, the Nasser government established new forms of public welfare provision. The new welfare regime was explicitly committed to promoting women's equality in Egypt (Hatem 1992: 231). The welfare state came under concerted attack during the 1980s. The Sadat and Mubarak governments undertook a programme of economic and political market liberalisation. Such market liberalisation led to a substantive reversal of welfare provision and of state-directed support for women. These changes undermined the prospects of lower middle-class and working-class Egyptian women, bringing socio-economic divisions amongst Egyptian women in general. The suggestion here, as already noted, is that the state is less an automatic instrument of patriarchy than it is in a position of relative autonomy from patriarchy.

Poststructural feminist theory highlights how the fragmented state generates opportunities for gender politics. And yet, for postmodern gender theorists, the state may be contradictory and open to challenges but it still remains an influential social and cultural entity, with the power to set boundaries, especially gender boundaries. So as well as being a site of multiple resistance and contradiction, state activities and policies give shape to, and define, women's identities.

The fracturing of femininity: the end of a feminist political agenda in the state arena?

From a poststructural perspective, it is not only state institutions that remain fragmented, uneven and disjointed but also gender itself. Postmodern feminist theory has challenged one of the shibboleths of patriarchal theory: that women share the same identity and interests because of their status as the second sex. Here, gender is not fixed, feminine identity is diverse, it is disparate, it is subject to constant renegotiation: women's political interests are not one and the same. But what does identity have to do with the state?

The existence of multiple gender identities and diverse interests amongst women is traced by certain postmodern feminist to the state. Rather, more specifically, it is traced to the system of law. Postmodern feminist legal scholars have been sensitive to how the law constitutes 'multiple categories of difference' amongst women. From this perspective, the law is a set of discourses rather than a series of formal conventions and regulations that constitute persons, that set social and gender boundaries (Haney 2000: 647). So gender identity and interests when before the law are subject to constant negotiation, but they are subject, also, to various strictures. The work of postmodern feminists such as Dixon (1995) demonstrates how gender interests are rarely unified before the law. The legal system is formed around complex discourses that fix gender categories but also suppress women along the lines of race, class and sexuality (see Dixon 1995: 372–4).

From Nancy Hirschmann's point of view, the discursive basis of gender can have quite far-reaching consequences: the idea that gender identity is something which is not necessarily common to all women leads to an evaporation of the term or concept of 'woman' (1992: 29). Questioning the very essence of gender as something that can be shared undermines a feminist analysis of politics and of the state. The argument here is that if women's identities are so fractured and divided, there is little prospect of women having collective political interests to advance. This is the argument made by the leading social theorist, Bob Jessop. The feminist attempts to reverse the patriarchal policies of the state, argues Jessop, are not straightforward, because there are many different types and versions of femininity. In other words, women are characterised by divergent interests and agendas. There are differences, as Jessop suggests, among women as a social group. Women are divided socio-economically, racially, culturally and generationally. But where does this proliferation of femininities leave a gendered theory of the state? For Jessop, it means that the pursuit of women's political interests may lack coherence – it may, ultimately, result in strategic tensions. Different femininities and identities produce divergent standpoints and horizons of action, as well as the pursuit of contrasting tactics and strategies (Jessop 2001b: 7). To support his case, Jessop points to the lack of consensus over the pursuit of women's interests through international conventions on human rights. Despite the progress achieved in pursuing women's interests internationally, there are feminists who criticise the feminisation of human rights discourse. But if, as Jessop suggests, women's political interests are so fractured and divided, a gendered theory of the state, to paraphrase Connell, will find it difficult to understand why women have collective interests to promote. And it will also be difficult to explain why men also have a collective interest to be defended in the state structure (Connell 1990: 513).

The idea that men form a homogeneous group contra women, who also form a homogeneous collective entity, is analytically suspect. There are differences among men and women as a social group. They are divided, as we have already seen, by class, race, culture and age. There are also different versions of femininity and masculinity within similar social groups. Whether men and women form a distinct collective grouping is problematic and difficult to comprehend. But, as Pringle and Watson (1992: 68) argue, 'many feminists would be reluctant to let go of some core of common identity which unites women across class, ethnic and racial boundaries'. Collective gender categories remain socially and politically significant. This line of reasoning is pursued by Brittan (1989) as he explores the question of whether men form a collectivity. He notes that the category of 'man' or 'woman' is not just a useful system of classification. It is more than a category. Gender is a factor responsible for the distribution of resources, wealth power, privilege and status. In accordance with this distributive influence, all manner of empirical surveys and academic studies have demonstrated that men are socially dominant *vis-à-vis* women. By the same token, women form a subaltern group. Following this, Connell (1987: 183) observes that there are different versions of masculinity and femininity but gender relations nevertheless centre 'on a single structural fact, the global domination of men over women'. The implication here is that men and women do not necessarily constitute social classes but they do 'stand in a political relationship to each other' (Brittan 1989: 110).

What is central to the political interests of both men and women, what is decisive in shaping the structures of gender domination, notes Brittan, is the mode of reproduction. Here, Brittan is drawing from Jeff Hearn's theorisation of masculinity. For Hearn, the realm of reproduction covers various processes. From sexual union, to marriage, to childcare, to the assumption of breadwinner responsibilities: these processes are controlled by men (Hearn 1987: 63–5). In other words, if there are distinct collective identities and interests based on gender, they revolve around the issue of reproduction. Men and women, it is possible to say, albeit with certain reservations, do form distinct collective groups, each with mutual interests and ideological identifications in common. Men and women as loose collectivities will pursue their common political interests through the institutions of the state. And the state, to use Jessop's terminology, is a site where these gender struggles are played out; for the state, due to its relative formlessness, is an arena where different social relations struggle for ascendancy.

Conclusion

It has been said that feminism has no theory of the state. This has much to do with the fact that the traditional focus and analytical strengths of feminist scholarship have been far from the conventional field of state theory. That said, feminist theorists have engaged with mainstream political thought and its attendant concerns. In so doing, they have challenged the gender ignorance of much state theory. For this alone they should be applauded and celebrated within mainstream political analysis – which they are not necessarily. More significantly, feminist political theory has also produced notable insights about the state. Although these contributions are written from a gendered perspective, they are far from homogeneous and encompass a range of theoretical perspectives. As shown in this chapter, gendered theories of the state have gone through different phases of development. Early feminist analyses largely drew from established state theories, particularly those inspired by Marxism; a 'second wave' of radical feminism portrayed the state as an inherently patriarchal institution; and, finally, state-centred feminist perspectives were based, in part, on detailed empirical analyses of how governments shape the relative life chances of men and women. Each respective contribution, however, is some way from establishing a gendered theory of the state that is wholly acceptable and adequate. Recent gendered approaches have embraced contemporary revisions of political power, especially those of a poststructural and Foucauldian persuasion, to underline the state as a fragmented, contingent and contradictory institution and as a site of social and political struggle. Such arguments show that gendered political interests located in the state are splintered and fragmented. At the same time, a gendered theory of the state still needs to demonstrate that men and women do have collective political interests which may be pursued through the state. The state still matters as something which impacts on women's lives both individually and collectively.

CHAPTER 5

THE CULTURAL TURN IN STATE THEORY

Introduction: the birth of culture

Everywhere we turn to nowadays in the human sciences we seem to find culture. The intellectual stature of culture has grown immeasurably since the late 1960s, standing as an equal alongside established ideas such as class, race, power, gender and bureaucracy. For this we have the so-called 'cultural turn' to blame. The turn to culture has challenged shibboleths and long-held assumptions in the social sciences. I say 'challenged' because the embrace of culture has invoked a relativist *fait accompli*: a scepticism of grand theory design; a fundamental re-evaluation of the materialist mindset in understanding social structures. Few disciplines and areas of study in the social sciences remain untouched by the cultural turn. This includes one of the cornerstones of social and political theory: the state. Our aim in this chapter is to explore how state theory has responded to the cultural turn.

Social and political theorists have long grappled with the state's relationship to society, especially the extent to which the former is independent of and autonomous from the latter. Much has been written about state–society relations; the cultural turn has taken this debate in new and interesting directions. The new *cultural enlightenment* has given analysts the intellectual red light to interrogate the foundations of the state – its authority and also its very existence. Such questions against the state have already been posed. Throughout the 1950s and 1960s, American political scientists with a behavioural predilection were at pains to argue that the state was a mere abstraction – an assemblage of institutions and various political actors (see Chapter 1). The affinity between behaviourists and cultural analysts ends at this particular juncture: with a healthy dose of scepticism over whether we can really talk about *the state*.

Cultural theorists of the state have pursued a more telling and richer course of analysis than the American behavioural tradition. Whereas behaviourists wished the state away out of a deep ideological antipathy, cultural theorists have been determined to overhaul and revise many taken-for-granted assumptions within state theory. As part of this revision, analysts have shown that there are definite cultural dimensions – often ignored by extant theories – to the modern state. For some this means the cultural realm actually constitutes the state, that it is a *cultural entity*. Other analysts take a more considered approach and see the state and culture lying in a mutually dependent, dialectical relationship. Before we examine how culture has entered contemporary state theory, we need to do some ground work: to consider the origins of the cultural turn in the social sciences and those formative attempts to bring a cultural dimension to state theory.

The cultural turn in social theory

Conventional social science opinion would have it that structures are *sui generis* to culture: the cultural realm is a product of, and prior to, objective social entities that endure across time and space. Intermediate structures such as bureaucratic hierarchies or institutional settings, or grand structures such as global markets and state authorities, have analytical priority over culture. But this orthodoxy, which has consigned culture to a secondary status, has been challenged. The main source of the challenge has come from the cultural turn within the social and human sciences. This new intellectual movement, unlike conventional social science wisdom, demands that culture is more than a mere 'superstructure', more than a symptom of deeper underlying forces. From this point of view, culture forms a context for action and thought. Alexander and Smith (1993: 156) 'propose that culture be thought of as a structure composed of symbolic sets ... This is to say that, when they are interrelated, symbols provide a nonmaterial structure. They represent a level of organisation that patterns action as surely as structures of a more visible, material kind'. So culture is seen to have structural properties. And structures are seen to be cultural.

The cultural turn was a spin-off from various intellectual developments that began and continued after the early 1960s. This included extant theoretical activities on the margins of mainstream socio-political thought and a range of nascent ideas. Poststructuralism, discourse theory, Foucauldian 'genealogy', hermeneutic phenomenology, symbolic interactionism, the symbolic anthropology peddled by such luminaries as Mary Douglas and Herbert Mead, and the new philosophy of science associated with Georges Canguilhem and Gaston Bachelard: these intellectual movements were the inspirational vanguard of the cultural turn (Norris 1997: 16). The cultural turn may be associated with new and innovative social theories from the postwar era, but its origins really stretch back to an earlier time. The formative, and some would say critical, influence was the classical sociology of Emile Durkheim, as already mentioned. It was Durkheim who produced these culturally informed writings late on in his career, during the late nineteenth and early twentieth centuries. The importance of Durkheim is routinely overlooked by the modern purveyors of cultural theory, even though, according to Alexander and Smith (2005: 17), the cultural turn owes everything to his legacy.

Much of this newfangled cultural thinking was European in origin, filling the vast void left by the political and intellectual disaffection with Marxism in the late 1960s. But to this brief 'intellectual genealogy' of the cultural turn a caveat should be added. Although Europe was the epicentre for such new wave philosophers, developments in American academe were also to play their part in the *discovery culture*. A distinct form of cultural analysis was paraded by the neo-pragmatist philosophy of Richard Rorty. In addition, there was the Durkheimian-informed social anthropology and socio-logics pioneered by Clifford Geertz and Robert Bellah.

The cultural turn in the social sciences prioritised the non-material. This meant that ideas, symbols, personal identity, discourse, norms and values as well as everyday mundane practices were given, at the very least, parity with material structures. The privileging of the cultural sent intellectual shockwaves across disciplines in the humanities and social sciences. Philosophy, literary criticism, history and sociology were all affected. Cultural analysis also had a deep impact on specialist subdisciplinary fields: feminist theory, contemporary psychoanalysis, social movement studies and the sociology of scientific knowledge all willingly embraced culture. The cultural turn even helped to popularise new subject disciplines – take cultural studies and semiotics.

We should now ask: did the cultural turn in the social sciences have any impact on state theory? The theoretical analysis of the state, when compared to other social science fields – feminist theory and the sociology of science to name a couple – has proven less receptive to the revival of culture. This conclusion is the view put forward by cultural sociologist George Steinmetz. As one of the few contemporary analysts to explore the interplay between state theory and cultural analysis in any detail, Steinmetz (1999: 3) notes that 'the study of the state has remained relatively aloof from' discussions about culture. When culture has come up for discussion, it has been seen as an epiphenomenon of the state. Culture is placed at the margins. It is a dependent rather than an independent variable in relation to the state.

Early forays into 'political culture'

There have been occasions, admittedly few, when culture was given prominence in formative discussions of state formation. But these discussions took place – argues Steinmetz – within narrow conceptual parameters. They were conceptually limited in part because culture was equated with distinct national values and beliefs, which were then grafted on to political systems. The archetypal example of this attempt to link different national cultures with governing systems was the political culture approach pioneered by Gabriel Almond and Sidney Verba in their book *The Civic Culture*. For these authors, culture is defined as, or rather is reduced to, 'psychological orientation toward social objects', namely, attitudes about the political system and its policy outputs (1963: 14). The political cultures of five democratic countries (Britain, the USA, Mexico, Italy and Germany) were studied, using mass survey questionnaires and statistical post-data analysis. Underlying this international survey is a definite theoretical position on the direction of causality between political culture and political system: that political culture affects democratic government. In particular, Almond and Verba wanted to reveal the extent to which political culture helps to cultivate and maintain a stable democracy. Stability depends on governing structures but is also contingent upon the attitudes of people towards the political process (Almond and Verba 1963: 498). In other words, the political culture – as measured in terms of popular attitudes towards government – shapes the destiny of the democratic political system and its institutions.

Whilst giving causal priority to culture, Almond and Verba's analysis has little affinity with the *topoi* of the cultural turn. To begin with, the authors are committed to a behaviourist approach. They see culture as little more than the preferences and attitudes of individuals (Steinmetz 1999: 19). The way such attitudes relate to political structures can appear at best perplexing and at worst lacking any real analytical depth. Whilst exploring a fit between political culture and governing structures, they caution against the assumption that both are somehow congruent (Almond and Verba 1963: 34). This is an odd position, argues Pateman (1980). And it is easy to see why, if we dig beneath the surface of Almond and Verba's book. There is a taken-for-granted notion within *The Civic Culture*, one influenced by Parsonian functionalism, that political culture and political structures develop together (Pateman 1980: 67–9). This is taken to be a given which makes the previous quote by Almond and Verba slightly perplexing and symptomatic of a fundamental weakness: there is a lack of real insight into and explanation of how culture and political structures are actually related. It would take a later generation of thinkers to explore the connection between the two in greater theoretical depth.

Early postwar theorisation of the state was to an extent conceptually conservative, making it resistant to or unreceptive to fresh and original innovations in the social sciences such as emerging cultural theories. Such observations seem a little misplaced for contemporary state theory. Even Steinmetz (1999: 3) makes an interesting concession: 'A partial erosion of the barriers to cultural theories and processes is nevertheless visible even in the field of state studies'. In part this is due to the ubiquity of the cultural turn in the social sciences. State theory could no longer ignore the force of its popularity throughout the social sciences. In addition to the popular diffusion of cultural analysis, there were developments specific to state theory, resulting in a greater openness to cultural explanations.

The call for a cultural appreciation of the state was made by Thomas and Meyer (1984). For these commentators, the state is more than a bureaucratic entity and its sphere of influence has grown beyond recognition since the Second World War (1984: 475–6). Because the state has grown and its influence extends through society, culture should naturally enter the equation; for the state is, in Thomas and Meyers thinking, a cultural entity. The recognition that the state's influence extends beyond political administration gradually made state theory open to cultural analysis. A good example of this is what happened to Marxian approaches to the state – so prominent during the state theory revival of the early 1970s. The intellectual decline of Marxism and the subsequent rebranding of Marxian scholarship during the 1970s broadened the parameters of state theory (Brenner 2004: 24). The work of neo-Gramscian Marxists led the way in terms of showing how cultural processes are integral to the way states regulate capitalist societies. There were other developments afoot that opened the door to culture.

Modern state theory has evolved into an eclectic and highly interdisciplinary activity. We can see this for ourselves by looking at recently published books on the state (see the Introduction). This is a far cry from the formative days of Hobbes and Locke in which the state was the moral and intellectual preserve of political theorists. Joining the established political tradition of state theory are thinkers operating across a range of disciplines and subdisciplines in the humanities and social sciences. Historians, anthropologists, feminists, socio-geographers, literary analysts and sociologists have contributed to state theory in recent years; and they are of course operating in fields that have been traditionally receptive to the cultural turn. Following the obvious disciplinary versatility of contemporary scholarship on the state, there is an implicit argument within this chapter: disciplinary inclusiveness has made contemporary state theory increasingly open to culturally orientated analysis.

Theorists offer a diverse range of interpretations and explanations about the relationship between the state and culture. To explore these various theoretical permutations, this chapter eschews a formulaic romp through key state theories and what they have to say about the state–culture connection. Rather my objective is to stress how different dimensions of culture have been implicated in studies of the state. Here, I intend to put the onus back on culture. It emphasises the way culture is a sphere worth analysing in its own right in relation to the state. For those studying how the culture impinges on the state, there is a tendency to focus on distinct dimensions of culture, or to argue that certain aspects of culture are more important than others. This is to be expected. As the realm covering the non-material, different understandings and explanations of culture abound. For some, culture is understood in linguistic terms, whilst for others symbols are everything. In this chapter, I will focus on two broad dimensions of culture: first, the influence of ideas and ideology; second, the contribution of ritual and symbols. Within each area, there exist different theoretical interpretations of how the cultural dimension in question relates and is linked to the state.

Ideas, ideology and the state

Our focus now turns to a key constituent of the non-material, cultural realm: the ideational. This is an elegant term encompassing ideas and ideology. There are those schools of thought that equate culture, wholly or in part, with belief systems and ideas. One school that stresses the cognitive dimension of culture is a branch of anthropology known as ethnoscience. This discipline is associated with the works of Ward Goodenough and Ino Rossi, for both of whom culture essentially boils down to being a creation of the human mind, a mind that is subject to rules and logic (Smircich 1983: 348). The equation between culture and ideas or cognition is also made by sociological theorists. A relatively early sociological contribution is Talcott Parsons' general theory of social action. This model of social action, as outlined in *The Social System* (1951), included a cultural dimension, amongst others. Culture, from a Parsonian perspective, is defined in cognitive terms, consisting of ideas and beliefs. Following Parsons's model of social action, contemporary organisational theorists Walter Powell and Paul DiMaggio make the case for culture as a cognitive form (see Powell and DiMaggio 1991: 14–15). Their now ubiquitous brand of neo-institutionalist organisational theory is critical of what is seen as Parsons's rational, *homo economicus* view of behaviour. Yet they concede that Parsons's appreciation of culture provides a rich and exhaustive schema for understanding action.

Of course, values and beliefs have a potent influence on political institutions and practices. There now exist noteworthy cultural explorations of the state that have focused on the influence of ideas, although some of these efforts, according to Kathryn Sikkink (1991), lack theoretical rigour. The contribution of ideas in political matters is hotly disputed. The key battleground centres on the extent to which ideas have a constitutive role, independent of the state and other material entities (Hay 2002: 205). I intend, in this section, to consider how ideas, as a form or expression of culture, are implicated in creating, sustaining and reproducing the state. How ideas maintain the state, creating a sort of cultural scaffold, is a matter of theoretical speculation. In the rest of this section three theoretical positions – Weberian, neo-Marxist and constructivist – are outlined, each offering radically different interpretations of the way ideas potentially contribute to the maintenance of the state.

Ideas versus the institutional and socio-economic context

There are studies which look at the influence of ideas on various facets of the state that have a theoretical affinity – implicitly or otherwise – with the sociology of Max Weber. Although these Weberian-influenced studies cover different social and historical contexts, they emphasise the role of ideas, rather than objective conditions and material interests, in the actions of the state (see Sikkink 1991: 242–3). One formative example is Peter Hall's historical study of British and French economic policy following the Second World War. Specifically, the study compares the relative decline of the British economy with the French economic miracle after the war. This comparative analysis, argues Hall (1986), shows how different facets related to ideas are implicated in politics. Take attitudes. These can assume an 'exogenous character', in that they may have an influence on political action, independent of the immediate organisational context. Hall notes that such autonomous attitudes are best described as ideologies. The principal ideologies that have shaped postwar economic policy are monetarism and Keynesianism. These ideologies helped to establish preferred courses of economic policy action. Whilst emphasising the autonomous standing of ideology, Hall maintains that the impact of ideas and their dissemination is dependent upon organisational settings. The emergence of certain policy ideologies may be linked to organisational interests (Hall 1986: 277–8). For instance, monetarist ideology found fertile ground in the British Treasury due to the long preoccupation of elite officials in this department with budgetary control. There was also the influence of the financial centre, the City of London. The City's historical predilection for tight controls over government spending – all in the name of maintaining the value of the pound as a marketable currency – made London's financial centre a natural cheer-leader for monetarist economics.

It would be difficult to disentangle the close interplay that runs through ideas and institutional contexts in the political realm. The mutual interchange between ideas and political context is similarly acknowledged by Bruce Carruthers in a study of government economic policy. This study of American and British Treasury policy in the 1930s acknowledges the importance of structural properties and individual action. And yet it places great store on culture as a means of explaining the twists and turns of economic policy – more so than Hall did in his earlier study of economic policy. Carruthers explains divergent courses of economic policy by recourse to an organisation's ability to generate independent cultural forms. These cultural forms amount to an organisation's identity and belief system, they amount to features that enable the organisation to interpret and make sense of the world. Organisations that have strong, well-developed cultures are likely to have greater policy autonomy (Carruthers 1994: 24). A case in point is the British Treasury in the 1930s. It possessed a distinctive quality which was independent of 'the preferences, expressed or otherwise, of British capital' (Carruthers 1994: 24). The independence of the Treasury was due to its pre-eminent status within the government bureaucratic machine. But cultural factors also come into play. The high level of commonality in the educational background and professional career development amongst Treasury officials proved significant. The shared *alma mater*, for instance, made for a highly integrated collective ideology amongst Treasury officials, resistant to influences from within and without government.

The tension that exists between the political context and belief systems is also evident in those studies that look to ideology to explain state actions. This is true of James Scott's 1998 book, *Seeing Like a State*. Here, Scott traces the historical origins of atrocities resulting from state-led programmes of social engineering. Scott's case histories of the state's inhumanity to man include the drive to agricultural collectivisation in the former Soviet Union, the forced villagisation in Tanzania and modern city planning schemes, especially the building of Brasília. These grand schemes took place at distinct historical junctures, in quite different national milieus, under diverse political regimes. And yet, these examples of state-originated hubris have a single common denominator: they were shaped, informed and influenced by an unflinching faith in the ability of science and technology to progress the human cause (Scott 1998: 4). This faith-like belief is borne out of what Scott terms 'high modernist ideology'.

Modernist ideology may form an influential context for state action, but its effect on the state is far from unidirectional or deterministic. There are contingencies involved, there are differential outcomes. Although highly critical of what has been committed in the name of modernisation, even Scott acknowledges that it would be wrong to characterise the modernist drive as inherently malevolent and brutish. Those modernist social experiments have proven beneficial and even promoted egalitarian policies (Scott 1998: 5). Such positive outcomes of modernism tend to be found in liberal parliamentary democracies, where there is public consultation between citizens and planners. When the cultural dominance of high modernism coincides with authoritarian regimes and weak civil societies, these factors make for a potentially lethal combination. With authoritarian governments, there is the political will and ability to place the coercive powers of the state at the disposal of high modernist designs. The point of these differential outcomes is that there are political and social considerations which explain state fiascos. The culture of high modernism is one, albeit significant, element.

But there are commentators for whom ideas are able to constitute, as opposed to being constituted by, governing institutions. What we see here is a strong thesis on the contribution of ideas. For these thinkers, in contrast to Hall's comparative historical analysis, ideas precede material structures and interests. Take Christopher Hood's book *The Art of the State* (2000); for him different ideas about public management – the so-called art of the state – result in a variety of policies and actions in relation, principally, to service provision. The influence of ideas in the political world for theorists such as Hood is seen less in terms of ideologies tied to powerful and elite interests. Another notable example of the strong thesis on ideas is Kathryn Sikkink's study of developmental politics in Latin America. The principle underlying the study is expressed as follows: 'We frequently focus on the material constraints but less often on the ideological constraints' (Sikkink 1991: xiv). For Sikkink policy ideas shape political actions. Ideas precede material structures and interests, 'shaping not only actors' perceptions of possibilities but also their understanding of their own interests' (1991: 243). Ideas, from this point of view, hold sway within the political field as free-floating, autonomous entities. They act as structures in their own right, though loosely coupled with other, namely, socio-economic structural properties. This loose coupling between ideas and socio-economic structures became apparent, for Sikkink, in the way developmentalism was embraced in Brazil and Argentina during the 1950s. In these countries the developmental policy decisions of political elites were a response to the opportunities and constraints of the global economic order (1991: xiv). But decisively, these policy choices were also fashioned by 'historical memory' and ideas about the economy. Policy decisions were based, in large part, on how key actors perceived and interpreted the international economy.

The discussion so far has mulled over how far ideas direct the activities of the state, over how ideas form a structural context, delimiting the actions of the state. Without ideas, states are hollow, they are a meaningless entity. Although the ideological is given certain priority, Sikkink, Scott and others acknowledge in their respective ways that ideas cannot be treated in isolation. Political processes, as well as social and economic factors, come into play. But what Sikkink and other authors in this section have said about the interrelationship between ideas and context will have failed to go far enough for other commentators. A critique of this nature would certainly find some resonance with Marxist theorists, who have taken a particular interest in ideology and the state. For neo-Marxist theorists, ideology and the interests of the social elite – big business, the state apparatchiks – are inextricably bound. A notable example of such thinking appeared briefly in the work of British neo-Gramscian social scientists and cultural analysts.

A neo-Gramscian approach to ideology and the state

The cultural Marxism of Antonio Gramsci established an influential legacy for modern state theory. Gramsci's writings gave neo-Marxian theorists of the state such as Nicos Poulantzas a lifeline out of the deterministic impasse left by the economic fixation of instrumental Marxism. Instead of economic reductionism, Gramsci emphasised the importance of purposeful action and ideas in what he termed the 'philosophy of praxis'. The project to redefine Marxian theory was influenced by the Hegelian philosophy of Benedetto Croce and Marx's early philosophical works. As well as refocusing on agency and ideas, Gramsci's work also opened up a broader cultural vista to Marxian scholarship. Gramsci examined the contribution of culture, but more specifically ideology, to bourgeois domination.

Anglo-sociologists proved especially receptive to this version of Marxism. Amongst the most enthusiastic of Gramsci's devotees were those sociologists based at the interdisciplinary Centre for Contemporary Cultural Studies (CCCS) at Birmingham University. Members of the CCCS were amongst the earliest trail-blazers of cultural theory around the postwar academic scene. The Centre's research was forged around a distinctive post-Gramscian intellectual manifesto. The Centre led the way in terms of a politicised form of cultural analysis, focusing on popular media outputs and their relationship to centres of power – whether the state or the capitalist economy. In addition to Gramsci, there is a clear Althusserian streak running through the CCCS's work. The Centre's work portrayed the mass media – in true Althusserian fashion – as an ideological state apparatus involved in the reproduction of dominant ideologies that help maintain existing power relations in society (see Woollacott 1982: 108–10).

Some of the CCCS's key studies emphasised the role of ideology in maintaining and legitimising the modern state. The CCCS's own dalliance with state theory can be found in the seminal text, *Policing the Crisis*, a text which boasted as one of its co-authors the name of Stuart Hall who would become a leading figure of British cultural theory. Hall and his colleagues, in *Policing the Crisis*, produced a no-holds-barred critique of the liberal welfare state. The critique rests on the supposed liberal state's role in periods of political turmoil and crisis, especially times when the existing class system of domination is challenged. As dominant powers are defied and confronted, the state's normal modus operandi, which relies on consent, is suspended and coercion becomes the norm (Hall *et al.* 1978: 217). The coercive practices of the state are extended through, and augmented by, a close coupling between ideological strategies and the forces of law and order.

This coercive alliance between the penal and the ideological was particularly apparent in the public reaction to one particular crime – mugging. Mugging and the shadowy figure of the mugger were hyped into a moral panic by a frenzied right-wing press gang. The media collectively helped to manipulate public perceptions, to stir the public imagination into believing that mugging was out of control. In reality fear of mugging outstripped the actual incidence of this particular crime. Moreover, according to Hall *et al.* (1978: 328), the media and public authorities equated the origins and perpetrators of mugging as a 'racial problem':

'"mugging" has come to be unambiguously assigned as a black crime, located in and arising from conditions of life in the black urban areas'. The ideologically driven creation of this racial moral panic held political implications. The propensity to racialise mugging was exploited by state authorities, being used as a justification for creating a more proactive form of policing against working-class communities, especially black communities. As well as justifying state coercion, this apparently racial crime had a more subtle function. It helped to create a material and ideological division of the working class along racial lines. White and black members of the working class, instead of finding a common cause and enemy in capitalism, came to see themselves as groups whose interests are divided.

Hall and his colleagues in *Policing the Crisis* make a typically Gramscian-inspired case: that the state and culture exist in a dialectical, mutually reinforcing relationship. On the one side of this dialectical relationship, culture is an independent force that can determine state practices. On the other side, the state and sub-state agencies such as the police are autonomous bureaucratic entities engaged in reinforcing the inequitable status quo; they do so in part through the cultural sphere. In its relationship to culture, the state reveals quite illiberal credentials. Hall *et al.*'s critique of the liberal state, according to certain commentators, goes beyond Gramsci. It reaches over Gramsci and even Poulantzas by portraying the state as a fully autonomous actor, which exploits cultural media to maintain the consent on which its authority depends. In fact, Sullivan (2000) goes as far as to suggest that for Hall *et al.* in *Policing the Crisis* the state has an absolute rather than a relative autonomy. The autonomy of the state was augmented through the emergence of the welfare capitalist state in postwar Britain. Gradually, after the war, the state assumed control over ever-growing areas of the economy and, most importantly, the ideological sphere (Sullivan 2000: 115–16). Culture is in the last instance subservient to the state.

The dependency of culture on the state is, for particular commentators, a weak spot. One critic argues that sociological thinkers who share an intellectual genealogy with Marx are out of their depth in dealing with the interface between culture and the state (Steinmetz 1999: 22–3). They suffer from a particular shortcoming, reflects Steinmetz. If these studies endeavour to furnish a cultural analysis of the state, the former is deemed reducible to an epiphenomenon of some superordinate and ubiquitous body – namely, the state. Here, and even for many of the analyses considered above, there is a clear division between ideas and the state. Whether from a quasi-Weberian or neo-Gramscian perspective, ideas and the state are distinct. For radical cultural analysts this distinction is collapsed, as we shall discover below.

The hyperreality of the state

One of the most radical cultural analyses of the state is associated with the work of Philip Abrams, specifically in a renowned article entitled 'Notes on the difficulty of studying the state', written in 1977 and published posthumously in 1988. The Abrams thesis is based on a familiar argument: there is little to be gained from suggesting that the state is the aggregate form of various institutional apparatuses or the sum of various decision-making processes. But Abrams adds a distinct ideational twist to this sceptical critique. He notes that the state as a superordinate, freestanding entity is an illusion. Or to use Baudrillard's brilliant concept: the state is a hyperreality. In essence, this means that ideas or simulations of the state are often more real than the thing itself (Lemert 1997: 27–8). The state is an exaggerated reality. Our thoughts are dominated by a *copy* of what we think the state actually is in reality.

The case made by Abrams draws its inspiration, in part, from A. R. Radcliffe-Brown's anthropological critique of political theory. In the preface to his classical anthropological text, *African Systems of Kinship and Marriage*, Radcliffe-Brown (1970: xxiii) notes: 'In writings on political institutions there is a good deal of discussion about the nature and origin of the State, which is virtually represented as being an entity over and above the human individuals ... The state in this sense does not exist in the phenomenal world; it is a fiction of the philosophers' (cited in Taussig 1993: 219). Following Radcliffe-Brown, Abrams denies the material existence of the state. He makes the bold assertion 'that any attempt to study the state either as concrete or abstract object should be abandoned' (Abrams 1988: 75). The reason for taking this extreme position is that the state is viewed as an imaginative construction. The *idea* of the state is constructed out of an array of political institutions which form the state system. In effect, there is an actual state system, which begins life as a set of ubiquitous institutions and political practices that centre on government. But the state system becomes reified into an all-powerful unified and centralised institution in the mind of the public – an idea divorced from reality and practice (1988: 82). In effect, the state is an ideological project.

As well as its strong constructivist connotations, Abrams's ground-breaking piece does embrace power. And in connecting power and ideology, Abrams credits Marx and Engels's *The German Ideology* as an influence on his thinking. The central thesis of *The German Ideology* is that the state contributes to an ideological distortion of reality. The state hoodwinks the public into believing that civil society is a fair, equitable and democratic body. Following Marx and Engels's lead, Abrams notes that the state in modern society is an ideological device through which the exercise of power is legitimated. The job of critics should be to dismantle the idea of the state in order to reveal those power relations that are hidden behind this powerful illusion. In terms of legitimating power relations, there is the familiar matter of economic power: the ideological construct of the state legitimates the exploitative relations between classes in capitalist society. But the power relations legitimated by the state also cover a whole multitude of sins regarding the moral and social regulation of society (Abrams 1988: 76). The institutions of the state legitimate different forms of coercion. Armies, secret services, the police, prisons and even fiscal policies: their association with the idea of the state excuses the use of force and over-zealous regulation. What is it about the idea of the state that has this effect? Ideology portrays the state as integrated expression of the commonweal and of the general public interest rather than as a body which cosies up to various sectional interests, whether class, race, gender or religious in origin.

The political scientist Timothy Mitchell shares the Abrams cultural constructivist manifesto. For a radical cultural constructivist like Mitchell, the state and its power are more apparent than real, more fiction than fact. Whilst questioning the reality of the state, he is wary of the Abrams telos: that of the state as a mental construct or ideological effect. This ideological critique depicts the state as a universal abstraction, dissociated from the historical context – a free-floating idea. Mitchell raises a query: is the state a pure ideological construction? For this particular constructivist theorist, the state is still grounded in real material processes. The material processes he has in mind are not grand institutions or structures, as suggested in part by Abrams. Rather these material structures depend on the minuscule, the incidental and the taken-for-granted features of everyday life. The state is 'an effect of mundane processes of spatial organization, temporal arrangement, ... supervision and surveillance, and representation that create the appearance of a world fundamentally divided into state and society' (Mitchell 1999: 95). As this quote suggests, there is something of the Foucauldian in Mitchell's cultural analysis (see Chapter 2). From the Foucauldian perspective, the state effect – its appearance as an external power – results from various disciplinary and regulatory practices.

The state seems hidden, argues Mitchell, because its presence is so intertwined with the fabric of our daily lives. From CCTV cameras to roadside warnings, from government buildings to the humble postage stamp: we take these observable artefacts of the state for granted, we assume them to be a normal and natural part of our everyday routine. Mitchell himself uses the example of territorial border controls as an example of how governmental powers extend and proliferate throughout our lives. The policing of frontiers involves a variety of modern and often routine practices: continuous barbed-wire fencing, passport controls, immigration laws, vehicle searches, inspections by customs officers, currency controls. Such arrangements were unheard of a century ago but 'they help manufacture an almost transcendental entity, the nation-state', creating the effect of the state as a formal, superimposed, superodrinate structure

(Mitchell 1999: 90). These routine practices create this image for the simple reason that they appear to instruct and give meaning to people's lives. The power of the state – or what we presume to be the state authority – is a chimera, created out of mundane and ordinary practices that inhabit daily existence.

Although there are differences between Abrams and Mitchell, they each offer *strong constructivist* accounts of the state system, which contrast markedly with the other approaches considered in this section. Although the neo-Gramscians and neo-Weberians attach quite different values to the influence of ideas, the separation between the realm of ideas and the state is taken as given. The distinction between state and ideas, from a radical constructivist perspective, is artificial, it should be dissolved. The state is essentially a cultural idea or an ideological form. The constructivist position shares a theoretical affinity with, and draws theoretical cues from poststructuralism. For poststructuralists, the social world does not have an independent, objective existence outside systems of meaning and communication – texts and discourse. In a similar vein, for radical cultural constructivists, the state has no independent existence outside the realm of ideas, ideology and culture itself. The state in itself is a fully cultural form and, as Mitchell intimates, it is also a symbolic form (Steinmetz 1999: 27). The relationship between the symbolic realm and the state has been subject to some concerted theoretical attention.

Drama, signs and rituals: the symbolic representation of the state

Anybody committed to a strong cultural perspective would be excused if they showed an interest in symbolic imagery and ritualistic behaviour. The symbolic and the ritualistic have become increasingly prominent in social theory under the aegis of the cultural turn. Both a symptom and a cause of the cultural turn has been the popularisation of semiotic theory. Books such as *Mythologies* (Barthes 1973) and Umberto Eco's 1975 essay on the American subculture of hyperrealism titled 'Faith in Fakes' (see Eco 1990) were influential cross-over texts, bridging the gap between the intricate technicalities of semiotic theory and mainstream social science. So, the study of symbols and rituals is well established in the social sciences. But can we also think about the symbolic as something that is also part and parcel of governmental activities and institutions?

The idea that the political is inherently symbolic is well established in classical social theory. Amongst the classical patriarchs of sociology, a leading proponent of the symbolic realm was Emile Durkheim. In many ways an embryonic and formative cultural theorist, Durkheim treated culture as an autonomous dimension, but one coupled with social and political processes. Such ideas became apparent in his later sociological work on the religious activities of tribal societies. Durkheim found that tribal culture is an intricate assemblage of symbols, representations, beliefs and values. These cultural features help tribal members to make sense of a confusing and threatening world. These collective efforts to understand the world take on an emergent or external quality that orders social behaviour, communal bonds and ties between individuals. In other words symbols, signs and rituals quickly become the outward rules and norms that dictate behaviour in the tribe. The possible contribution that symbols can make to systems of authority has not been lost on other guiding intellectual figures in history. There is Freud's study of totemism and Lévi-Strauss's exploration of marriage. Both contributions, in different ways, touched upon the way symbols and rituals act to glue societies together and to regulate the behaviour of individuals. These formative efforts, especially the work of Durkheim, have left an influential legacy. The question is whether it is possible to make a conceptual leap from the rich symbolism of tribal societies to how modern political systems can be understood. It was the American social anthropologist, Clifford Geertz, who helped to pave the way for a culturally orientated, theoretical connection between the state and the symbolic.

A cultural anthropology of the state: power serving ritual

As would be expected from an anthropologist, Clifford Geertz's methodological modus operandi gives primacy to culture. This cultural anthropology focuses on the outward symbolic and ritualistic dimensions of culture. It is these observable 'public texts', which for Brint (1994: 7) 'can unlock the secrets to the distinctive sensibilities and ethos of a people'. Geertz would baulk at the idea that culture is a superstructure or the outward surface appearance of some deeper underlying structural force. Hence, ideology, religion, politics, and stratification are cultural (Alexander 1990). The same case is made in relation to the state.

The state and political institutions are featured with some prominence in the Geertzian oeuvre. The study of political institutions goes somewhat against the disciplinary grain of anthropology. But Geertz is no anthropological purist, occupying a distinguished chair at Princeton in the social sciences. In fact, there is a distinct interdisciplinary feel to his work, with Durkheim being a notable but barely mentioned influence.

Much of the raw material that was used by Geertz in his cultural anthropology of the state comes from the pre-colonial nineteenth-century Balinese state, otherwise known as the *negara*. This anthropology of the Balinese state turns the conventional wisdom of political theory on its head. The classical political thought of Hobbes and Juvenal would contend that spectacle serves power. For Hobbes, political rituals intimidate subjects of the state. They let them know who is in charge (Geertz 1980: 122). Contrary to the prevailing wisdom of classical political philosophy, Geertz argues that the nineteenth-century Balinese state was dominated by an expressive conception of politics. This refers to 'the conviction that the principal instrumentalities of rule lie less in the techniques of administration than in the arts of the theatre' (Geertz 1993: 331). Here, symbolic expression of political power is an end rather than a means. In the negara, it seems, there is no power without ritual.

The celebration of ritual over the naked pursuit of power was a constant throughout the history of the Balinese state. The vast concentration of political and administrative authority vested in the negara was treated with indifference by key political figures. Either that or they were too incompetent to govern. Instead of power, the key protagonists of the Balinese state – punggawas, perbekels, kawulas, and parekans – were motivated by ritual above all else. These political actors were especially enamoured with dramatising their main ruling preoccupations, which involved the valorisation of status differentials and inequalities. Governance, as such, was about performance, with ceremonies being the driving force of Balinese politics. Cremations, teeth-filing, temple dedications, blood sacrifices: these rituals, which often involved the mobilisation of thousands of people and vast resources, were less about supporting the state. Rather the state was a vehicle for enacting mass rituals: 'Power served pomp, not pomp power' (Geertz 1993: 335).

Just a couple of observations need elaboration. What we have with Geertz is an anthropologically informed theory of the state, where culture makes an integral contribution to political activities. Primacy is given to the cultural foundations of political activities and institutions. But Geertz's cultural description of the Balinese state begs the question: what about modern Western societies? The dramaturgical basis of a state like the nineteenth-century negara may come as no surprise. Pre-twentieth-century Bali society was in many ways an anachronistic throwback, a ritual-heavy and culturally exotic community, largely cut off from outside influences.

Geertz acknowledges that modern state craft still depends upon Juvenal's dictum about bread and circuses. He observes: 'though Weber promised us ... specialists without spirit in a bureaucratic iron cage ... the course of events since, with its Sukarnos, Churchills, Nkrumahs, Hitlers, Maos, Roosevelts, Stalins, Nasser, and de Gaulles, suggests' that there is still room for grand ceremony in modern politics. He goes on to add: 'The extraordinary has not gone out of modern politics, however much the banal may have entered; power not only still intoxicates, it still exalts' (Geertz 1983: 143). Pomp and ceremony continue to be a part and parcel of the modern state's armoury in large-scale, complex industrialised societies and democracies. The circus side of the contemporary state has expressed itself in many different ways. We often find it in set-piece spectacles and state-sponsored celebrations, heavily laden with symbolism and ritual. The camp pomposity of the state opening of Parliament in Britain, with its Black Rod and the Queen in full regalia, is a case in point.

From a Geertzian perspective, the purpose of the state is to serve ritual, rather than ritual serving the state. But it is possible for the state theatre to be instrumentally linked to the maintenance of political power. Geertz admits in a later book on the negara that state ritual has some instrumental payback. For him, dominant theories of the state since the sixteenth century have emphasised that public spectacle reinforces the state's monopoly over the means of violence. The Balinese state can easily be fitted into this familiar model of the state, although this position, Geertz concedes, would divert attention from the more interesting aspects of the negara. He notes: 'The state drew its force, which was real enough, from its imaginative energies, its semiotic capacity to make inequality enchant' (Geertz 1980: 123). It is possible to take a cultural approach to state ritual, whilst being aware that the symbols and theatre contiguous to the state are also instrumentally linked to the exercise of political power. One such endeavour to combine cultural analysis with an 'orthodox' treatment of political ritual can be found in Philip Corrigan and Derek Sayer's study of the English state.

The drama, ritual and power of the modern state

In their book *The Great Arch* (1985), Corrigan and Sayer trace the historical origins of the English state between the eleventh and nineteenth centuries. But this is no orthodox history. It is a cultural history. The authors go behind the 'idea of the state', revealing its constructiveness, decoding its 'message of domination'. As part of this process of historical deconstruction, the formation of the English state is portrayed, first and foremost, as a cultural revolution. Here, the activities and institutions associated with the state are 'cultural forms', and these forms are state-regulated. Rituals are central to the cultural basis of the state. The contention about the cultural basis of the state has its intellectual foundations in the works of Marx and Weber, but also Durkheim (Corrigan and Sayer 1985: 9–10). From Durkheim, Corrigan and Sayer embrace the idea of moral authority. The moral authority of the state is integral to its ability to regulate society. The machinery of government takes on a moral quality through the cultural symbols and bourgeois-influenced rituals performed by the state.

Both the mundane and the spectacular rituals of the state 'define, in great detail, acceptable forms and images of social activity and individual and collective identity; they regulate, in empirically specifiable ways, much ... of social life' (Corrigan and Sayer 1985: 3). By demarcating what is socially acceptable behaviour and identity, the state normalises social divisions. As such, age, gender and class divisions are made to seem normal and natural. In maintaining these divisions, rituals and symbols serve powerful interests. This is a matter of regulation through ritual.

Ceremony and pageantry were an essential part of state authority during the period of the Tudors and Stuarts from the fifteenth to the eighteenth century. This began with Henry VII and reached its apogee with Elizabeth I. During the Elizabethan period, portraits of saints were removed from churches and replaced with the royal coat of arms. Elizabeth I encouraged, but carefully managed, the use of her own portrait in private and public settings. In addition to the careful use of the monarchical image, the royal court stage-managed spectacular public events to celebrate coronations and special anniversaries. What was the rationale behind such pomp and ceremony? These rituals were organised to valorise the crown and therefore the state. In fact, after the 1570 celebrations of Elizabeth I's coronation in 1559, her image became a quasi-divine icon, being compared to the Virgin Mary. Little has changed, if recent events are anything to go by. Nearly 400 years later pop stars – Madonna – would be doing the same in their MTV music promo videos. Take the protracted and over-the-top celebrations commemorating the Queen's Golden Jubilee in 2003, from torches being lit throughout the land to the pop concert at Buckingham Palace. These celebrations represented a 'hegemonic moment', argues Duffett, for there took place a symbolic rapprochement – an identification – between the monarchy and its subjects (see Duffett 2004: 494–6).

How did the ritual state of the sixteenth and seventeenth centuries survive the advent of modernising economic forces? With full-blown industrialisation, and faced with a growing population, a rapidly expanding economy, new forms of private wealth and social problems linked to urbanisation, the English state was forced to intervene. Governments also undertook major economic reforms during the 1780s, with the extension of property rights a flagship policy. As economic management became an increasingly pressing issue, there would seem little room for dramatic sentiment, for rituals and ceremonies. If the irrational cultural practices of the past age survived, they existed as useless relics, peripheral to the main business of the modern state. Or so the argument goes. Although industrialisation demanded a more businesslike and rational form of political rule, Corrigan and Sayer (1985: 102) highlight 'the peculiarly ritualised, theatrical qualities of eighteenth-century rule'.

For theatrical expressions of the eighteenth- and nineteenth-century state, one need look no further than the penal system and its houses of justice – the law courts. There was the drama and theatre of public executions and the quasi-religious practices of the law courts, emphasising the law's divine otherness (Corrigan and Sayer 1985: 99). Penal spectacles were matched by the symbolic baggage of the central executive. Organisations within the central state remained largely 'unbureaucratised' throughout the eighteenth century; that is, they still displayed some of the symbolic paraphernalia of the past. Throughout this period, for instance, the Exchequer continued to make use of Roman numerals, courthand and tallies (Corrigan and Sayer 1985: 93).

With the cultural spectacle of the eighteenth-century English state, there was a socio-economic imperative at work. Or to paraphrase Corrigan and Sayer: the symbolism of the state was integral to the moral regulation of a nascent capitalism. Such theatrical displays could mask dramatic, wholesale economic changes under way, and in so doing help usher them in. By arguing that there is an economic rationale to these state rituals, the authors are clearly revealing their Marxist credentials. Employing a Marxian-informed economic logic to understand the cultural activities and expressions of the eighteenth-century English state only goes so far. There were non-economic considerations, too.

The rituals immanent in the eighteenth-century English state helped to unify and establish a fledgling industrial elite. They also contributed to the creation of an English national identity. To comprehend these broader social functions, Corrigan and Sayer summon Durkheim's concept of collective representation. The idea of collective representation refers to those cultural constructs or social symbols that have a collective meaning, which give meaning to individual existence (Corrigan and Sayer 1985: 103). In effect, cultural artefacts that are widely shared in a community help to define a set of beliefs, norms and values. In other words, they cultivate a moral order. The argument that there exists a close association between moral codes and the symbolic sphere has some illustrious backers. Take Mary Douglas's anthropology on primitive cultures. In her work on the treatment on hygiene, she demonstrated how symbolic activities such as religious rituals create powerful moral boundaries (Douglas 2002: 74–5). It should be mentioned that Douglas's work itself was also informed by Durkheim's classical sociology.

The Durkheimian concept of collective representation is employed by Corrigan and Sayer to make this case: that public rituals in the political arena serve powerful interests. State-sponsored rituals and events help to legitimate and maintain the existing social and political order. Although state theatre and powerful interests coalesce, Corrigan and Sayer say very little about how the ideologies of state-centred rituals are transmitted to the public. There is limited understanding of the way the symbolism of the state begins to influence the public at large. If the dramaturgy surrounding the state is to have wider reverberations, consideration should be given to those practices that act as cultural transmitters and institutional intermediaries that penetrate everyday life. For instance, Ben-Amos and Ben-Ari (1995) note how the state funerals in the French Third Republic held symbolic resonance with the public at large because of the education system. The administrative organisations overseeing the education system formed local, micro-level networks. These networks connected the state's cultural practices with society. Such matters need to enter the equation. Coverage of these processes and organisations – the cultural transmitters – in the *Great Arch* is limited, although both Corrigan and Sayer, in later writings (see Sayer 1994), examine the cultural practices involved in the everyday construction of the state. For a systematic coverage of the way state cultural practices are passed on to the wider population, we need to look elsewhere.

Symbolic capital, the field and habitus: state/culture and Bourdieu

One place where we can potentially find an answer is in the sociology of Pierre Bourdieu. Although known more as a cultural sociologist than as a theorist of the state, his later works shows how the state penetrates society at large. The state is able to infiltrate society through culture or, more specifically, through recourse to the symbolic realm.

The symbolic features prominently in Bourdieu's social theory. In fact, the emphasis on symbols, and culture generally, is in part what distinguishes this particular Gallic brand of sociology. Bourdieu began theorising around the idea of symbolic violence in his formative contributions to the sociology of education. The theory of symbolic violence is outlined in the initial sections of the 1974 book, *Reproduction in Education, Society and Culture* (see Bourdieu and Passeron 1977). This book on the sociology of education shows how in modern industrial societies physical coercion and direct repression are less prominent in the regulation of populations. Rather social regulation is conducted by surreptitious cultural processes. In other words, control is invisible. People are largely unaware that their behaviour is being closely managed and directed. Or they take state control for granted. These indirect processes of domination depend on symbolic systems, which are transmitted through the education system.

In Bourdieu's later writings on the French education system, cultural analysis and the state coalesce and intermingle. Such disparate themes are covered in a book about France's elite secondary school sector centred on the *grandes écoles*. These educational institutions serve as preparation for prestigious universities and ultimately a working life in the elite strata of French society. *La Noblesse d'État* (Bourdieu 1989), later published in English as *The State Nobility* (Bourdieu 1996), offers what Wacquant terms a 'political sociology of symbolic forms'. Here, symbolic domination is grounded in different forms of capital (Wacquant 1993: 3), namely, cultural capital and economic capital. With these diverse types of capital, this study links the bourgeois intelligentsia (cultural capital) and the corporate establishment (economic capital) to France's elite school institutions. The social pre-eminence of both classes is sustained and perpetuated – through symbolic mechanisms – by France's elite school system. In reproducing elite power, these schools reinforce social divisions through their testing regimes. As well as the examination process, the didactic and training practices of the *écoles* is likened by Bourdieu to the ordination process for clergy. Such training is highly ascetic, rigorous and relentlessly competitive. An educational curriculum as intensive and austere as that of the *grandes écoles* produces individuals that see themselves as a race apart.

This ascetic schooling also cultivates a symbolic capital that is collectively shared, forming the basis of future class-wide networking and cooperation (Bourdieu 1989: 160–1, cited in Wacquant 1993: 8).

If the elite school system secures the 'production of a nobility', the state underwrites this production line of society's economic and cultural establishment. The state legitimates the cycle of social advantage by formally recognising the qualifications and credentials of the elite schools. The state actively maintains the extant social hierarchy in its own administration: it smoothes the paths of those alumni from France's superior schools to the higher reaches of the civil service and, therefore, the state administration.

How can the state act as the middleman between educational and social privilege? It is able to do this, says Bourdieu, because the modern state forms into an autonomous field. The term 'field' refers to those objective structures and relations of power which form the context for purposeful individual action, or what Bourdieu terms 'habitus' (Bourdieu and Wacquant 1992: 39). As a distinct field, the state possesses, and judiciously distributes, its own home-grown 'social capital'. But the state is not just one field amongst numerous fields – though we might get this impression from Bourdieu's work. It is not even a first among equals. The state is the first. It has no equals. It has – much like the economic field – a pre-eminence over other fields, including the cultural sphere. In *The State Nobility*, the state is described as an autonomous bureaucratic field. Such pre-eminence comes as no surprise, given that Bourdieu embraces Weber's description of the state as an institution with monopoly control over the means of violence. Arguments about the state's monopoly are further extended by Bourdieu in a 1994 article, in which he notes that different species of capital are concentrated in the state – coercive, informational, symbolic, economic and cultural capital. This makes the state 'the holder of a sort of meta-capital' (Bourdieu 1994: 4). These species of capital include instruments of coercion, economic capital, informational (cultural) capital and symbolic capital. This process of concentration enables the state to control different fields and various forms of capital.

In Bourdieu's thought, chasms do appear between what is intended and what is actually said. Discrepancies appear in his writings on culture and the state. With culture, the intention was to produce a non-reductive analysis, where it is equal to the material realm. This 'strong view of culture', though intimated in certain publications, is difficult to square with Bourdieu's general sociological worldview. As we have seen, the state, in the last instance, has a determining role in relation to culture and other social fields. And in addition to the state's pre-eminence, the economy is probably the *über*-field. Both cultural and social capital can be converted into economic capital; different forms of capital can be derived from economic capital, for economic capital is at the root of all other types of capital (Bourdieu 1986: 252). Bourdieu may deny all accusations of being a structural reductionist. Yet, he comes up with 'deterministic models of social process' (Jenkins 2002: 175–6). Pointing out this Bourdieuian double-speak is a legitimate criticism to make. But Bourdieu is far from being a naïve or one-dimensional thinker.

A double-speak does occasionally afflict Bourdieu's work, although this was something he acknowledged (see Bourdieu *et al.* 1991: 259). These residual lacunae are the price to pay for the strengths of Bourdieu's theoretical analysis. A positive feature of such theoretical work is the coverage given to culture. His treatment of culture, in turn, was all the richer for the way that struggle is inscribed within culture – both in ancient and modern society (Jenkins 2002: 179–80). The weight attached to cultural struggles makes for a subtle and contingent reading of the interaction between culture and the state. Hence, culture's impression on the state is not as a pre-eminent force in society. Rather culture – whether as a symbolic, linguistic or educational form – is a type of capital over which there is stiff competition between various protagonists as they vie for dominance and control. Those competing for cultural capital will include various agents, operating in particular local fields within or without the state. Hence, politicians aware of media power will compete for press coverage to gain tactical advantages over opponents (Couldry 2003: 8–9). We just have to look at the way politicians slavishly court the editors and proprietors of right-wing publications such as the *Sun* or the *Daily Mail*. As such, culture will help set the rules, standards and objectives for agents of the state. The cultural realm, by influencing the rules in this way, shapes the aspirations, expectations and goals of these agents. What we have here is a localised or 'weak' version of culture as an independent and constitutive force over society and the state.

Conclusion

This chapter has reviewed theories that have made an explicit attempt to draw on cultural processes to understand the workings of the state. Early attempts to explore the culture–state interface were far from satisfactory. A far richer analysis has emerged form those efforts to incorporate the ideas, concepts and methodologies associated with the cultural turn in the social sciences, which owes something to the growing intellectual stature of poststructuralism. This intellectual movement went against the grain of conventional academic thinking about culture. Prevailing social science opinion would insist that culture is a product of, and prior to, objective social structures that endure across time and space. With the cultural turn, culture is seen as an independent structure. Cultural theory in the political field has been used in various ways: to interrogate the reality of the state, to widen understanding of state regulation and reproduction. The influence of modern cultural thinking in state theory is far from uniform. For those studying the way culture impinges on the state, there is a tendency to focus on distinct dimensions of culture, or to argue that certain aspects of culture are more important than others. This is to be expected. As the realm covering the non-material, different understandings and explanations of culture abound. For some, culture is understood in linguistic terms, whilst for others, dramaturgy everything. This chapter has focused on two broad dimensions of culture: the influence of ideas and ideology, and the contribution of ritual and symbols. Under each area, there exist alternative interpretations of how the cultural dimension in question is independent from institutions like the state. And yet what these different perspectives have in common is that they attempt to take culture seriously. Here, culture is treated as an objective structure that provides a context for behaviour and thought just as much as material or socio-economic structures. This has provided the field of state theory with a rich and diverse body of ideas and empirically driven theoretical insights. But more importantly cultural takes on state theory have established an alternative understanding to mainstream state theory of how the state works and how state power is reproduced. Cultural perspectives on the state, though, are far from being on the margins and are now part and parcel of the work conducted by renowned thinkers in the field of state theory.

CHAPTER 6

THE STATE IN A GLOBAL CONTEXT

Introduction

The globalisation debate is one academic wrangle that is difficult to ignore. It is a theme which has even enjoyed notoriety beyond academic discourse. On the back of the globalisation debate, the state has become vital, or at least interesting, to social scientists once again. Globalisation analysis has transformed, and to an extent rejuvenated, one of the perennial issues in contemporary state theory. The enduring debate surrounding the relationship between state and society has found something of a new lease of life through recent discussions of globalisation. Except that the debate here is about the relationship between the state and a *globalised* society. We would have to question the existence of a truly 'globalised world'. Some writers have gone as far to describe 'globalisation theory' as a folly because of its tendency to reify space and ignore the explanatory schemas of classical social thought (Rosenberg 2000: 14). Clearly, globalisation is a problematic, and contested, concept. And yet, social processes are undoubtedly organised at a worldwide, international or what might be termed transnational level. The reality of globalisation presents a distinct challenge to state theorists. There has been intense theoretical speculation over the state's powers, influence and position within a world that has become more internationally integrated. Most discussions have concentrated on the transformation of the state through economic integration across the world. There are of course different opinions as to how economic globalisation has impeded the sovereignty of the state. These views will be covered in the course of this chapter. But there is more to such discussions about state autonomy than economic globalisation. The process of globalisation also has a political dimension. And the second half of this chapter will consider this: the extent to which political globalisation has created alternative centres of governing authority to that of the state.

Economically-led globalisation and the state

There is a strong tendency in the literature to equate globalisation with economics – or rather economic processes, institutions and agents. Globalisation is seen to be fundamentally driven by processes of modern economic activity: industrial production, commercial trade and natural resource exploration. For instance, world exports in 1950 equalled 7 per cent of world output; by the mid-1990s the figure was 17 per cent (Held *et al.* 1999: 168). Globalisation has also been spearheaded by more recent economic innovations: the growth of financial speculation, the liberalisation of currency markets and the expansion of brand-led marketing. Take, for example, the international diversification of global financial flows. 'From negligible levels in the 1960s, private capital flows grew so that in 1997 the total net new issues of international loans and bonds amounted to $890 billion while stocks of outstanding loans and bonds totalled $7,635 billion in March 1998' (Held *et al.* 1999: 202–3).

The intensification of global integration is for many theoreticians an economically driven process. The economic imperative of globalisation was stressed by some of the earliest proponents of a global system. A prime example in this respect is Immanuel Wallerstein. For Wallerstein, and others of his ilk, it has proven impossible for capitalism to remain self-contained within neat, national units. The very nature of the modern capitalist beast is that it needs to expand across national borders in order to survive and prosper. By doing so, new markets are created and sources of profit widened.

The stress on globalisation as an economic system has given rise to high-profile discussion about the future of the state; for economically-led globalisation has profound implications for the nation state. The impact of economic globalisation on the sovereignty of the nation state is one of the key theoretical skirmishes within the globalisation literature. Indeed, it could be said to be *the* main theoretical skirmish. The main warring factions are split between two distinct but far from internally homogeneous camps. On the one hand, there is the camp which believes that economic globalisation has done irreparable damage to the sovereignty of the state. Here, individual state units are effectively swallowed up by global forces – primarily economic in nature. In the opposing corner, there are those authors for whom the sovereignty of the state remains largely intact, and the overwhelming power of economic integration has been wildly exaggerated. This interpretation offers a globalised variation on the theme of state-centred analysis, as exemplified by authors such as Theda Skocpol and Nordlinger (see Chapter 1). Below we shall attempt to consider the arguments, perspectives and thinkers associated with these opposing camps on the economic globalisation versus state-sovereignty divide.

The borderless economy versus the sovereign state

There is evidence which shows that the world economy is becoming more and more integrated. But there is a theoretical issue at hand. It is necessary to read into and interpret the available evidence. From this deeper perspective, theoretical questions have been driven by the prospect that global economic integration has produced a wholesale transformation of modern societies. The argument goes something like this: contemporary economic development has witnessed an intensification and proliferation of global economic integration. Such integration has helped to usurp existing forms of social organisation that were a firm part of the modernist landscape. Globalisation, in other words, is one of the prime forces responsible for what contemporary social theorists have termed 'detraditionalisation'. Of the changes that are afoot, the forces of detraditionalisation unleashed by the world economy have significant implications for contemporary statehood. The sovereignty and autonomy of the state have fallen victim to, or have been undermined by, the global economy. Within the literature this particular theoretical interpretation has been termed the 'hyperglobalist' or 'transformationalist' perspective (see Held *et al.* 1999).

Under the hyperglobalist umbrella can be found pro-globalisation, neo-liberal boosterists as well as anti-globalisation, quasi-Marxist critics of global capitalism. Although the range of ideological views represented under the hyperglobalist school of thought are quite disparate, they all converge on one specific point: denationalisation. That is, the prospective disappearance of the nation state as a result of the global forces of economic integration. These economic forces have scant respect for national boundaries and are able to side-step local democratic accountability. The argument about the impact of the borderless economy on state sovereignty does have a long gestation. Raymond Vernon in the early 1970s wrote about the political uncertainties in a world where multinational enterprises were beginning to grow in number and power. As such, multinational enterprises are less easy to control than national business organisations. In the future, Vernon (1971: 257–8) concedes, multinational enterprises may come into conflict with nation states. The growing power of multinational enterprises would also begin to embroil nation states deeper in international agreements and discussions. This prediction is largely true if we consider postwar trade agreements such as the World Trade Organisation and North American Free Trade Agreement (NAFTA). Charles Kindleberger, writing in 1970, proclaimed that the railroad destroyed the regional state and led to the emergence of national government. By the same token, international investment and the multinational corporation 'may well be preparing the same fate for the nation state' (1970: 53–4). Although figures such as Kindleberger and Vernon showed an early awareness of the potential threat posed by international capital to national sovereignty, the hyperglobalist approach very much has a contemporary ring to it.

The recent popularisation of ideas related to the borderless economy is far from being the sole preserve of academic commentators. The name of Kenichi Ohmae, a Japanese *über*-consultant and management guru, is synonymous with hyperglobalisation. Ohmae's key assertion is that the state has become defunct or, to use his words, 'an unnatural business unit'. It is unnatural in the sense that, within an increasingly integrated global economy, the state is an impotent economic actor, unable to exploit and determine what happens in the market. Ohmae (1995: 2) observes that in the era of the borderless economy 'nation states no longer possess the seemingly bottomless well of resources from which they used to draw with impunity to fund their ambitions'. The state has become a 'nostalgic fiction'. The state, in order to meet public demand, should cede economic control to the natural agents of the global market. These natural agents include capital markets, corporations, information technology and consumers, which have the flexibility and mobility to tap into the global market without the assistance of the traditional 'middleman' – the nation state. For example, the financial markets possess the capability to reinvest internationally the vast reserves of private wealth such as pension funds that remain stored away within individual nation states. The system of global finance created a vast network of private capital flows across national boundaries. But here is the nub of Ohmae's argument: individual nation states have little or no jurisdiction and influence over these-cross border flows of capital investment.

The capitulation of national sovereignty to the global economy is welcomed by Ohmae. The new global economy, if harnessed in the correct way, can potentially add to human progress and prosperity. In the Ohmae thesis, globalisation has unified disparate national markets and economies, resulting in the global trickle-down of material prosperity to non-Western countries. As well as the material benefits, the denationalisation effect also unites diverse cultures and groups, bringing prosperity, peace and freedom. These political and social benefits are evident in China, where the discipline of the market has made the Chinese government less likely to utilise repressive measures against civil society (Ohmae 1995: 72). The same observation about globalisation being the handmaiden of peace is nicely illustrated by the *New York Times* foreign correspondent and apostle of the global free market, Thomas Friedman (2000). His 'golden arches theory of conflict prevention' states that no two nations possessing a McDonald's restaurant ever went to war with each other – until the US-led air attacks on Yugoslavia, that is. And Mike Moore, the former director-general of the World Trade Organisation, pursued related sentiments in his apologia for global capitalism, *A World Without Walls* (2003). According to Moore, the world's best hope for security and prosperity is globalisation, hand in hand with democratic internationalism.

The view that we are entering a new global period of existence, where worldwide markets predominate, is also shared by commentators on the radical left. But for these thinkers, globalisation is far from bringing prosperity and freedom to humanity. Ritzer (2004), for example, argues that state sovereignty is undermined by global capitalism at the expense of distinctive and locally controlled patterns of social life and economic activity: the family-owned *trattoria* versus the fast-food restaurant chain; the local grocer versus the supermarket giant; the arts screen cinema versus the multiscreen multiplex. One notable example of an anti-capitalist advocate of the hyperglobalisation thesis is the international political economist, Susan Strange. In *The Retreat of the State* (1996), she notes that there is an inherent paradox in the balance of power between state and market. It seems that state intervention in the micromanagement of society seems to be increasing. But at the same time, the power of the state is in terminal decline. Strange reconciles these two seemingly contradictory developments by making a telling statement. The state may be interfering more in day-to-day life, but it has become a less effective provider of basic public services. By the same token, the market's star is very much in the ascendancy.

The pendulum which has swung in favour of the market at the state's expense is an outcome of global economic forces. The global economic impetus for this shift from state to market dominance is attributed by Strange to the transformation of the production structure of the world economy. The world production structure has changed under the influence of rapid technological innovation and the expansion of financial markets. The change in production is less about the rise of the multinational company than the denationalisation of the market: the change from production designed for the local market, to production centred on the world market (Strange 1996: 44). The end result of this shift to international production is that the multinational corporation has become both a central organiser of the world economy and a key political actor. But does this spell the end of the nation state? Strange adds that it would be an exaggeration to suggest the days of the state are numbered as it becomes usurped by powerful transnational corporations. Rather than the disappearance of the state, 'the progressive integration of the world economy, through international production, has shifted the balance of power away from states and toward world markets' (1996: 46). In fact, Strange (1994: 236) contends, in an earlier book, that those countries which are closely integrated within the global economy, through cross-border trade and financial investments, are more likely to have their sovereignty threatened.

Hyperglobalisation or (hyped) globalisation?

A theoretically and empirically robust critique of the globalisation thesis was developed by the sadly late social theorist, Paul Hirst, and the political economist, Grahame Thompson. In their influential text, *Globalization in*

Question (1996), they have in their critical sights the extreme globalisation position or hyperglobalisation thesis: that there has been a distinct historical shift towards economic globalisation, which has brought to an end the autonomy and independence of the nation state. Although essentially sceptical globalists, they do see a grain of truth in the political arguments of hyperglobalists such as Ohmae. In political terms, there is an acknowledgement that the state has changed since the Keynesian era of the 1930s and 1940s. For them, the state has not remained the same powerful, centralised institution over the years. It has not continued to exist as a unified institution, with full executive power and sovereignty intact. For Hirst and Thompson, states have succumbed to modern economic pressures, enjoying less independence and becoming less adept at controlling economic activities within their national territories (Hirst and Thompson 1996: 177). Hence state governance of the national macro-economy has weakened as a result of the borderless economy – a by-product of international markets.

It is one thing to argue that the state has changed and that it possesses less control over social and economic functions than in the past. But it would be quite another to equate these developments with the terminal decline and growing irrelevance of the nation state. Hirst and Thompson take issue with Ohmae and other hyperglobalists over the demise of the welfare state, the deregulation of state-based financial controls and the consequent decline of national sovereignty at the expense of global forces. For Hirst and Thompson, the state continues to be a regulatory force which global institutions rely upon for continued expansion and liberalisation; it persists as the prime law-maker which national territories depend upon for social and political integration (1996: 269–80). In other words, the state continues to hold its own within an international free market economy. Hirst and Thompson's predilection for defending the nation state against predictions of its demise is shared by Linda Weiss in *The Myth of the Powerless State* (1998). From contemporary case studies, Weiss concludes that domestic political institutions still make a vital contribution in a country's adjustment to global economic forces. Indeed, the intervention of the state in the world economy has grown and expanded in the global era.

As part of their defence of the nation state, Hirst and Thompson question whether economic globalisation actually exists. For these authors, from their survey of empirical and historical data, the level of economic globalisation has been exaggerated. This analysis reveals that the present integration of national economies is far from unprecedented. More than this, the extent of contemporary globalisation is less extensive than it was during the classical era of the Gold Standard between 1879 and 1914. Hirst and Thompson use comparative historical evidence to examine the extent of global economic integration across time. A pointer of note concerns the level of international financial integration, as indicated by offshore markets, parity of interest rates and asset prices. Taking parity of interest rates, there is a revealing comparison to be made between the contemporary era and the Gold Standard period. Whilst little headway was achieved in the early 1990s, the earlier Gold Standard era revealed that short-term interest rates were closely matched internationally. Hirst and Thompson (1996: 49) note that the level of national autonomy under the Gold Standard period 'was much less for the advanced economies than it is today'. The international economy has changed. But according to the data amassed by Hirst and Thompson, there are reservations over whether economic activities are truly globalised. Rather than a globalised economy there exists a 'highly internationalised economy', where companies are firmly rooted within national boundaries (Hirst and Thompson 1996: 185).

There also exists intensive cross-border trade and investment. But the point is that it takes place under the tutelage of nation states, which continue to make a fundamental contribution to the governance of the international economy. Indeed, there is a school of thought for which the state, far from being paralysed by globalisation, acts to buttress globalisation, at least in its economic manifestation. Here, the state is integral to globalisation. According to Weiss (1998: 2004), 'states may at times be facilitators (even perhaps perpetrators) rather than mere victims of so-called "globalization"'. Here, external global forces are shaped by the state rather than the other way round. Similar views were central to the later works of the French sociologist, Henri Lefebvre. Between 1976 and 1978 Lefebvre produced an extensive four-volume work entitled *De l'État*, which theorised the spatial geography of the state across the world. This work has never been translated into English and, as such, remains largely ignored in the clamour to rediscover his work by urban geographers and sociologists (Brenner 2001: 791). And yet *De l'État* manages to encompass his key ideas on the modern state and spatial politics. The third and fourth volumes of *De l'État* develop the idea of state productivism, of how the state has become more directly engaged in the management of capitalist growth. The state has made a pre-eminent contribution to the management capitalism on a grand scale, that is, at a global level. Rather than being subject to the dictates of global capitalism, the state is regarded by Lefebvre to be 'the major institutional framework in and through which the contemporary round of globalization is being fought out' (Brenner 2001: 794). For instance, the state is integral to the mediation between national and worldwide markets, the growth of commodity circulation, and the internationalisation of industrial production. That said, the state for Lefebvre is not wholly subservient to or an instrument of global capitalism – as some critics, especially those of a Marxist persuasion, would argue. The state, for this school of thought, is highly contested and subject to diverse socio-political forces.

Between the global and the local: the search for a compromise

Something of a sectarian divide has emerged in the literature on economic globalisation. The extent of economic globalisation and its effect on the nation state has been subject to quite stark interpretations, as shown above. There is little common ground and no meeting of minds between hyperglobalists and the critics of globalisation. Despite the radically different interpretations, it would be an oversight to argue that both positions are mutually exclusive, or completely irreconcilable. As we have seen, proponents from both the hyperglobal or critical camp do acknowledge the need to moderate their arguments. For example, critics of the extreme globalisation thesis such as Hirst and Thompson do accept that the autonomy of the nation state has been eroded by global economic forces.

Each camp has an inclination toward partisanship, leading to exaggerated claims or the impressionistic use evidence. Globalists, for Weiss, have exaggerated the powers of the state in previous eras, with the postwar Keynesian state being the apogee of a fully functioning and powerful central political body (Weiss 1998: 190). This has been done in order to contrast contemporary state weaknesses brought about by modern global economic pressures. Similarly, critics of globalisation – Hirst and Thompson most notably – stand accused for their embellished use of statistical evidence. These authors use quantitative historical data to show that trade gross domestic product ratios were higher in the 1890s than one hundred years later; thus making the point that the world economy was more integrated in the past than the present day. These statistics are used as a critical battering ram against the hyperglobalist contention that we have now entered a new global era. The use of quantitative data – especially economic data – fails to do justice to the qualitative shifts brought about by globalisation (Held *et al.* 1999: 11–12). For instance, globalisation involves more than simply economic integration. Globalisation has influenced or is manifest in various social activities: military affairs, culture, politics, the environment and even organised crime.

Some major thinkers in the field have reached for the middle ground between the hyperglobal and critical interpretations of economic globalisation. This includes recent publications by Georg Sørensen and Bob Jessop, who are prominent contributors to the globalisation and state theory literature. These authors attempt to reconcile change and continuity in the remorseless march of the global economy. They embrace the prospect that economic globalisation has changed the world but without dislodging the nation state. Herein is the basic tenor of recent contributions by Jessop and Sørensen: they have looked to reconcile distinct ideological and analytical positions on the global economy.

The Danish political scientist Georg Sørensen, in his recent work, has looked to theorise how far the modern state has changed. In weighing up the transformation of the state, globalisation enters the equation. *The Transformation of the State* (2004) attempts, as the subtitle of this book intimates, to go 'beyond the myth of [state] retreat', to question the alleged evaporation of state sovereignty. And yet the book does entertain the prospect that the modern capitalist state has been caught up in the global maelstrom. Here, the state has undergone fundamental change as a result of global forces such as the borderless economy. This seems to be a paradoxical position, one that reflects the complexity of contemporary globalisation. In an endeavour to reconcile these seemingly contradictory positions − hyperglobalisation and global sceptic approaches − Sørensen considers different perspectives on state power: there is the state-centric or realist position, represented by such figures as Hirst and Thompson and Weiss, respectively; the liberalist approach associated with Ohmae, amongst others; and finally the critical perspective, of which the British social theorist Bob Jessop is a clear proponent. These perspectives, according to Sørensen, are neither right nor wrong. Each one focuses upon certain essential aspects of a complex reality, whilst leaving aside or overlooking other features of the globalisation–state relationship. For instance, the realist perspective emphasises the centrality of the state in most forms of social and economic life; the liberal perspective is concerned with the constraining influence of economic and other civil actors on the state; and critical theory emphasises the close links between politics and economics in understanding the state (Sørensen 2004: 21). Although these approaches to globalisation seem to be far removed from each other, there is some degree of overlap. The similarities appear because they attempt to grapple with how the state has changed over time. In searching for such overlaps, Sørensen's aim is to reach for the middle-ground between retreatist and state-centric theories of the state. The buzz concept in reaching for the middle-ground is that of *state transformation* rather than retreat.

In putting the state in a global context, Sørensen is looking for an *open theoretical* approach. What he means by this is that analytical options on the relationship between globalisation and the state are effectively kept open. In other words, there is a conscious effort to stay clear of siding with either the state-centred or retreatist camp. Sørensen manoeuvres his way between each faction by emphasising that the state is in constant flux or transition in the global era. In fact, transformation is central to the history of the state, which affects the state's authority and influence relative to other stakeholders in the global system. Because of global pressures, the state − or specifically state sovereignty − is open to change in either direction: either in retreat or in ascendance. Within the global system, modern states have to live with the prospect that sovereignty is always in the balance. The precarious nature of modern state sovereignty is borne out by economic globalisation.

The state is both a winner and loser when it comes to economic globalisation and the attendant transformation of sovereignty. Take the *losing* element. Economic globalisation is real for Sørensen. There is little scepticism here. The extent of economic globalisation can be gauged in several different ways. There is, for instance, the deepening integration of *national economic spaces*. One outcome of such integration is the formation of regional economic blocs – take the European Union and NAFTA as prime examples – encompassing various national economies. There is also the growth of multinational companies, transnational financial institutions and the increased flow of foreign currency transactions. What is the outcome of such economic globalisation on the role and function of the modern state in industrial societies? The state, from the vantage point of Sørensen's open theoretical approach, has changed considerably under modern economic globalisation. The role of the state during the early postwar years was to address market failures within specific national boundaries. By contrast, within the cut-throat modern global market, the function of the state is to secure a competitive advantage for capitalistic entities based within its national borders (see Jessop 2002: 96). Of course there are differences in how advanced states handle the demands of the emerging global economy. There also exist differences between the way advanced and post-colonial, developing states have dealt with economic globalisation. Despite these differences, 'the general trend that can be discerned is one of moving towards a competition state' (Sørensen 2004: 36).

The idea that there has been a historical break in the competitive functions of the state is well established in the contemporary globalisation literature. In one formative instance, Cerny (1990) traced the changing structures of the late twentieth-century state, making the case for a transition from the *welfare* to the *competition state*. The emergence of the competition state, notes Cerny, is a product of a world that has become economically, as well as politically, interdependent. Another recent author in the historical rupture tradition is Bob Jessop. In fact Sørensen cites Jessop's recent book on *The Future of the Capitalist State* extensively, especially his chapter on the global economy. In this book, Jessop conceptualises the changes afoot in the functions of the state as a shift from the Keynesian welfare national state to the Schumpeterian competition state. The central narrative here is that Atlantic Fordism, the dominant system of capital accumulation in the postwar period, was able to coexist with a Keynesian welfare state for some time. Eventually, Fordism and the Keynesian system of regulation became incompatible due to the global expansion of the economy and the emergence of post-Fordist capitalism, an accumulative regime based on flexible production and lean organisations. This historical shift has required the state to adopt new guises and sets of functions. For instance, the prevailing activities of the state have changed from macroeconomic management such as nationalisation to the microeconomic concerns of trade liberalisation.

Does the rise of the competitive state – fashioned by the dictates, whims and fancies of the global market – mean a reduced role for the state? States now, as a matter of routine, face exposure to the economic forces of the world market. Despite globally induced trends such as denationalisation, the state is still a key political actor which has resisted displacement by the market (Jessop 2002: 211). Rather than the nation state losing out completely, it is the Keynesian welfare state that has been eroded. Jessop notes that as the Keynesian welfare state is rolled back, certain generic functions of the national state continue to remain. The state has also extended its authority into other new areas. The state's relevance matters in *political* terms above all else: the state is still best placed to handle conflicts, safeguard democracy and oversee redistributive policies. For Jessop, the state and its functions have been redefined by the competitive dictates of the global market. But the state remains a significant political actor within the global marketplace.

Interestingly, equal billing is given to political and economic processes by Jessop and Sørensen in their respective analyses of the modern state. By doing so, such thinkers demonstrate that globalisation is more than an economic process; globalisation encompasses the political realm which, like economic globalisation, can make an impression on the state. In the sections that follow, we examine debates that revolve around the relationship between globalisation and the state, except the emphasis is on *global political* actors, institutions and practices.

Globalisation as a political process

Those with even a passing interest in globalisation would be forgiven if they regarded globalisation as something which revolves around economics. It is economic matters and issues that dominate the way globalisation comes to manifest itself. There are the regular news features covering the daily fluctuations of international currency values. There are the consumer durables that are assembled and produced in far-flung places, mainly East Asia nowadays. There is the national mourning and hand-ringing whenever regionally based companies, such as Rover at Longbridge and Sony at Bridgend, decide to relocate to those parts of the world where labour is cheaper and more expendable. From the NASDAQ to the Nikkei index, globalisation seems to be about economics.

The dam in globalisation theory, though, has long since burst – the dam in this case being the fixation with globalisation as an exclusively economic phenomenon. Noteworthy social thinkers such as Ulrich Beck and Roland Robertson have long claimed that globalisation involves more than mere economic processes. For Albrow (1996), globalisation involves a complex set of social arrangements. Globalisation also encompasses culture, forms of communication, identity and, most importantly, politics. In fact, global political developments are of equal significance to economic globalisation. Peterson (1992: 372), for one, points out how the spread of democracy has given rise to the idea that economic globalisation is being shadowed by political and cultural process of globalisation. The political nature of globalisation matters just as much as economics when it comes to discussions of state sovereignty. The urgent issue now becomes one of how we come to conceptualise the state in the context of global events and developments of a political or even cultural nature. In discussions of political globalisation, there exists a rich source of competing traditions and schools of thought. These can be found across different social science disciplines but especially in that offshoot of political science, international relations. In fact, the political subdiscipline of international relations has been at the forefront in theorising how the state operates within and through a transnational political system.

Realism versus anti-realism: the state in the international arena

International relations theorists have been at the forefront in theorising how the state operates within and through a transnational political system. As an emerging discipline in the early twentieth century, the field of international relations was dominated by liberal idealists. Liberal internationalists saw appeals to reason and notions of mutual cooperation over a slavish attachment to national interest as the only means for achieving international peace and stability. The liberal panacea for international conflict had its firm advocates in Britain (Norman Angell and Alfred Zimmern) and the United States (Pitman Potter and James Shotwell). But liberal idealism was largely discredited by the rise of fascism and the proliferation of conflict throughout the interwar years. However, it was only in the late 1930s that alternative schools of thought, or rather one single school of thought, rose to prominence: realism (Donnelly 2000: 26–7). If there is a dominant approach within the modern study of international relations, realism fits that bill. For realist practitioners, international politics revolves around the nation state, or a system of competing nation states. The state is assumed to be the central and principal actor within the international system of political governance.

Amongst the initial exponents of realism was the historian, Edward Carr. His classic work *The Twenty Years' Crisis* attempted to explain away the causes of international conflict, especially the events leading to the Second World War. Here, Carr is less interested in laying the blame at the feet of leaders and individual politicians than in the fundamental political causes of wars, or what he terms the 'power politics' between states (1946: 102–4). The thesis pursued in *The Twenty Years' Crisis* furnished the intellectual foundations of what is known as the English school of realism in international relations. The English school, following the Carr tradition, drew from the classical writings of law (Hobbes and Machiavelli), philosophy (Kant) and history (Grotius). These influences become apparent in the writings of prominent alumni of the English school, key among them being Martin Wright and Herbert Butterfield (Viotti and Kauppi 1999: 6). For such acolytes of the English school, international politics is essentially anarchical. The international arena is an anarchical system made up of sovereign states intent on maximising their interests. Because states are unable to transcend their own self-interests, internecine conflict and war are inevitable.

The anarchical international system portrayed by the English school also became a template for American commentators on international affairs. The Chicago University political scientist, George Kennan, in his critique of US foreign policy reflected that foreign policy is a thankless task dominated by conflict and violence between nation states. The tendency has been to approach these international problems by adopting a legal-moralistic strategy. This in effect involves the subordination of nation states to some form of overarching international law. For Kennan, the belief that international law is able to curb the lawlessness of foreign affairs is misplaced. Why? Many international borders are disputed and the cause of endless flashpoints. Moreover, international law would prove too inflexible and too rigid to keep up with the constant evolution of nation states. Kennan reached a bleak conclusion. Whilst international law must be respected, individual states should become detached from foreign affairs and 'have the modesty to admit that our own national interest is all that we are really capable of knowing and understanding' (Kennan 1969: 103). The central tenets of realism – anarchy and the sovereignty of the nation state – became the bedrock of the international relations discipline during the 1950s and early 1960s. Some commentators observed that such was the dominance of realism that bona fide anti-realists were thin on the ground or non-existent (see Fox and Fox 1961: 343).

Academic challenges bedevilled the realist school from the 1960s onwards. Claims made, for example, by Hans Morgenthau about the essentially self-interested nature of state action, and the reduction of international politics to a zero-sum game where only the fittest survive, failed to withstand close scrutiny (Donnelly 2000: 29). These arguments seemed excessive for critics. As a result of these growing challenges, realism began to haemorrhage support and influence, signalling its fall from grace amongst international relations scholars. The decline of realism left a vacuum that was filled in the 1970s by a liberal humanist approach to international relations. In the vanguard of this anti-realist, liberal offensive in the mid-1960s was David Mitrany (1966). He enlisted what he saw as the growing significance of non-governmental organisations to challenge the state-centric model of international affairs (Wapner 1995: 316–17). Mitrany's example was followed by other thinkers.

In this more holistic take on international relations, Robert Keohane and Joseph Nye became key theoreticians. Their landmark book, *Power and Interdependence* (1977), made the case for approaching the world polity as a complex set of interdependencies. The model of 'complex interdependence', when compared to realism, approaches the political machinations of the global arena quite differently. International relations are fragmented, revolving around a diverse and motley collection of agents – among which the autonomous state rubs shoulders with a variety of international players. And from this fragmentation two consequences ensue. Firstly, the political agenda internationally is rarely controlled by centralised institutions such as nation states. Secondly, international politics is less dominated by force, with states increasingly unable to 'get their way' economically through military might. The interdependence model, although it never gained a dominant foothold, began to squeeze realism out from the international relations field. That said, it was later claimed by Keohane and Nye (1987: 727–8) in a review essay on *Power and Interdependence* that their ideas sought to revise as opposed to usurping realism; both realism and liberal interdependence theory complement each other. Be that as it may, their book offered a substantive alternative to the realist school, both in Britain and America.

But it would be premature to say realism was dead and buried. Nothing could be further from the truth. Wider political events and disciplinary-specific machinations in the late 1970s and early 1980s attest to such claims. At the time, there was something of a neo-realist revival. The later revival was aided and abetted, in part, by the lay of the political land at the time. The reintensification of the Cold War during the late 1970s was one thing. And the attendant emergence of local internecine conflicts throughout the world led to a preoccupation with security issues in the literature. All this concern with security, of course, brought the state back into play once again. These neo-realist concerns were influentially articulated by Hedley Bull's (1977) *The Anarchical Society*, a study which portrayed the global superpowers as vying for supremacy by steadily and suicidally upping the ante in the nuclear arms race. And the return to realism was given a further shot in the arm by Ronald Reagan's foreign policy. Reagan's aggressive pursuit of American national interest, as underlined by the Iran-Contra Affair, became a guiding principle long before the neo-conservative revival under Paul Wolfowitz and others. For all that the cut and thrust of history at the time favoured realist ideas, internal disciplinary concerns were also responsible for the neo-realist revival of the 1980s.

In the disciplinary field of international relations, a new generation of thinkers were intent on reinventing realism for a modern context and audience. The leading neo-realist revivalists emerged from American universities. Weighty contributions were made by Kenneth Thompson and, especially, Kenneth Waltz. For these American neo-realists, the international polity existing as a harmonious system, revolving around interdependent state and non-state actors, is at best a 'marginal affair' (Waltz 1970: 206). To rebut such claims and assert a methodologically coherent alternative, neo-realists looked to economic theory, or more specifically rational choice theory. Waltz, in particular, drew parallels between the workings of the commercial market composed of various profit-maximising firms and international affairs, although he conceded that there were limits to the comparison. In a chapter on national independence, Waltz (1979: 91) observes: 'International-political systems, like economic markets, are formed by the action of self-regarding units'. These self-regarding units are, of course, independent nation states. The state, for neo-realists such as Waltz, is regarded as a unified and coherent institutional entity – an institution that, to boot, operates as a rational, interest-maximising actor. By highlighting the essentially self-serving nature of state behaviour in the international arena, the potential for conflict is ever present: 'the state of nature is a state of war' (Waltz 1979: 102). This means that war can occur at any time. And within this faction-ridden system, economic supremacy and military might are intertwined. The most powerful states, even if they are dependent on other actors for vital economic and material supplies, will use their military strength to secure access to these material necessities (Waltz 1978: 222). For instance, the second Gulf war was fought on the pretext of locating weapons of mass destruction, but for critics, such as the film maker Michael Moore, this is an 'oil war' – a military campaign contrived by the neo-conservative Bush administration to secure vital oil supplies for America.

The theoretical and empirical status of the state-centric realist paradigm experienced another dip in its popularity within the international relations field during the late 1980s and early 1990s. Key events during the decade, most notably the international deregulation of financial markets and the collapse of the Iron Curtain, showed what an important contribution non-state actors have made to geopolitics (Peterson 1992: 371). The state must have seemed more peripheral than ever. But the impact of all this transnational activity on state autonomy is still a matter of some dispute and differing interpretations. When it comes to globalisation as a political process, it would be an exaggeration to say that anti-statists or liberal pluralists now have it all their own way. This is true despite the growth of transnational cooperation and activism during the past fifty years. In other words, realism is still in the game, despite having fallen from grace within international relations (Donnelly 2000: 31). And as such, the state is still regarded as a unit of some influence within the international relations literature. If anything, the state, in the increasingly security-conscious climate since 11 September 2001, has tightened its grip on areas such as cross-border security. And even the internet, supposedly free from the constraints of time, space and the arm of regulation, has been a victim of state paranoia and interference. The internet companies Yahoo! and

Google famously capitulated to pressures from the despotic Chinese state to censor the release of politically sensitive information on its search engines. Hence, tensions between realists and anti-realists, statists and pluralists, state-centred and anti-statist thinkers are still evident in the study of international relations. Such theoretical tensions form part of current discussions about transnational politics and institutions, a key area being that of multilevel governance, as we shall investigate below.

The rise of multilevel governance

The international polity has taken on new characteristics in the postwar era. The modern history of international politics is characterised by the strengthening of global political institutions. It is clear for all to see. Intergovernmental organisations flex their muscles like never before. And nation states become so deeply embroiled with each other that it is sometimes difficult to see where national sovereignty begins and where it ends. An interesting feature of global governance is the intensification of cross-border transactions, contacts and cooperation. Bilateral and multilateral agreements have grown dramatically for Western states. Take the USA and Britain as examples. In the USA the number of bilateral agreements increased from 696 between 1960 and 1964 to 1250 between 1975 and 1979. In Britain, the number of multilateral agreements grew from 144 during the 1950–4 period to 197 in 1970–4 (Sørensen 2004: 60–1). Reflecting the greater degree of solidarity amongst states, there was also the postwar growth of intergovernmental organisations. Such institutions, crucially, have formed geopolitical sites where nation states collaborate and work together. As well as their numerical growth, intergovernmental bodies have become increasingly assertive – the United Nations and the OECD to name two major players on the international stage.

The evolving order of global governance is some way off from being a world government, with ultimate legal and military sanction; and neither is it a loose cooperative arrangement between nation states. Rather 'it comprises a vast array of formal suprastate bodies and regional organizations ... as well as regimes and transnational policy networks embracing government officials, technocrats, corporate representatives, pressure groups, and non-governmental organizations' (Held and McGrew 2002: 59). This global political order is described as a system of multilevel governance by Sørensen. The multilevel governance institution par excellence is the EU. In other words, this is an institution where national power is decentralised and dispersed. Through transnational decentralisation, key regulatory powers have moved from individual nation states to 'a complex network of supranational, national and subnational' bodies (Sørensen 2004: 65). European multilevel governance has gone hand in hand with growing societal integration between individual member states, although key European partners such as Britain continue to drag their feet over monetary union. Under the EU, nation states, regions and cities collaborate at various levels – economic, political and cultural.

Instances of intergovernmental cooperation other than European model are plentiful (as are the acronyms). There is the Mercado Commún del Sur (Mercosur), a free trade agreement between South American countries. In Africa, structure for economic cooperation has been sought by the Southern African Development Community (SADC) and the Economic Community of West African States (ECOWAS). These examples of intergovernmental cooperation across national borders follow what can be termed a 'traditional' pattern: strictly delimited cooperation on specific policy areas, particularly trade. In contrast to such partial forms of cooperation, the EU has taken multilevel governance to new heights and degrees of intensity. Since the creation of the EU, European nations have gradually pooled their sovereignty on specified policy areas. Monetary union is probably the most far-reaching example of where sovereignty is voluntarily ceded, with individual states giving up their currency and control over key economic policies. Cases of multilevel governance where sovereignty is affected are regarded by Sørensen (2004) as examples of deep integration. Another notable instance of deep integration is the World Trade Organisation, where signatories (individual national governments) are brought into binding trade agreements.

These are the hard facts of political globalisation or multilevel governance: the number of bilateral and multilateral agreements, the growth of intergovernmental organisations, and the increasing depth of multilevel governance across national borders. Such empirical indicators manage to capture the extent and reach of the global polity. But the nub of the argument, as far as state theory is concerned, is how these facts of political globalisation are interpreted theoretically.

Theorising multilevel governance: the rise of the global polity?

The extent of multilevel governance, it seems, offers more grist to the mill for those perennial warring factions in the globalisation debate surrounding the state – the statists and the retreatists. This is the observation made, at least, by Sørensen. For retreatists, the extent of political integration at a global level has, like economic globalisation, rendered the state increasingly less powerful and dependent on sharing sovereignty. A notable proponent of politically driven retreatism is James Rosenau. In his book *Turbulence in World Politics*, Rosenau argues that changes in global politics are rare occurrences but that when they do happen they are likely to be highly disruptive. The transformation of global politics under way since the 1950s is one such turbulent event. It has resulted in the replacement of a state-centric order with an autonomous multicentric world. This multicentric polity has come about, in part, through the emergence of transnational political issues such as global terrorism, drug trade and environmental pollution, the technologically driven compression of political spaces and the rise of what Rosenau terms 'sub-groupism' such as nationalist political groups. Because of these global political developments, national governments have become less able to generate compliance and ultimately their legitimacy has been questioned (Rosenau 1990: 398).

Anti-retreatists put a less pessimistic spin on the state's prospects in a politically globalised world. But for those on the statist side of the fence, global cooperation and the pooling of sovereignty in transgovernmental bodies only serve to strengthen individual nation states. A similar argument is developed by Marks *et al.* (1996) in relation to the EU. For these authors, the sovereignty of individual states within the EU has been diluted by collective decision-making and the operation of supranational law-making institutions. Moreover, European states are finding that they enjoy less representation in the international arena. But why do states allow powers and competencies to move upwards to supranational bodies such as the EU policy machine? Marks *et al.* note that states do receive something in return, a sort of sovereignty quid pro quo. They may give up some external control, but individual nation states find that their domestic powers are strengthened in turn by the process of integration (Marks *et al.* 1996: 347). Nation states, when involved in the process of integration, transfer power so as to not harm but ultimately preserve the power of the nation state. Indeed, any loss of power from this deliberate sharing of sovereignty has been superficial.

My view is that Sørensen exaggerates the controversy between statists and retreatists in the contemporary debate surrounding political globalisation. Present-day discussions of political globalisation are less characterised by turf wars between statists and retreatists. And the hyperbole predicting the end of the state is also less prominent nowadays. These extreme positions marked the globalisation literature in the 1980s and early 1990s, especially for those debating economic globalisation. But the political globalisation debate has moved on somewhat. It has matured, becoming less reactionary and more considered. Typical of these increasingly measured impulses within the political globalisation debate are emerging discussions about the global polity.

The global polity perspective attempts to go beyond the traditional sectarian divide in international relations, that between realism and liberalism. It attempts to side-step the 'methodological nationalism' of realism and the anti-realist insistence that the state is haemorrhaging influence to global forces. Certainly, these are the arguments put forward by Morten Ougaard, a leading proponent of the global polity approach, in his book *Political Globalization* (2004). From a global polity perspective, acknowledges Ougaard, we are unlikely to witness the rise of a worldwide government that supersedes an international structure made up of individual nation states. We are unlikely to have a global equivalent where the emergence of the nation state during the eighteenth and nineteenth centuries eventually superseded feudal kingdoms. The political situation globally is nicely captured by the notion that international politics involves *governance with many governments*, rather than a system of governance without government (see Zürn 2002: 81). To develop the concept of a global polity, researchers have adapted concepts from democratic political systems or from state theory.

A homogenous global state covering the world remains a pipe dream or unlikely nightmare scenario, depending on your point of view. And yet the global polity system is not made up of hermetically sealed nation states. For advocates of the global polity perspective, such as McGrew (2002) and Keck and Sikkink (1998), the global polity is made up of political entities (states) which occasionally reach agreements or cooperate on specific policy issues. But it is more than a matter of cooperation. Globalisation has made a difference to national politics. Recent discussions of the global polity have stressed, amongst other things, the growing influence of non-state actors, organisations and activities within international politics. For instance, McGrew (2002: 210–25) observes how the global associational revolution, as manifested in the expansion of the activity of non-governmental organisations, may be the beginnings of a democratic system of global governance. The prospect of international relations involving a plurality of interests – both state as well as non-state interests – has been an integral part of the anti-realist rearguard. In fact, international relations theorists during the course of the 1990s paid increased attention to how society outside the state flexed its muscles within the global political arena. We close this chapter by considering the possible emergence of a global civil society and the implications of a global civil society for the state and state theory.

The globalisation of civic society: the end of nationhood?

Globalisation theorists have taken concepts normally equated with the domestic, national context and used them to understand global politics. A concept traditionally delimited to national boundaries, which has been used to explore globalisation, is that of civil society. Employing civil society in the context of globalisation research has produced a welter of literature and debate beyond the subdiscipline of international relations. The argument is that what Robertson (1992) terms the objective conditions of globalisation – the rise of global markets, travel, communications, immigration and so on – are transforming the subjective conditions of globalisation – cultural identities, communities and forms of association. In particular, the growth of international civil links across national boundaries poses significant challenges to the state.

Civil society as traditionally dealt with by political and social theorists is rooted within national territorial settings. It is regarded as 'society minus the state'. A more critical definition would exclude commercial and economic entities, noting that 'between the economic structure and the state with its legislation and coercion stands civil society' (Gramsci 1982: 208). Several political theorists, with an international focus, have applied the concept of civil society to a global context. As in the national state, the key actors of a global civil society include non-governmental organisations, trade unions, social activists and private enterprises and social movements. But in a global context, these civil actors have connections and interests and partake in activities that are mainly transnational rather than national in scope. In making these claims, theorists are responding to real world developments. Evidence suggests that the number of international organisations, outside the scope of national and global governing authorities, has grown significantly in recent decades. Such growth is highlighted by data from the Union of International Organizations, showing that the number of formal international non-governmental organisations had increased from 13,000 in 1981 to 47,000 in 2001 (Anheier and Themundo 2002: 194). Similar trends are identified by Jackie Smith who found, using information from the *Yearbook of International Organizations*, that more than 60 per cent of transnational social movement organisations active in 1993 were established after 1970. In fact, between 1973 and 1993, their numbers increased from around 200 to over 600 organisations (Smith 1997: 46–7).

With the explosion of civil actors on the global stage, what are the implications for the state and state theory? According to Shaw (1994: 647–8): 'Within International Relations, there has been particular interest in these movements which have been seen as especially significant forms through which society outside the state is represented in the global and international arenas'. For others, the growing density of connections between social movements and non-governmental organisations across national boundaries has produced a transnational network independent of the nation state. This is not so much a retreat of the state as the creation of a parallel system of democratic representation. For Lipschutz (1992), a global civil society is emerging at this historical juncture, partly as a response to the more limited role of the state in matters of welfare and public provision – a reaction to the New Right agenda of the 1980s. The rise of a global civil society is also part and parcel of an evolving international resistance against the hegemonic structure of global capital (Lipschutz 1992: 399).

There are other proponents of a global civil society, albeit with more reservations than Lipschutz. An interesting example is the Gramscian international relations theorist, Robert Cox, who points to the emergence of a nascent 'global civil society' in which the increasingly transnational scope of social movements constitutes the basis of an alternative world order (Cox 1999: 11). The wave of strikes organised in France in 1995 and South Korea in 1997; the growth of non-governmental and mutual agencies in Asia; community-led women's relief organisations in Africa;

the claims by indigenous groups in such areas as the Mexican state of Chiapas: these are all instances of an emerging civil counterweight to the hegemonic power of global capitalism (Cox 1999: 13–15). Cox acknowledges that the prospect of a global civil society as the harbinger of emancipation is an aspiration to be achieved (see Cox 1999: 11, footnote). Similar arguments are made by Shaw, for whom the activities of transnational social movements and non-governmental agencies are bringing the reality of a global civil society closer. They have done this by creating links between people in the Northern and Southern Hemispheres. But such developments are limited – a global civil society is still more a potential than an actual reality (Shaw 1994: 655).

The global reach of modern civic activism may be symptomatic of processes other than the rise of a fully fledged global civil society. This is the point made by O'Brien *et al.* (2000) in their study of international opposition in the late 1990s to the Multilateral Agreement on Investment (MAI) – a treaty organised between members of the OECD to smooth the path for cross-border financial investment. For these authors, the globalisation of social movements is the outcome of *complex multilateralism*. The concept of complex multilateralism alludes to how global governance is gradually moving from a system centred exclusively on states to an entity that is more inclusive of different actors from civil society, be they non-governmental organisations, trade unions, social activists and private enterprises. The authors are careful not to portray this as a fundamental and comprehensive shift toward a pluralistic global polity. Rather, complex multilateralism has 'incrementally pluralized governing structures' (O'Brien *et al.* 2000: 3). A number of significant changes in how the global political economy is regulated and governed were responsible for the pluralisation of global governance.

There is good reason why a global civil society is still in its infancy. So-called transnational social movements and activist organisations that are in the vanguard of this global civil movement are still very much attached to and dependent upon specific geographic territories and nation states (see Rohrschneider and Dalton 2002). To think about transnational political activism as if it exists within the parameters of one international society is premature. Peterson prefers to conceive of transnational activity in terms of several internationally linked civil societies. In addition, the notion of an international as opposed to a 'global civil society' does not explain away the reality of national borders (Peterson 1992: 377–8). To talk of a global civil society is to enter the realms of the hyperbolic. One issue is clear: a truly global civil society is yet to usurp the nation state. And yet when civil society is caught in the global maelstrom, it often leads to further questions rather than a definite resolution of issues.

Any discussion of globalisation and civil society would be incomplete without a consideration of national identity – or nationhood. Nationhood cannot be ignored by state theory, especially those globally-tinged analyses of the state. In fact, at the non-economic end of the globalisation literature, there exist some interesting attempts to understand the impact of globalisation on national identity. As the nation state became a firm and permanent fixture in Europe during the eighteenth and nineteenth centuries, it transformed cultural politics and notions of place and belonging. There emerged a new collective political identity. Those people and communities who came under the jurisdiction of a state became political citizens. State citizens began to identify with, or see themselves as belonging to, a particular nation. Of course the changes to political identity were, initially, uncertain, and far from definite. But over time political identities became firmly established. Eventually people saw themselves as being French, Prussian or English. Although ethnic-political identities are now a solid mainstay across nation states, the process of globalisation has complicated matters. To be more precise, it is cultural globalisation which has posed a series of questions for national identity – or at least conceptions of national identity as a fixed, permanent and unified characteristic of modern society.

An obvious challenge to nationhood comes from labour migration. An attempt to explore how migration can disrupt traditional notions of national identity and citizenship is made in Yasemin Soysal's (1994) study of non-EU migrant guest workers across Europe. For example, guest workers in countries such as Germany did not enjoy citizenship and yet the legal system conferred certain basic rights on these workers such as social security and protection in work (Soysal 1994: 122–3). In other words, certain basic human rights are conferred on these migrant workers irrespective of their nationality. Of course, the EU is not an out-and-out paradise for migrants and asylum seekers. But this is another issue. Nevertheless, Soysal's study manages to capture the way migrant labour flows have transformed citizenship. Citizenship has moved from something that is particular and specific to nationhood to a more universal form of political membership based on personhood. Soysal (1994: 161) argues that 'as particularistic identities are transformed into expressive modes of core humanness, thus acquiring universal currency, the "nation" looses its charisma and becomes normalized'. In other words, national citizenship is now being eclipsed by a postnational form of citizenship based on universal human rights.

National identity forms the cultural DNA for any political state institution. So how do states cope with the fragmentation of nationhood brought about by cultural globalisation? Can the state survive the way national identity has been thrown into the detraditionalising maelstrom of globalisation? The state will of course survive, but it survives with its pre-eminence and authority severely challenged. This is the opinion of David Held, certainly no dilettante of a global commentator and theorist. He notes that global 'processes can weaken the cultural hegemony of nation-states and re-stimulate the ethnic and cultural groups which compose them' (Held 1995: 126). This process of restimulation may lead to pressures for subnational and regional autonomy – a case in point being the UK and the recent setting up of devolved political institutions for the Celtic peripheries. The break-up of national identity can also prove foreboding for nation states. We do not have to look far back into history to witness examples of how ethnic groupings begin to treat the nation state less as a host than as an enemy. In so doing, such groups may challenge the very legitimacy and authority of the state, as has recently happened in France. The nondescript and largely anonymous suburb of Clichy-sous-Bois was unknown to most people in Paris, let alone anyone outside of France. But this mainly immigrant housing estate shot to world attention in October 2005 when two weeks of sustained rioting broke out on its streets. Initially the riots were ignited by the accidental deaths of two teenagers, but this unprecedented unrest spread to other Paris suburbs and locations across France (Lille and Toulouse) with dense immigrant populations. If ever there was an example of the way nationhood and political citizenship can be challenged, this was it. The immediate causes of the riots were local in nature, but the structural causes were to be found in the policies, or lack of policies, of the French state. Successive French governments have shown an indifference to the socio-economic plight experienced by immigrant communities. Events of this nature have been predicted in films like Mathieu Kassovitz's film *La Haine* or by French rap artists such as La Fonky Family. To an extent, the French state is reaping what its particular brand of nationhood has sown.

Conclusion

The presence of globalisation in social analysis is ubiquitous, standing as an equal alongside established ideas such as class, power, gender and bureaucracy. It is a theme not only confined to academic discourse. Broadcasters and journalists, politicians and policy-makers, novelists and cultural commentators, business leaders and management gurus: all elements of the free-floating intelligentsia have embraced globalisation as their own. But this recognition of the global is far from being unproblematic, certainly within academe. The key issues of globalisation research – its historical phasing, socio-economic causes and repercussions for humanity – have been subject to intense speculation. Different interpretations abound. As shown in this chapter, this has been especially so in those attempts to theorise the state in a global context. In fact, globalisation research has brought the state back into greater prominence within the social sciences. The debate about globalisation has reinvigorated interest in the state. This is to an extent ironic as one of the key debates in the globalisation literature is over the issue of whether global forces have rendered national boundaries, and therefore the state, superfluous. In this chapter, we have seen how initial discussions about the effects of globalisation on national sovereignty concentrated on economic forces. But globalisation is also fuelled by cultural, social and political processes. And these different forms of globalisation have a bearing on the state. But various interpretations on how globalisations impacts on the nation state abound – and this chapter has attempted to cover these ideas. For example, transnational political institutions depend on the pooling of national sovereignty. This can spell the end of the state for some commentators, but for others these very same institutions can strengthen individual state units. Global processes also influence ideas of nationhood and a sense of belonging, which can potentially undermine the legitimacy of the state. And yet despite the force of power of globalisation at different levels, the state retains a presence in reality and in the theoretical language of the social sciences.

CONCLUSION: THE PAST, PRESENT AND FUTURE OF STATE THEORY

The 'Nietzschean legacy'

We have tried during the course of this book to provide a taste and an overview of contemporary efforts to construct theories of the state, or specifically, the liberal democratic state in Western capitalist societies. These existing theories inevitably reflect, and are closely informed by, modern currents of social and political thought: feminist thought, globalisation studies, governance theory, cultural analysis, poststructuralism and so on. As such, during the course of this book, a wide range of approaches and theoretical opinions on the state have been covered. That said, one recurring motif throughout the book has been a tendency to write off the state, or a certain ambivalence, antipathy even, towards the state. Thinkers have written about the fragmentation of the state, the process of denationalisation and the state as a cultural illusion.

Of course, philosophical critiques aimed against the state have a long and very honourable tradition. It could be said that Friedrich Nietzsche is one of the 'founding fathers' of anti-statist theory. Nietzsche was an ardent critic of the fledgling mass culture of the nineteenth century and the institutions of modernity. The modern nation state was a prime candidate for his anti-modernist broadsides. The modern state bureaucracy – specifically, the German state under Bismarck is what Nietzsche principally has in mind – has been responsible for cultural homogeneity, for reducing individual difference and promoting social regimentation. The state is also responsible for reactionary hysteria, whether in the form of nationalism or anti-Semitism (Kellner n.d.). And democracy? For Nietzsche the democratic state was simply a mask for authoritarian rule.

In *Thus Spake Zarathustra*, published in 1883, Nietzsche launches one of the first critiques of the modern state (Kellner n.d.). *Zarathustra* adopts colourful and often acerbic language to describe the modern state. Nietzsche writes how everything about the state is false, it devours, chews and rechews its citizens (Nietzsche 2003: 37). The state is portrayed as a 'cold monster', which ultimately annihilates its citizens: 'State I call it, where all are poison drinkers, good and bad: state, where the slow suicide of all – is called "life"' (2003: 37). The modern state stands in contrast to individual people with their traditions, culture and customs. And Nietzsche's solution to the impending manipulation and doom of the state ushered in by modern society? *Zarathustra* recommends withdrawal from mass society, splendid isolation over participation, which is tantamount to complicity in its destructive ways: 'Flee, my friend, into your solitude! I see you deafened by the noise of the great men and stung all over by the stings of the little men' (2003: 38). In certain respects the Nietzsche of *Zarathustra* brings to mind the actions and recommendations of contemporary environmentalists who recommend going back to some past idyll to reverse the destructive trends of modern living.

As well as the vitriol aimed at the state, Nietzsche made interesting predictions in *Twilight of the Idols*, published in 1888, his final productive year before madness and illness rendered him incapable. He observes: 'Culture and the state ... are antagonists: "cultural state" is just a modern idea. The one lives off the other, the one flourishes at the expense of the other. All great periods in culture are periods of political decline: anything which is great in a cultural sense was unpolitical, even *antipolitical*' (Nietzsche 1998: 39). By this we deduce political decline to also refer to the decline of the state. Of course the Nietzschean legacy still lives on in different ways, as we can see in the theoretical antipathy levelled at the state by certain schools of thought in contemporary social and political theory. It was his critique of mass culture and the state that inspired later thinkers across the political spectrum, including Heidegger and the Frankfurt School.

Well over a century has passed since Nietzsche made his prediction about culture and the decline of the state. From an ardent critique of mass culture and modern society, his anticipation of the state's demise was possibly a matter of wishful thinking. For in the century since he wrote *Twilight of the Idols*, Nietzsche's prediction is yet to materialise. Nor is it likely to – certainly in our lifetime. If anything, this book has shown that the state still matters. Most importantly, it continues to matter as a topic for theoretical discussion and debate amongst social scientists, political commentators and philosophers. It is also true that even for those writers who operate with some anti-theory of the state, it still retains sufficient import. The state continues to be of sufficient interest for them to comment on its nature and activities, even if it is to remark on the break-up and fragmentation of the state or its imminent passing into history. The continued interest in the state is symptomatic of its staying power. The state may not be the omnipresent and integrated force portrayed in classical social theory, but it is a powerful regulatory force; and even some anti-state theorists acknowledge this fact. It is still worth the effort of theoretical speculation.

State theory: a post-disciplinary affair

The continued interest in the state is also a product of developments internal to social and political theory. The subject of the state has stirred important debates and spearheaded significant innovations in social and political thought. Just as the state was central to the emergence of modern political thought in the works of such luminaries as Locke and Mill, so it continues to provoke theoretical excursions and flights of fancy. Take the issue of globalisation. The whole debate surrounding globalisation took off around concerns about whether state sovereignty and autonomy have been undermined by the global integration of economic markets and productive forces. As we saw in Chapter 6, globalisation theory, to an extent, is dominated by the shadow of the state. There is the school of thought for which economic globalisation has rendered the state powerless: it enjoys limited autonomy and sovereignty, for key political decisions are taken by economic actors and institutions. Contrary to this position, there are those authors for whom economic globalisation is exaggerated and the sovereignty of the state remains largely intact. The state-centred versus anti-statist perspectives are repeated in discussions other than economic globalisation. They are found in debates about the globalisation of political governance, in the field of international relations and in deliberations over the transnational reach of social movements.

As well as globalisation, the state has featured prominently in writings and theories about the way culture acts as a social glue. In the past, the likes of Hegel, Weber and Durkheim have considered how the state helped to form communities and to provide the stability required for ordered societies. Durkheim (1984) makes a simple evolutionary connection between the emergence of industrial society and the growth of the state. Whilst industrial society offers ever greater individual freedom, the state becomes ever more powerful and, by implication, ever more controlling over individuals. The rise of both individualism and the power of the state is not necessarily paradoxical; for the state guarantees individual rights and promotes social solidarity – or the status quo at least (Giddens 1986: 2–3). As outlined in Chapter 5, later contributions from the likes of Geertz and Bourdieu looked to the cultural functions of the state which act to reproduce and support modern societies. So the state continues to be at the forefront of theoretical innovations. And, partly for this reason, it will have something of a sustained shelf-life.

In many respects the present condition of state theory is relatively healthy. Numerous books have been written on the subject. The state is covered in university courses at both undergraduate and postgraduate level.

And academics still carve out illustrious careers from their learned writings and thoughts about the state. State theory still has plenty of mileage – that is certainly the hope for the sales and professional reception of this particular book. This whole book has shown, above all else, the disciplinary scope and theoretical depth of much contemporary state theory. We would be hard pressed to say of state theory that it is confined to a dingy ghetto of political science. Theories of the state have emerged across a range of disciplines and subdisciplines. In addition, state theory has been subject to various perspectives and philosophical standpoints, from poststructuralism to postpsychoanalytic theory, from symbolic analysis to systems theory. State theory has moved on since the days of the 1970s when it was a battleground dominated by different factions within Marxist theory. Undoubtedly, theoretical discussions of the state have flourished because this whole enterprise has opened itself up to a range of perspectives and approaches. And what this has done is give rise to a new wave of post-Marxist analysis of the state.

State theory has diversified and in the process maintained its interest for the academic community. According to Jessop (2001a: 165): 'Recent state theorizing and state research are much more diverse than that which occurred during the 1970s'. But he observes that various currents of contemporary state theory have gone on to mirror the analytical fault-lines of Marxist debate about the relationship between state and society. For instance, there are those patriarchal theorists of the state, as shown in Chapter 4, who simply rely on the same crude, deterministic logic which has dogged instrumental Marxist approaches to the state theory. On the other hand, there emerged gender theories that saw the state as having a more independent position in relation to the patriarchal system. This relative independence would allow the state to make progressive interventions in promoting gender equality.

The fact that contemporary state theories are still preoccupied with trying to comprehend the relationship between state and society is not necessarily a problem. Far from it. Whilst contemporary state theory has been unable to resolve the state–society issue, it has done more than simply go over old ground. With contemporary state theories, the societal forces that form a context for state action encompass more than economic relations. For some thinkers, societal structures are cultural in nature. For others, structures are essentially gendered. Still others argue that the social forces which the state has to deal with operate at a global level.

Mass democratisation and the new wave of state theory

The new wave of state theories implicitly embraced a certain Nietzschean antipathy towards their subject matter. Although, for many contemporary thinkers, the state may be a 'liar' and a 'monster', it is a convoluted liar and monster, operating in an uncertain and complex social context. There is an effort to deconstruct the state, to unmask what really lies behind its authority and power.

The state has changed with the times. Dario Melossi (1990) captures usefully how the state has responded to modern social conditions and, as a result, has been transformed. Melossi distinguishes between two phases in the development of the modern state in European society. Up until the early nineteenth century, the social order in Europe was secured by the state acting as a force of social unification. The state was a focal point which dispossessed social groups could rally around. Here the state acted as a distant but benevolent paternalist to the masses excluded from economic prosperity and political participation. The state under these social conditions would also employ a reactive form of social control, where prohibition was the order of the day. But the democratisation of western Europe during the course of the nineteenth century brought demands from the masses for their inclusion in the democratic system. Mass democracy for the state 'shifted the issue of order and order making from the political to the social sphere' (Melossi 1990: 3). The shift to the social sphere is a reference to the way social control has become diffuse throughout society. This is seen as necessary. In modern democracies, with mass political participation, systems of communication are more sophisticated and the populace is generally better educated. Here the type of state control that prevails, argues Melossi, is an active form of control. This is a form of control that produces rather than coerces. According to Melossi, modern forms of social control are decentred. Durkheim makes a similar point: that repressive modes of control have a limited place under modern democratic conditions. Government in primitive societies was absolute and its powers coercive. With the development of more complex forms of society ushered in by industrialisation, states could not simply rely on coercion (see Giddens 1986). With the decline of coercion and outright repression, the political order was maintained through cooperation and individualised forms of control.

In effect, the ideas, discussions and theories covered in this book attempt to capture the complexities and intricacies of modern state power. They have endeavoured to achieve a more nuanced and subtle reading of how the modern state grapples with the whole task of regulating and administering society. The lesson is that the state may still be alive and well but the process of governance is a highly complex and elaborate business.

There are theorists – especially those belonging to the postmodern camp – for whom liberal democratic states are just as coercive and repressive as their medieval forebears (see Chapter 2). Take the Slovenian philosopher, Slavoj Žižek. His 2001 book *Did Somebody Say Totalitarianism?* fires a hard-hitting broadside against liberal democracy. For Žižek, totalitarianism is an ideological concept, which grew out of the democratic tradition. It is an ideological tool that prevents the public from engaging critically with the modern democratic system. 'Throughout its entire career, "totalitarianism" was an ideological notion that sustained the complex operation of "taming free radicals", of guaranteeing the liberal-democratic hegemony, dismissing the Leftist critique of liberal democracy as the obverse, the "twin", of the Rightist Fascist dictatorship' (Žižek 2001: 3). Liberalism does encourage freedom of thought and action, but only within certain limits. Liberal democracy is to a degree, for Žižek, totalitarian. The reason why he views liberal states as totalitarian boils down to a matter of economics, or rather capitalist economics. Individual citizens are deprived by the capitalist economic system of certain choices and rights in the name of 'freedom'. And yet the tendency has been for liberal conservative ideologists of the postmodern society to suspend the importance of material production, with all its inequalities. But the modern capitalist system is intimately bonded to material wealth. Today's proletarians, argues Žižek (2001: 140), 'are subjects reduced to a rootless existence, deprived of all substantial links'. It seems the postmodern worm has turned once again – to Marxism, once again.

'Keeping up with the state theory literature'

State theory today is written from a variety of disciplinary perspectives and is subject to a myriad of theoretical approaches. This has given state theory a certain depth of analysis and coverage. It has also made state theory interesting once again and given it some mileage in academic circles. So, state theory has undoubtedly benefited from moving outside the confines of the political science discipline. But are the ideas and theories of the state too dominated by professional academics? That is, should state theory be written by non-specialist intellectuals and public scholars as well as professional academics?

In terms of the historical genesis of state theory, Lloyd and Thomas (1998) make an interesting observation. They argue that from the end of the eighteenth century to the late nineteenth century there emerged in Europe a convergence between theories of the state and culture, between ideas of the state and cultural criticism. The English poets and cultural critics Matthew Arnold and Samuel Coleridge as well as the German dramatist and philosopher Friedrich Schiller, amongst others in this era, were prone to pontificate and develop ideas about the state. In different ways, they were concerned with how culture, especially a liberal education system, contributes to the formation of citizens for the state. The role of cultural critics as state theorists, observe Lloyd and Thomas, continued into the twentieth century. The novels of George Orwell and the cultural criticism of Raymond Williams have contributed to our understanding of the state. However, the story of state theory after the Second World War is a field that became dominated by professional academe.

We could say that the colonisation of state theory by academe is only a recent phenomenon. But is it a development that we should welcome with open arms? Why ask this question in the first place? We just have to look at the history of political thought to appreciate the colossal contribution made by non-professional generalists to our understanding of the state. Ricci makes the intended point well. The ideas that form the historical basis of political thought, and by implication state theory, come from writings by the likes of Plato, Aristotle, Bodin, Locke, Burke, Mill and Marx. According to Ricci (1984: ix), these writings 'were not themselves mainly the product of an academic environment. Some of the authors taught for a living, but most were busy with practical affairs, and their tradition of discourse therefore owed more to experience in the realms of culture and society than to enthusiasm for a narrow and scholarly view of public life'. Ricci poses the question: who are the great thinkers of today? He concludes that the last truly great political thinkers in the Western tradition were around over one hundred years ago. This is possibly a little unfair on some of the great intellectuals that have appeared in the twentieth century. Nevertheless, it is a point worth making.

During the course of the twentieth century university bureaucracies have grown and academics have become undeniably more professional and productive. And yet the quality of ideas and thought may be short on true inspiration. Much of the literature that appears on reading lists or that professional academics find themselves having to read are, according to Ricci not inherently impressive but are important because they allow us and our students to 'keep up with the literature'. Ricci (1984: 313) says: 'Let us remember that keeping up with the literature means following a small conversation, based on specialized terms and expressed largely in jargon, which is itself shifting ground constantly as novelty wins out over wisdom and quantity of publication triumphs over quality'. The practice of theorising and debating the state does not belong simply to specialists, to academic professionals. Indeed, the continued development and relevance of state theory depends on intellectual inclusiveness and the encompassing of diverse traditions. Certainly, figures such as Aristotle, Marx and Hume would have something to say about that if they were available for comment today. Which, of course, they are not.

REFERENCES

Abrams, Philip (1988) Notes on the difficulty of studying the state (1977), *Journal of Historical Sociology*, 1(1): 58–89.

Agamben, Giorgio (1998) *Homo Sacer: Sovereign Power and Bare Life*, trans. Daniel Heller-Roazen. Stanford, CA: Stanford University Press.

Agamben, Giorgio (2000) *Means Without End: Notes on Politics*, trans. Vincenzo Binetti and Cesare Casarino. Minneapolis: University of Minnesota Press.

Albrow, Martin (1996) *Global Age: State and Society Beyond Modernity*. Cambridge: Polity Press.

Alexander, Jeffrey C. (1990) Analytical debates: understanding the relative autonomy of culture, in Jeffrey C. Alexander and Steven Seidman (eds) *Culture and Society: Contemporary Debates*. Cambridge: Cambridge University Press.

Alexander, Jeffrey C. and Smith, Philip (1993) The discourse of American civil society: a new proposal for cultural studies, *Theory and Society*, 22(2): 151–207.

Alexander, Jeffrey C. and Smith, Philip (2005) Introduction: the new Durkheim, in Jeffrey C. Alexander and Philip Smith (eds) *The Cambridge Companion to Durkheim*. Cambridge: Cambridge University Press.

Allen, Amy (1999) *The Power of Feminist Theory: Domination, Resistance, Solidarity*. Boulder, CO: Westview Press.

Allen, Barry (1998) Foucault and modern political philosophy, in Jeremy Moss (ed.) *The Later Foucault: Politics and Philosophy*. London: Sage.

Allen, Judith (1990) Does feminism need a theory of 'the state'? in Sophie Watson (ed.) *Playing the State: Australian Feminist Interventions*. London: Verso.

Almond, Gabriel A. and Verba, Sidney (1963) *The Civic Culture: Political Attitudes and Democracy in Five Nations*. Princeton, NJ: Princeton University Press.

Anheier, Helmut and Themundo, Nuno (2002) Organizational forms of global civil society: implications of going global, in Marlies Glasius, Mary Kaldor and Helmut Anheier (eds) *Global Civil Society 2002*. Oxford: Oxford University Press.

Arac, Jonathan (1986) Introduction, in Jonathan Arac (ed.) *Postmodern Politics*. Minneapolis: University of Minnesota Press.

Aron, Raymond (1950) Social structure and the ruling class: part 1, *British Journal of Sociology*, 1(1): 1–16.

Aronowitz, Stanley and Bratsis, Peter (eds) (2002) *Paradigm Lost: State Theory Reconsidered*. Minneapolis: University of Minnesota Press.

Bakvis, Herman (1997) Advising the executive: think tanks, consultants, political staff and kitchen cabinets, in Patrick Weller, Herman Bakvis and Rod A. W. Rhodes (eds) *The Hollow Crown: Countervailing Trends in Core Executives*. Basingstoke: Macmillan.

Barrett, Michèle (1986) *Women's Oppression Today: Problems in Marxist Feminist Analysis*, 5th edition. London: Verso.

Bartelson, Jens (2001) *The Critique of the State*. Cambridge: Cambridge University Press.

Barthes, Roland (1973) *Mythologies*, trans. Annette Lavers. London: Cape. First published in 1957.

Ben-Amos, Avner and Ben-Ari, Eyal (1995) Resonance and reverberation: ritual and bureaucracy in the state funerals of the French Third Republic, *Theory and Society*, 24(2): 163–91.

Benhabib, Seyla (1995) Subjectivity, historiography, and politics: reflections on the 'feminism/postmodernism exchange', in Seyla Benhabib, Judith Butler, Drucilla Cornell and Nancy Fraser (eds) *Feminist Contentions: A Philisophical Exchange*. New York and London: Routledge.

Benyon, John and Edwards, Adam (1999) Community governance of crime control, in Gerry Stoker (ed.) *The New Management of British Local Governance*. Basingstoke: Macmillan.

Best, Steven and Kellner, Douglas (1991) *Postmodern Theory: Critical Interrogations*. Basingstoke: Macmillan.

Bevir, Mark (1999) Foucault, power and institutions, *Political Studies*, 47(2): 345–59.

Birch, Anthony H. (1964) *Representative and Responsible Government: An Essay on the British Constitution*. London: Allen & Unwin.

Borchorst, Anette (1995) A political niche: Denmark's Equal Status Council, in Dorothy McBride Stetson and Amy G. Mazur (eds) *Comparative State Feminism*. Thousand Oaks, CA: Sage.

Bourdieu, Pierre (1986) The forms of capital, in John G. Richardson (ed.) *Handbook of Theory and Research for the Sociology of Education*. Westport, CT: Greenwood Press.

Bourdieu, Pierre (1988) *Homo Academicus*. Cambridge: Polity Press.

Bourdieu, Pierre (1989) *La Noblesse d'État: Grandes Écoles et Esprit de Corps*. Paris: Editions de Minuit.

Bourdieu, Pierre (1994) Rethinking the state: genesis and structure of the bureaucratic field, *Sociological Theory*, 12(1): 1–18.

Bourdieu, Pierre (1996) *The State Nobility: Elite Schools in the Field of Power*, trans. Lauretta C. Clough. Oxford: Polity Press.

Bourdieu, Pierre and Passeron, Jean-Claude (1977) *Reproduction in Education, Society and Culture*, trans. Richard Nice. London: Sage.

Bourdieu, Pierre and Wacquant, Loïc J. D. (1992) *An Invitation to Reflexive Sociology*. Chicago: University of Chicago Press.

Bourdieu, Pierre, Chamboredon, Jean-Claude and Passeron, Jean-Claude (1991) *The Craft of Sociology: Epistemological Preliminaries*, trans. Richard Nice. Berlin: Walter de Gruyter.

Brenner, Neil (1994) Foucault's new functionalism, *Theory and Society*, 23(5): 679–709.

Brenner, Neil (2001) State theory in the political conjuncture: Henri Lefebvre's 'Comments on a New State Form', *Antipode*, 33(5): 783–808.

Brenner, Neil (2004) *New State Spaces: Urban Governance and the Rescaling of Statehood*. Oxford: Oxford University Press.

Brint, Steven (1994) Sociological analysis of political culture: an introduction and assessment, in Fredrick D. Weil and Mary Gautier (eds) *Research on Democracy and Society: Political Culture and Political Structure – Theoretical and Emprical Studies Volume 2*. Greenwich, CT: JAI Press.

Brittan, Arthur (1989) *Masculinity and Power*. Oxford: Basil Blackwell.

Brittan, Samuel (1975) The economic contradictions of democracy, *British Journal of Political Science*, 5(2): 129–59.

Bryson, Valerie (1999) *Feminist Debates: Issues of Theory and Political Practice*. Basingstoke: Macmillan.

Bull, Hedley (1977) *The Anarchical Society: A Study of Order in World Politics*. New York: Columbia University Press.

Burstyn, Varda (1983) Masculine dominance and the state, in Ralph Miliband and John Saville (eds) *The Socialist Register 1983*. London: Merlin Press.

Butler, Judith (1997) *Excitable Speech: A Politics of the Performative*. New York: Routledge.

Callinicos, Alex (1989) *Against Postmodernism: A Marxist Critique*. Cambridge: Polity Press.

Callinicos, Alex (1990) *Trotskyism*. Milton Keynes: Open University Press.

Callinicos, Alex (1999) *Social Theory: A Historical Introduction*. Cambridge: Polity Press.

Carr, Edward H. (1946) *The Twenty Years' Crisis, 1919–1939: An Introduction to the Study of International Relations*, 2nd edition. London: Macmillan.

Carruthers, Bruce G. (1994) When is the state autonomous? Culture, organisation theory and the political sociology of the state, *Sociological Theory*, 12(1): 19–44.

Catlin, George E. G. (1964) *The Science and Method of Politics*. Hamden, CT: Archon Books.

Cawson, Alan (1982) *Corporatism and Welfare: Social Policy and State Intervention in Britain*. London: Heinemann.

Cerny, Philip G. (1990) *The Changing Architecture of Politics: Structure, Agency, and the Future of the State.* London: Sage.

Charles, Nickie (2000) *Feminism, the State and Social Policy.* Basingstoke: Macmillan.

Clegg, Stuart R. (1989) *Frameworks of Power.* London: Sage.

Connell, Robert W. (1987) *Gender and Power: Society, the Person and Sexual Politics.* Cambridge: Polity Press.

Connell, Robert. W. (1990) The state, gender, and sexual politics: theory and appraisal, *Theory and Society,* 19(5): 507–44.

Connolly, William F. (1993) *The Augustinian Imperative: A Reflection on the Politics of Morality.* Newbury Park, CA: Sage.

Coole, Diana H. (1993) *Women in Political Theory: From Ancient Misogyny to Contemporary Feminism,* 2nd edition. Hemel Hempstead: Harvester Wheatsheaf.

Cooper, Davina (1995) *Power in Struggle: Feminism, Sexuality and the State.* Buckingham: Open University Press.

Corrigan, Philip and Sayer, Derek (1985) *The Great Arch: English State Formation as Cultural Revolution.* Oxford: Basil Blackwell.

Couldry, Nick (2003) Media, symbolic power and the limits of Bourdieu's field theory. MEDIA@LSE Electronic Working Papers No. 2, London School of Economics.

Cox, Robert W. (1999) Civil society at the turn of the millennium: prospects for an alternative world order, *Review of International Studies,* 25(1): 3–28.

Cravey, Altha J. (1998) Engendering the Latin American state, *Progress in Human Geography,* 22(4): 523–42.

Curtis, Bruce (1995) Taking the state back out: Rose and Miller on political power, *British Journal of Sociology,* 46(4): 575–89.

Dahl, Robert A. (1956) *A Preface to Democratic Theory.* Chicago: Chicago University Press.

Dahl, Robert A. (1978) Pluralism revisited, *Comparative Politics,* 10(2): 191–203.

Dahl, Robert A. (1985) *A Preface to Economic Democracy.* Cambridge: Polity Press.

Daly, Mary (1987) *Gyn/Ecology: The Metaethics of Radical Feminism,* 5th edition. London: Women's Press.

Daly, Mary and Rake, Katherine (2003) *Gender and the Welfare State: Care, Work and Welfare in Europe and the USA.* Cambridge: Polity Press.

Davies, Jonathan S. (2000) The hollowing-out of local democracy and the 'fatal conceit' of governing without government, *British Journal of Politics and International Relations,* 2(3): 414–28.

Dean, Mitchell (1995) Governing the unemployed self in an active society, *Economy and Society,* 24(4): 559–83.

Dean, Mitchell (1999) *Governmentality: Power and Rule in Modern Society.* Thousand Oaks, CA: Sage.

Dixon, Jo (1995) The nexus of sex, spousal violence, and the state, *Law and Society Review*, 29(2): 359–76.

Donnelly, Jack (2000) *Realism and International Relations.* Cambridge: Cambridge University Press.

Douglas, Mary (2002) *Purity and Danger: An Analysis of Concepts of Pollution and Taboo.* London: Routledge. First published in 1966.

Duffett, Mark (2004) A 'strange blooding in the ways of popular culture'? Party at the Palace as hegemonic project, *Popular Music and Society*, 27(4): 489–506.

Dunleavy, Patrick and O'Leary, Brendan (1987) *Theories of the State: The Politics of Liberal Democracy.* Basingstoke: Macmillan Education.

Dunleavy, Patrick and Rhodes, Rod A. W. (1990) Core executive studies in Britain, *Public Administration*, 68(1): 3–28.

Dupuy, Alex and Truchil, Barry (1979) Problems in the theory of state capitalism, *Theory and Society*, 8(1): 1–38.

Durkheim, Émile (1984) *The Division of Labour in Society*, trans W.D. Halls. Basingstoke: Macmillan. First published in 1893.

Easton, David (1966) *The Political System: An Inquiry into the State of Political Science.* New York: Alfred A. Knopf.

Eco, Umberto (1990) *Travels in Hyperreality: Essays*, trans. William Weaver. San Diego, CA: Harcourt Brace Jovanovich.

Eisenstein, Zillah (1979) Developing a theory of capitalist patriarchy and socialist feminism, in Zillah R. Eisenstein (ed.) *Capitalist Patriarchy and the Case for Socialist Feminism.* New York and London: Monthly Review Press.

Esping-Andersen, Gøsta (1990) *The Three Worlds of Welfare Capitalism.* Cambridge: Polity.

Foucault, Michel (1967) *Madness and Civilisation: A History of Insanity in the Age of Reason.* London: Tavistock. First published in French in 1961.

Foucault, Michel (1977) *Discipline and Punish: The Birth of the Prison.* Harmondsworth: Penguin. First published in French in 1975.

Foucault, Michel (1978) *The History of Sexuality: An Introduction.* Harmondsworth: Penguin. First published in France in 1976.

Foucault, Michel (1980a) The history of sexuality, in Colin Gordon (ed.) *Power/Knowledge: Selected Interviews and Other Writings 1972–1977.* Brighton: Harvester.

Foucault, Michel (1980b) Truth and power, in Colin Gordon (ed.) *Power/Knowledge: Selected Interviews and Other Writings 1972–1977.* Brighton: Harvester.

Foucault, Michel (1982) Afterword: the subject and power, in Hubert L. Dreyfus and Paul Rabinow, *Michel Foucault: Beyond Structuralism and Hermeneutics.* Brighton: Harvester Press.

Foucault, Michel (1989) *The Order of Things: An Archaeology of the Human Sciences.* London: Routledge. First published in French in 1966.

Foucault, Michel (1990) *Politics, Philosophy, Culture: Interviews and Other Writings 1977–1984*, trans. Alan Sheridan and others. New York and London: Routledge.

Foucault, Michel (1991) Governmentality, in Graham Burchell, Colin Gordon and Peter Miller (eds) *The Foucault Effect: Studies in Governmentality*. London: Harvester Wheatsheaf.

Foucault, Michel and Chomsky, Noam (1997) Human nature: justice versus power, in Arnold I. Davidson (ed.) *Foucault and His Interlocutors*. Chicago: University of Chicago Press.

Fox, William T. R. and Fox, Annette Baker (1961) The teaching of international relations in the United States, *World Politics* (April): 339–59.

Franzway, Suzanne, Court, Diane and Connell, Robert W. (1989) *Staking a Claim: Feminism, Bureaucracy and the State*. Sydney: Allen & Unwin.

Friedman, Thomas (2000) *The Lexus and the Olive Tree: Understanding Globalization*. London: HarperCollins.

Geertz, Clifford (1980) *Negara: The Theatre State in Nineteenth-Century Bali*. Princeton, NJ: Princeton University Press.

Geertz, Clifford (1993) *The Interpretation of Cultures*. New York: Basic Books. First published in 1973.

Geertz, Clifford (1983) *Local Knowledge: Further Essays in Interpretative Anthropology*. New York: Basic Books.

Giddens, Anthony (1986) Introduction, in Anthony Giddens (ed.) *Durkheim on Politics and the State*. Stanford, Cal.: Stanford University Press.

Giddens, Anthony (1987) *Social Theory and Modern Sociology*. Cambridge: Polity Press.

Goetz, Klaus H. and Margetts, Helen Z. (1999) The solitary center: the core executive in Central and Eastern Europe, *Governance*, 12(4): 425–53.

Gordon, Colin (1991) Governmental rationality: an introduction, in Graham Burchell, Colin Gordon and Peter Miller (eds) *The Foucault Effect: Studies in Governmentality*. Chicago: University of Chicago Press.

Gough, Ian (1979) *The Political Economy of the Welfare State*. London: Macmillan.

Gramsci, Antonio (1982) *Selections from the Prison Notebooks*, ed. and trans. Quintin Hoare and Geoffrey Nowell Smith. London: Lawrence and Wishart.

Grant, Wyn (1993) *Business and Politics in Britain*, 2nd edition. Basingstoke: Macmillan.

Grimshaw, Jean (1993) Practices of freedom, in Caroline Ramazanoğlu (ed.) *Up Against Foucault: Explorations of some Tensions between Foucault and Feminism*. London: Routledge.

Habermas, Jürgen (1986) *The Theory of Communicative Action, Volume I: Reason and the Rationalization of Society*. Cambridge: Polity Press.

Habermas, Jürgen (1994) Some questions concerning the theory of power: Foucault again, in M. Kelly (ed.) *Critique and Power: Recasting the Foucault/Habermas Debate.* Cambridge, MA: MIT Press.

Hall, John A. and Ikenberry, G. John (1989) *The State.* Milton Keynes: Open University Press.

Hall, Peter A. (1986) *Governing the Economy: The Politics of State Intervention in Britain and France.* Cambridge: Polity.

Hall, Stuart, Critcher, Chas, Jefferson, Tony, Clarke, John and Roberts, Brian (1978) *Policing the Crisis: Mugging, the State and Law and Order.* Basingstoke: Macmillan Press.

Haney, Lynne A. (2000) Feminist state theory: applications to jurisprudence, criminology, and the welfare state, *Annual Review of Sociology,* 26: 641–66.

Hanf, Kenneth (1978) Introduction, in Kenneth Hanf and Fritz W. Scharpf (eds) *Interorganizational Policy Making: Limits to Coordination and Central Control.* London: Sage.

Hartmann, Heidi (1981) The unhappy marriage of Marxism and feminism: towards a more progressive union, in Heidi Hartmann and Lydia Sargent (eds) *Women and Revolution: A Discussion of the Unhappy Marriage of Marxism and Feminism.* Montreal: Black Rose Books.

Hassard, John (1993) Postmodernism and organizational analysis: an overview, in John Hassard and Martin Parker (eds) *Postmodernism and Organizations.* London: Sage.

Hatem, Mervat F. (1992) Economic and political liberation in Egypt and the demise of state feminism, *International Journal of Middle East Studies,* 24(2): 231–51.

Hattenstone, Simon (2004) The man who doesn't exist, *The Guardian: G2,* 30 April.

Hay, Colin (2002) *Political Analysis: A Critical Introduction.* Basingstoke: Palgrave.

Hay, Colin and Richards, David (2000) The tangled webs of Westminster and Whitehall: the discourse, strategy and practice of networking within the British core executive, *Public Administration,* 78(1): 1–28.

Hearn, Jeff (1987) *The Gender of Oppression: Men, Masculinity and the Critique of Marxism.* Brighton: Wheatsheaf.

Heelas, Paul (1991) Reforming the self: enterprise and the characters of Thatcherism, in Russell Keat and Nicholas Abercrombie (eds) *Enterprise Culture.* London and New York: Routledge.

Held, David (1989) *Political Theory and the Modern State: Essays on State, Power and Democracy.* Cambridge: Polity Press.

Held, David (1995) *Democracy and the Global Order: From the Modern State to Cosmopolitan Governance.* Cambridge: Polity.

Held, David (1996) *Models of Democracy,* 2nd edition. Cambridge: Polity.

Held, David and McGrew, Anthony (2002) *Globalization/Antiglobalization.* Oxford: Polity Press.

Held, David, McGrew, Anthony, Goldblatt, David and Perraton, Jonathan (1999) *Global Transformations: Politics, Economics and Culture.* Cambridge: Polity Press.

Hennis, Wilhelm (1987) Max Weber's theme: personality and life orders, in Sam Whimster and Scott Lash (eds) *Max Weber, Rationality and Modernity.* London: Allen & Unwin.

Hernes, Helga M. (1987) *Welfare State and Woman Power: Essays in State Feminism.* Oslo: Norwegian University Press.

Hirschmann, Nancy (1992) *Rethinking Obligation: A Feminist Method for Political Theory.* Ithaca, NY: Cornell University Press.

Hirst, Paul Q. and Thompson, Grahame (1996) *Globalization in Question: The International Economy and the Possibilities of Governance.* Cambridge: Polity Press.

Hoffman, John (2001) *Gender and Sovereignty: Feminism, the State and International Relations.* Basingstoke: Macmillan.

Holliday, Ian (2000) Is the British state hollowing out? *Political Quarterly*, 71(2): 167–76.

Hood, Christopher (2000) *The Art of the State: Culture, Rhetoric and Public Management.* Oxford: Clarendon Press.

Htun, Mala (2003) *Sex and the State: Abortion, Divorce, and the Family under Latin American Dictatorships and Democracies.* Cambridge: Cambridge University Press.

Hughes, David and Griffiths, Lesley (1999) On penalties and the Patient's Charter: centralism v de-centralised governance in the NHS, *Sociology of Health and Illness*, 20(1): 71–94.

Jackson, Norman and Carter, Pippa (1998) Labour as dressage, in Alan McKinlay and Ken Starkey (eds) *Foucault, Management and Organization Theory: From Panopticon to Technologies of Self.* London: Sage.

Jenkins, Richard (2002) *Pierre Bourdieu*, 2nd edition. London: Routledge.

Jessop, Bob (1982) *The Capitalist State: Marxist Theories and Methods.* Oxford: Martin Robertson.

Jessop, Bob (1990) *State Theory: Putting the Capitalist State in its Place.* Cambridge: Polity Press.

Jessop, Bob (1997) Capitalism and its future: remarks on regulation, government and governance, *Review of International Political Economy*, 4(3): 561–81.

Jessop, Bob (2001a) Bringing the state back in (yet again): reviews, revisions, rejections and redirections, *International Review of Sociology*, 11(2): 149–73.

Jessop, Bob (2001b) The gender selectivities of the state. http://www.lancs.ac.uk/fss/sociology/papers/jessop-gender-selectivities.pdf (accessed 9 March 2007).

Jessop, Bob (2002) *The Future of the Capitalist State.* Cambrdige: Polity Press.

Kassim, Hussein (1994) Policy networks, networks and European Union policy making: a skeptical view, *West European Politics*, 17(4): 15–27.

Keck, Margaret E. and Sikkink, Kathryn (1998) *Activists beyond Borders: Advocacy Networks in International Politics.* Ithaca, NY: Cornell University Press.

Kellner, Douglas (n.d.) Nietzsche's critique of mass culture. http://www.uta.edu/human/illuminations/kell22.htm (accessed 9 March 2007).

Kennan, George F. (1969) *American Diplomacy, 1900–1950.* Chicago: University of Chicago Press. First published in 1956.

Keohane, Robert O. and Nye, Joseph S. (1977) *Power and Interdependence: World Politics in Transition.* Boston: Little, Brown.

Keohane, Robert O. and Nye, Joseph S. (1987) *Power and Interdependence* revisited, *International Organization*, 41(4): 725–53.

Kerr, Derek (1999) Beheading the king and enthroning the market: a critique of Foucauldian governmentality, *Science and Society*, 63(2): 173–202.

Khandwalla, Pradin N. (1999) *Revitalizing the State: A Menu of Options.* New Delhi: Sage.

Kindleberger, Charles P. (1970) *Power and Money : The Economics of International Politics and the Politics of International Economics.* London: Macmillan.

King, Anthony (1975) Overload: problems of governing in the 1970s, *Political Studies*, 23(2): 284–96.

Kooiman, Jan (1993) Findings, speculations and recommendations, in Jan Kooiman (ed.) *Modern Governance: New Government–Society Interactions.* London: Sage.

Krasner, Stephen D. (1978) *Defending the National Interest: Raw Materials Investments and U.S. Foreign Policy.* Princeton, NJ: Princeton University Press.

Kuhn, Annette and Wolpe, Ann Marie (eds) (1978) *Feminism and Materialism: Women and Modes of Production.* London: Routledge & Kegan Paul.

Larner, Wendy and Walters, William (2000) Privatisation, governance and identity: the United Kingdom and New Zealand compared, *Policy and Politics*, 28(3): 361–77.

Lash, Scott and Urry, John (1987) *The End of Organised Capitalism.* Cambridge: Polity Press.

Laslett, Peter (1956) Introduction, in Peter Laslett (ed.) *Philosophy, Politics and Society.* Oxford: Backwell.

Latour, Bruno (1987) *Science in Action.* Milton Keynes: Open University Press.

Law, John (1986) Power/knowledge and the dissolution of the sociology of knowledge, in John Law (ed.) *Power, Action and Belief: A New Sociology of Knowledge?* London: Routledge & Kegan Paul.

Leira, Arnlaug (1989) *Models of Motherhood, Welfare State Policies and Everyday Practices: the Scandinavian Experience.* Oslo: Institute for Social Research.

Lemert, Charles (1997) *Postmodernism Is Not What You Think.* Malden MA: Blackwell Publishers.

Lenin, Vladimir I. (1970) *The State and Revolution: The Marxist Teaching on the State and the Tasks of the Proletariat in the Revolution.* Peking: Foreign Languages Press. First published in 1918.

Lewis, Jane (1992) Gender and the development of welfare regimes, *Journal of European Social Policy*, 2(3): 159–73.

Lindblom, Charles (1977) *Politics and Markets: The World's Political-Economic Systems.* New York: Basic Books.

Lipschutz, Ronnie D. (1992) Reconstructing world politics: the emergence of global civil society, *Millennium*, 21(3): 389–420.

Lively, Jack (1975) *Democracy.* Oxford: Basil Blackwell.

Lloyd, David and Thomas, Paul (1998) *Culture and the State.* New York: Routledge.

Loader, Ian (2000) Plural policing and democratic governance, *Social and Legal Studies*, 9(3): 323–45.

London Edinburgh Weekend Return Group (1980) *In and against the State.* London: Pluto.

Lowe, Rodney and Rollings, Neil (2000) Modernising Britain, 1957–64: a classic case of centralisation and fragmentation? in Rod A. W. Rhodes (ed.) *Transforming British Government, Volume 1: Changing Institutions.* Basingstoke: Macmillan.

Lowndes, Vivien (1996) Varieties of new institutionalism: a critical appraisal, *Public Administration*, 74(2): 181–97.

Luhmann, Niklas (1982) *The Differentiation of Society.* New York: Columbia University Press.

Lyotard, Jean-François (1979) *The Postmodern Condition: A Report on Knowledge.* Minneapolis: University of Minnesota Press.

MacKinnon, Catharine A. (1989) *Toward a Feminist Theory of the State.* Cambridge, MA: Harvard University Press.

MacKinnon, Danny (2000) Managerialism, governmentality and the state: a neo-Foucauldian approach to local economic governance, *Political Geography*, 19(3): 293–314.

Mackintosh, John P. (1977) *The Government and Politics of Britain*, 4th edition. London: Hutchinson.

Malik, Kenan (1996) *The Meaning of Race: Race, History and Culture in Western Society.* Basingstoke: Macmillan.

Mann, Michael (1993) *The Sources of Social Power: The Rise of Classes and Nation-States, 1760–1914, Vol. 2.* Cambridge: Cambridge University Press.

Margolis, Michael (1983) Democracy: American style, in Graeme Duncan (ed.) *Democratic Theory and Practice.* Cambridge: Cambridge University Press.

Marin, Bernd and Mayntz, Renate (1991) Introduction: studying policy networks, in Bernd Marin and Renate Mayntz (eds) *Policy Networks: Empirical Evidence and Theoretical Considerations.* Boulder, CO: Westview Press.

Marks, Gary, Hooghe, Liesbet and Blank, Kermit (1996) European integration from the 1980s: state-centric v. multi-level governance, *Journal of Common Market Studies,* 34(3): 341–78.

Marsh, David, Richards, David and Smith, Martin J. (2001) *Changing Patterns of Governance in the United Kingdom: Reinventing Whitehall?* Basinstoke: Palgrave.

Marx, Karl and Engels, Fredrick (1965) *The German Ideology.* London: Lawrence and Wishart. First Published in 1932.

Marx, Karl and Engels, Fredrick (1977) *Selected Works: in One Volume.* London: Lawrence and Wishart. First published in 1932.

Mazur, Amy G. and Stetson, Dorothy McBride (1995) Conclusion: the case for state feminism, in Dorothy McBride Stetson and Amy G. Mazur (eds) *Comparative State Feminism.* Thousand Oaks, CA: Sage.

McGreggor Cawley R. and Chaloupka, William (1997) American governmentality: Michel Foucault and public administration, *American Behavioral Scientist,* 41(1): 28–42.

McGrew, Anthony (2002) From global governance to good governance: theories and prospects of democratizing the global polity, in Morten Ougaard and Richard Higgott (eds) *Towards a Global Polity.* London: Routledge.

McIntosh, Mary (1978) The state and the oppression of women, in Annette Kuhn and Ann Marie Wolpe (eds) *Feminism and Materialism: Women and Modes of Production.* London: Routledge & Kegan Paul.

McLellan, David (1995) *The Thought of Karl Marx: An Introduction,* 3rd edition. London: Papermac.

McLennan, Gregor (1984) Capitalist state or democratic polity? Recent developments in Marxist and pluralist theory, in Gregor McLennan, David Held and Stuart Hall (eds) *The Idea of the Modern State.* Milton Keynes: Open University Press.

McNay, Lois (1992) *Foucault and Feminism: Power, Gender and the Self.* Cambridge: Polity Press.

McNay, Lois (1994) *Foucault: An Introduction.* Cambridge: Polity Press.

McNay, Lois (2000) *Gender and Agency: Reconfiguring the Subject in Feminist and Social Theory.* Cambridge: Polity Press.

Melossi, Dario (1990) *The State of Social Control: A Sociological Study of Concepts of State and Social Control in the Making of Democracy.* Cambridge: Polity Press.

Middlemas, Keith (1979) *Politics and Industrial Society: The Experience of the British System since 1911.* London: André Deutsch.

Miliband, Ralph (1973) *The State in Capitalist Society.* London: Quartet Books.

Miller, Peter and Rose, Nikolas (1990) Governing economic life, *Economy and Society*, 19(1): 1–31.

Mills, Catherine (2003) Contesting the political: Butler and Foucault on power and resistance, *Journal of Political Philosophy*, 11(3): 253–72.

Milward, H. Brinton and Francisco, Ronald A. (1983) Subsystem politics and corporatism in the United States, *Policy and Politics*, 11(3): 273–93.

Mitchell, Timothy (1991) The limits of the state: beyond statist approaches and their critics, *The American Political Science Review*, 85(1): 77–96.

Mitchell, Timothy (1999) Society, economy and the state effect, in George Steinmetz (ed.) *State/Culture: State-Formation after the Cultural Turn.* Ithaca, NY: Cornell University Press.

Mitrany, David (1966) *A Working Peace System.* Chicago: Quadrangle Books.

Moore, Mike (2003) *A World Without Walls: Freedom, Development, Free Trade and Global Governance.* Cambridge: Cambridge University Press.

Morgan, Kevin, Rees, Gareth and Garmise, Shari (1999) Networking for local economic development, in Gerry Stoker (ed.) *The New Management of British Local Governance.* Basingstoke: Macmillan.

Müller, Wolfgang C. and Wright, Vincent (1994) Reshaping the state in Western Europe: the limits to retreat, *West European Politics*, 17(3): 1–11.

Murdoch, Jonathan (1997) The shifting territory of government: some insights from the Rural White Paper, *Area*, 29(2): 109–18.

Neocleous, Mark (1996) *Administering Civil Society: Towards a Theory of State Power.* Basingstoke: Macmillan.

Nettl, John P. (1968) The state as a conceptual variable, *World Politics*, 20(4): 559–92.

Nietzsche, Friedrich (1998) *Twilight of the Idols or How to Philosophize with a Hammer*, trans. Duncan Large. Oxford: Oxford University Press. First published in 1888.

Nietzsche, Friedrich (2003) *Thus Spake Zarathustra: A Book for All and None*, trans. Thomas Wayne. New York: Algora. First published in 1883.

Nordlinger, Eric A. (1987) Taking the state seriously, in Myron Weiner and Samuel P. Huntington (eds) *Understanding Political Development.* Boston: Little, Brown.

Norris, Christopher (1997) *Against Relativism: Philosophy of Science, Deconstruction and Critical Theory.* Oxford: Blackwell.

O'Brien, Robert, Goetz, Anne Marie, Scholte, Jan Aart and Williams, Marc (2000) *Contesting Global Governance: Multilateral Economic Institutions and Global Social Movements.* Cambridge: Cambridge University Press.

O'Connor, Julia S. (1993) Gender, class and citizenship in the comparative analysis of welfare state regimes: theoretical and methodological issues, *British Journal of Sociology*, 44(3): 501–18.

Ohmae, Kenichi (1995) *The End of the Nation State: The Rise of Regional Economics.* London: HarperCollins.

O'Malley, Pat, Weir, Lorna and Shearing, Clifford (1997) Governmentality, criticism, politics, *Economy and Society*, 26(4): 501–17.

Ougaard, Morten (2004) *Political Globalization: State, Power and Social Forces.* Basingstoke: Palgrave Macmillan.

Parsons, Talcott (1951) *The Social System.* New York: Free Press.

Pateman, Carole (1979) *The Problem of Political Obligation: A Critical Analysis of Liberal Theory.* Chichester: Wiley.

Pateman, Carole (1980) The civic culture: a philosophical critique, in Gabriel A. Almond and Sidney Verba (eds) *The Civic Culture Revisited: an Analytic Study.* Boston: Little, Brown.

Patterson, Alan and Pinch, Phil L. (1995) 'Hollowing out' the local state: compulsory competitive tendering and the restructuring of British public sector services, *Environment and Planning A*, 27: 1437–61.

Peters, B. Guy (1993) Managing the hollow state, in Kjell A. Eliassen and Jan Kooiman (eds) *Managing Public Organizations: Lessons from Contemporary European Experience*, 2nd edition. London: Sage.

Peterson, M. J. (1992) Transnational activity, international society and world politics, *Millennium*, 21(3): 371–88.

Petras, James (1977) State capitalism and the third world, *Development and Change*, 8(1): 1–17.

Pierson, Christopher (1996) *The Modern State.* London: Routledge.

Poggi, Gianfranco (1978) *The Development of the Modern State: A Sociological Introduction.* London: Hutchinson.

Poulantzas, Nicos (1973) *Political Power and Social Classes*, trans. Timothy O'Hagan. London: New Left Books.

Poulantzas, Nicos (1978) *State, Power, Socialism*, trans. Patrick Camiller. London: New Left Books.

Powell, Walter W. and DiMaggio, Paul J. (1991) Introduction, in Walter W. Powell and Paul J. DiMaggio (eds) *The New Institutionalism in Organisational Analysis.* Chicago: University of Chicago Press.

Pringle, Rosemary and Watson, Sophie (1992) 'Women's interests' and the post-structuralist state, in Michèle Barrett and Anne Phillips (eds) *Destabilizing Theory: Contemporary Feminist Debates.* Cambridge: Polity.

Radcliffe-Brown, Alfred R. (1970) *African Systems of Kinship and Marriage.* London: Oxford University Press.

Rhodes, Rod A. W. (1988) *Beyond Westminster and Whitehall: The Sub-central Governments of Britain.* London: Routledge.

Rhodes, Rod A. W. (1994) The hollowing out of the state: the changing nature of the public service in Britain, *Political Quarterly*, 65(2): 138–51.

Rhodes, Rod A. W. (1995), *The New Governance: Governing without Government*, The State of Britain Seminars (Swindon: Economic and Social Research Council).

Rhodes, Rod A. W. (1996) The new governance: governing without government, *Political Studies*, 44(4): 652–67.

Rhodes, Rod A. W. (1997) *Understanding Governance: Policy Networks, Governance, Reflexivity and Accountability.* Buckingham: Open University Press.

Rhodes, Rod A. W. (2000a) *Transforming British Government: Volume 2: Changing Roles and Relationships.* Basingstoke: Macmillan.

Rhodes, Rod A. W. (2000b) A guide to the ESRC's Whitehall programme, 1994–1999, *Public Administration*, 78(2): 251–82.

Rhodes, Rod A. W. and Dunleavy, Patrick. (eds) (1995) *Prime Minister, Cabinet and Core Executive.* Basingstoke: Macmillan.

Rhodes, Rod A. W. and Marsh, David. (1992) Policy networks in British politics: a critique of existing approaches, in David Marsh and Rod A. W. Rhodes (eds) *Policy Networks in British Government.* Oxford: Clarendon Press.

Ricci, David M. (1984) *The Tragedy of Political Science: Politics, Scholarship and Democracy.* New Haven, CT: Yale University Press.

Richards, David and Smith, Martin J. (2002) *Governance and Public Policy in the United Kingdom.* Oxford: Oxford University Press.

Ritzer, George (2004) *The Globalization of Nothing.* Thousand Oaks, CA: Pine Forge.

Robertson, Roland (1992) *Globalization: Social Theory and Global Culture.* London: Sage.

Rohrschneider, Robert and Dalton, Russell J. (2002) A global network? Transnational cooperation among environmental groups, *Journal of Politics*, 64(2): 510–33.

Rollings, Neil (1992) 'The Reichstag method of governing'? The Attlee governments and permanent economic controls, in Helen Mercer, Neil Rollings and Jim Tomlinson (eds) *Labour Governments and Private Industry: The Experience of 1945–51.* Edinburgh: Edinburgh University Press.

Rose, Nikolas (1992) Governing the enterprising self, in Paul Heelas and Paul Morris (eds) *The Values of the Enterprise Culture: The Moral Debate.* London: Routledge.

Rosenau, James N. (1990) *Turbulence in World Politics: A Theory of Change and Continuity.* London: Harvester Wheatsheaf.

Rosenberg, Justin (2000) *The Follies of Globalisation Theory: Polemical Essays.* London: Verso.

Rubin, Gayle (1975) The traffic of women: notes on the 'political economy' of sex, in Rayna Reiter (ed.) *Toward an Anthropology of Women.* New York: Monthly Review Press.

Ruggie, Mary (1984) *The State and Working Women: A Comparative Study of Britain and Sweden.* Princeton NJ: Princeton University Press.

Saward, Michael (1997) In search of the hollow crown, in Patrick Weller, Herman Bakvis and Rod A. W. Rhodes (eds) *The Hollow Crown: Countervailing Trends in Core Executives.* Basingstoke: Macmillan.

Sayer, Derek (1994) Everyday forms of state formation: some dissident remarks on 'hegemony', in Gilbert M. Joseph and Daniel Nugent (eds) *Everyday Forms of State Formation: Revolution and the Negotiation of Rule in Modern Mexico.* Durham, NC: Duke University Press.

Scharpf, Fritz W. (1978) Interorganizational policy studies: issues, concepts and perspectives, in Kenneth Hanf and Fritz W. Scharpf (eds) *Interorganizational Policy Making: Limits to Coordination and Central Control.* London: Sage.

Scharpf, Fritz W., Reissert, Bernd and Schnabel, Fritz (1978) Policy effectiveness and conflict avoidance in intergovernmental policy formation, in Kenneth Hanf and Fritz W. Scharpf (eds) *Interorganizational Policy Making: Limits to Coordination and Central Control.* London: Sage.

Schofield, Jill (2001) The old ways are the best? The durability and usefulness of bureaucracy in public sector management, *Organization*, 8(1): 77–96.

Schrift, Alan D. (1995) *Nietzsche's French Legacy: A Genealogy of Poststructuralism.* New York: Routledge.

Scott, James C. (1998) *Seeing Like a State: How Certain Schemes to Improve the Human Condition Have Failed.* New Haven CT: Yale University Press.

Shaw, Martin (1994) Civil society and global politics: beyond a social movements approach, *Millennium*, 23(3): 647–67.

Sicker, Martin (2003) *The Orthocratic State.* Westport, CT: Praeger.

Siim, Birte (1988) Towards a feminist rethinking of the welfare state, in Kathleen B. Jones and Anna G. Jónasdóttir (eds) *The Political Interests of Gender: Developing Theory and Research with a Feminist Face.* London: Sage.

Sikkink, Kathryn (1991) *Ideas and Institutions: Developmentalism in Brazil and Argentina.* Ithaca, NY: Cornell University Press.

Simons, Jon (1995) *Foucault and the Political.* London: Routledge.

Skelcher, Chris (2000) Changing images of the state: overloaded, hollowed-out, congested, *Public Policy and Administration*, 15(3): 3–19.

Skocpol, Theda (1979) *States and Social Revolutions: A Comparative Analysis of France, Russia, and China.* Cambridge: Cambridge University Press.

Skocpol, Theda (2000) *The Missing Middle: Working Families and the Future of American Social Policy.* New York: W. W. Norton.

Smircich, Linda (1983) Concepts of culture and organizational analysis, *Administrative Science Quarterly*, 28(3): 339–58.

Smith, Jackie (1997) Characteristics of the modern transnational social movements sector, in Jackie Smith, Charles Chatfield and Ron Pagnucco (eds) *Transnational Social Movements and Global Politics: Solidarity beyond the States*. Syracuse, NY: Syracuse University Press.

Smith, Mark J. (2000) *Rethinking State Theory*. London: Routledge.

Smith, Martin J. (1998) Reconceptualizing the British state: theoretical and empirical challenges to central government, *Public Administration*, 76(1): 45–72.

Smith, Martin J. (1999) *The Core Executive in Britain*. Basingstoke: Macmillan.

Sørensen, Georg (2004) *The Transformation of the State: Beyond the Myth of Retreat*. Basingstoke: Palgrave/Macmillan.

Soysal, Yasemin N. (1994) *Limits of Citizenship: Migrants and Postnational Membership in Europe*. Chicago: University of Chicago Press.

Spencer, Martin E. (1979) Marx on the state: the events in France between 1848–1850, *Theory and Society*, 7(1/2): 167–98.

Steinmetz, George (1999) Introduction: culture and the state, in George Steinmetz (ed.) *State/Culture: State-Formation after the Cultural Turn*. Ithaca, NY: Cornell University Press.

Stetson, Dorothy McBride and Mazur, Amy G. (1995) Introduction, in Dorothy McBride Stetson and Amy G. Mazur (eds) *Comparative State Feminism*. Thousand Oaks, CA: Sage.

Strange, Susan (1994) *States and Markets*, 2nd edition. London: Pinter. First published in 1988.

Strange, Susan (1996) *The Retreat of the State: The Diffusion of Power in the World Economy*. Cambridge: Cambridge University Press.

Sullivan, Robert R. (2000) *Liberalism and Crime: the British Experience*. Lanham, MD: Lexington Books.

Szakolczai, Apád (1993) *From Governmentality to the Genealogy of Subjectivity: On Foucault's Path in the 1980s*, European University Institute Working Paper SPS No. 93/4. Badia Fiesolana: European University Institute.

Taussig, Michael (1993) *Maleficium*: state fetishism, in Emily Apter and William Pietz (eds) *Fetishism as Cultural Discourse*. Ithaca, NY: Cornell University Press.

Taylor, Andrew (1997) 'Arm's length but hands on'. Mapping the new Governance: The Department of National Heritage and cultural politics in Britain, *Public Administration*, 75(3): 441–66.

Taylor, Andrew (2000) Hollowing out or filling in? Taskforces and the management of cross-cutting issues in British government, *British Journal of Politics and International Relations*, 2(1): 46–71.

Thomas, George M. and Meyer, John W. (1984) The expansion of the state, *Annual Review of Sociology*, 10: 461–82.

Threlfall, Monica (1998) State feminism or party feminism? Feminist politics and the Spanish Institute of Women, *The European Journal of Women's Studies*, 5(1): 69–93.

Truman, David B. (1981) *The Governmental Process: Political Interests and Public Opinion.* Westport, CT: Greenwood Press.

Tudor, Andrew (1999) *Decoding Culture: Theory and Method in Cultural Studies.* London: Sage.

Vernon, Raymond (1971) *Sovereignty at Bay: The Multinational Spread of U.S. Enterprises.* London: Longman.

Vincent, Andrew (1987) *Theories of the State.* Oxford: Basil Blackwell.

Viotti, Paul R. and Kauppi, Mark V. (1999) *International Relations Theory: Realism, Pluralism, Globalism, and Beyond*, 3rd edition. Boston: Allyn and Bacon.

Wacquant, Loïc J. D. (1993) On the tracks of symbolic power: prefatory notes to Bourdieu's 'state nobility', *Theory, Culture and Society*, 10(3): 1–17.

Walby, Sylvia (1990) *Theorizing Patriarchy.* Oxford: Basil Blackwell.

Walby, Sylvia (1999) The new regulatory state: the social powers of the European Union, *British Journal of Sociology*, 50(1): 118–40.

Waltz, Kenneth N. (1970) The myth of national interdependence, in Charles P. Kindleberger (ed.) *The International Corporation.* Cambridge, MA: MIT Press.

Waltz, Kenneth N. (1979) *Theory of International Politics.* Reading, MA: Addison-Wesley.

Wanna, John (1997) Managing budgets, in Patrick Weller, Herman Bakvis and Rod A. W. Rhodes (eds) *The Hollow Crown: Countervailing Trends in Core Executives.* Basingstoke: Macmillan.

Wapner, Paul (1995) Politics beyond the state: environmental activism and world civic politics, *World Politics*, 47(3): 311–40.

Waylen, Georgina (1998) Gender, feminism and the state: an overview, in Vicky Randall and Georgina Waylen (eds) *Gender, Politics and the State.* London: Routledge.

Weiss, Linda (1998) *The Myth of the Powerless State: Governing the Economy in a Global Era.* Cambridge: Polity Press.

Wilson, Elizabeth (1977), *Women and the Welfare State.* London: Tavistock Publications.

Woollacott, Janet (1982) Messages and meanings, in Michael Gurevitch, Tony Bennett, James Curran and Janet Woollacott (eds) *Culture, Society and the Media.* London: Methuen.

Yeatman, Anna (1994) *Postmodern Revisionings of the Political.* New York: Routledge.

Žižek, Slavoj (2001) *Did Somebody Say Totalitarianism? Five Interventions in the (Mis)use of a Notion.* London: Verso.

Zürn, Michael (2002) Societal denationalization and positive governance, in Morten Ougaard and Richard Higgott (eds) *Towards a Global Polity.* London: Routledge.

NAME INDEX

SUBJECT INDEX